ecprPRESS
classics

Series Editors:
Alan Ware (University of Oxford) and
Vincent Hoffmann-Martinot (Sciences Po Bordeaux)

territory and power
in the united kingdom

an interpretation

Jim Bulpitt

with a new introduction by Peter John

ecprPRESS

© Jim Bulpitt

First published in 1983
by Manchester University Press

First published by the ECPR Press in 2008

The ECPR Press is the publishing imprint of the European Consortium for
Political Research (ECPR), a scholarly association, which supports and encour-
ages the training, research and cross-national cooperation of political scientists in
institutions throughout Europe and beyond. The ECPR's Central Services are
located at the University of Essex, Wivenhoe Park,
Colchester, CO4 3SQ, UK

Typeset in Times 10pt by the ECPR Press
Printed and bound in the UK by the University of Essex Print Centre

British Library Cataloguing in Publication Data
A catalogue record for this book is available from the British Library

ISBN13 978-0-9552488-6-3

ecpr PRESS
classics

The ECPR Classics series is published by the ECPR Press, the publishing imprint of the European Consortium for Political Research (ECPR).

As an independent, scholarly institution, one of the ECPR's objectives is to facilitate research in political science among European universities. To that end, the ECPR has developed a strong publishing portfolio since the 1970s.

The policy to extend that portfolio by launching its own publishing imprint was discussed by the Executive Committee of the ECPR in 2002, and the decision to proceed was taken in early 2003.

It was decided that the first two series to be published under the imprint should be complementary. The ECPR Monographs series publishes major new research in all sub-disciplines of political science. The ECPR Classics series facilitates scholarly access to significant works from earlier eras of political science by re-publishing books that have been out of print. It believes this will enable contemporary students and researchers to develop their own work more effectively.

While every effort has been made to reproduce faithfully the original text, the pagination of this ECPR Classics edition differs slightly from the pagination in the original edition of the work; this follows from the decision to keep the size of page and font consistent across all titles in the series. To enable scholars to locate cited page references to the earlier edition, the original chapter pagination is stated at the beginning of the corresponding chapter in this ECPR Classics edition. The Index of this edition also includes both the original and the ECPR Classics edition page numbers for each entry.

contents

new introduction by Peter John[1]
territory and power
and the study of comparative politics

Jim Bulpitt was born in Wembley, London, in 1937. As an undergraduate, he studied Politics and History at the University of Exeter, followed by a MA in Politics at the University of Manchester. In 1965, after spending a year as a research fellow at the University of Milan and then a three-year appointment at the University of Strathclyde, he took up a lectureship at the newly-established University of Warwick, where he helped found the Department of Politics. He remained there for thirty-four years, most of his academic career, becoming Professor of Politics in 1992. He died in 1999.

He was a very lively and sociable individual, who liked a good argument. He was engaged with debates in contemporary politics, partly because he was an activist, having first been a Labour Party agent in the 1960s before moving over to the Conservative Party in the 1970s. Students used to love his lectures, which were full of anecdotes, jokes and insights. Academics of his generation are usually able to tell a story about him, which often involves a comic event highlighted by his trenchant political opinions.

Jim Bulpitt's lasting reputation has so far remained mainly with British scholars, largely because he was a scholar of UK politics and operated mainly within its academic circles. He tended to work on his own, rather than in collaborations. Nor did he write that much; but what he did was always very good, particularly his book, *Territory and Power in the United Kingdom*, which has had such a profound influence. This book shows he was scholar in the true sense of the word: he was engaged with big intellectual themes and he worked within historical studies as well responding to debates in political science. His research topics were local and territorial politics, political parties, economic policy and foreign affairs, to which he directed questions about the operation of statecraft, the salience of elite interests, the development of territorial identity and the contradictions of political power, all of which are central to the study of comparative politics. By placing nation states in their historical contexts, examining the constraints and limitations on central decision-makers and the scope for political choice and autonomy, he belongs to the institutional political science tradition, which has rediscovered the state and observes the path of history just as he did (Ware 1987: 75, Bradbury 2006).

Territory and Power in the United Kingdom is not a dry history of central-local government relations characterised by changes in legal powers and policies; it is about the nature of the UK state, where it came from and where it is going. Bulpitt sought to summarise the political code and statecraft that helped govern the territories of the United Kingdom for much of the twentieth century, though it had its antecedents many years before. This polity was characterised by informal brokerage and the reluctance of the centre to deal with the detail of decentralised administration. The system of governance had specific historical origins, a persistent institutional culture, and a logic that delivered benefits to both the centre and the periphery. Bulpitt provided an account of its emergence, operation and decline, which summarised an important phase in the United Kingdom's history and marked out why the country stood out from its continental neighbours in its territorial organisation and state tradition.

Territory and Power is not a time-limited country-bound project. It has lessons about how to study territorial politics, setting out the nature of this kind of decision-making and showing how historical factors play out as part of it. Most of all, Bulpitt showed that the practice of territorial politics is an integral part of the general exercise of power and authority in nation states, influencing how central elites seek autonomy and influence over economic and foreign policy matters by managing the affairs of the periphery in a strategic manner. While states vary in the way they do this, the underlying problem is the same – how to develop a form of statecraft that allows the central authority to sustain itself over time and to reward the interests of its governing elites. Bulpitt's analysis shows comparative scholars just how such a study can be done. And it is the intention of this introduction to explain just how he did it, first summarising Bulpitt's conceptual scheme, especially his discussion of political power, then moving through the argument of the book chapter by chapter. The discussion concludes by outlining and responding to some possible objections to Bulpitt's analysis and approach.

THE CONCEPTS

Territory and Power introduces many new terms that were not so familiar when Bulpitt set them out, but whose commonplace occurrence may now be attributed to the influence of the book. Bulpitt's use of language allowed him to construct a theoretical account of a certain kind of politics, even though he was never wedded to universal definitions and he recognised the slippery nature of these concepts and the practices they represented. The first is the term 'territorial politics' itself, which was not in common use at the time of the publication of the book, but Bulpitt can claim the credit for developing it. This concept does not just refer to intergovernmental relations; it is a much broader phenomenon than institutional interactions. Territorial politics is about how spatially-located decision-makers play out their strategies and realise their values and interests. Institutions may give central and peripheral elites their formal roles; but territorial politics is more often about the informal and political relationships. It concerns economic interests, pressure groups and the political parties, which are differently constituted in the various territories of the nation state. This term, and the analysis behind it, has stimulated a stream of work in UK political science (e.g. Rhodes 1988), which is now labelled as 'territorial politics' (Bradbury 2006). Territorial politics scholars fully acknowledge the importance of the state as a concept to understand the exercise of power and authority and places historical context at the centre of political analysis. The approach also implies a comparative framework which can understand how similar sets of power exchanges take place in different state traditions and political contexts. With most of the academics working in the field the debt to Bulpitt is implicit rather than direct. The exception is Bradbury (2006, 2008) who uses the epithet 'neo-Bulpittian' to indicate his approach to UK politics.

The second set of terms is 'centre' and 'periphery'. The centre is the concentration of political interests, identity and power occurring primarily in the capital, London, where the political and administrative elites had control over the levers of power. Their close proximity to each other fostered their sense of political interest. Their common values and assumptions influenced how they exercised authority. Bulpitt used the phrase 'the official mind' to represent the centre's sets of values and assumptions, which have been solidified by key historical events and passed down the generations from one politician and civil servant to another. The periphery is the rest of the country – outside the centre's loop – which has its own elites and power holders who seek influence and need – to a greater or lesser extent – an accommodation with the centre. For it is the centre that has the finance and laws needed for sub-national administration to be carried out effectively and efficiently.

Bulpitt drew on the 1950s sociologist Edward Shils to understand the practice of centre and local politics. Bulpitt referred to Shils' idea of the central value system as opposed to those of the non-elite outside the centre. But essentially these terms are common sense ones that indicate the link between the spatial location of the elites, the institutions they occupy and the power they have, even if it is hard to define and identify the two realms. UK political scientists did not often use these concepts at that time and they usually ignored the territorial dimension to power (or left it to the Marxists). They focused on the character of central and local institutions, like central government departments and local authorities, and treated Scottish, Welsh and Irish politics as separate topics in their own right. Bulpitt took the whole of the UK as the space within which central-local politics is played out.

Bulpitt's approach has more in common with discussions of territorial politics in the study of comparative European politics, such as Tarrow's (1977) account of local and central elites in France and Italy, Rokkan and Unwin's (1982) analysis of the territorial basis to political cleavages, and Grémion's (1976) seminal study of French central-local relations. Like these classic comparativists, Bulpitt deployed a political definition of the centre and periphery, where the role of elites is central to explaining the operation of the system. Both central and local elites have their own interests and work within a powerful set of constraints. They operate within political institutions, and across and around them as well.

Bulpitt deployed the terms 'court' and 'country', which are more particular to England. These descriptors indicate the character and the values of the elites in both the centre and the periphery, and also the longevity of pre-modern institutions in UK politics. The court is in the centre, characterised by a circle of power, originally around the monarch, which then moved to senior politicians and civil servants. The court has a common stock of knowledge and sense of superiority and difference from the country, which it governs. Country refers to the periphery, with its less urban bias and its focus on the territories outside London and the South East. These terms indicate the sense of superiority the court feels it has, which derives from its common culture, international links and economic interests. In contrast, the periphery is parochial and has a spatially limited point of reference. The implicit meaning of these terms suggest the court has little interest in the country – it is not concerned about dominating the periphery as its preoccupations are elsewhere; it tends not to have much knowledge of what happens there, but it has to get involved in periods of crisis.

Bulpitt also used the terms 'high' and 'low' politics, which relate to the centre and periphery, with the centre having the high and the periphery the low. High means matters of state, international policy and the economy; low is about administration and public services. Bulpitt argued that the centre wants to focus mainly on high politics, which it considers is more important and connected to its prestige, and does not want to get involved with low politics unless it has to. These preoccupations become part of the reason the central state withdraws from much of sub-national politics, accounting for its willingness to let go of power. British politicians and civil servants were content for multifarious territorial settlements to emerge across the United Kingdom. Bulpitt deployed the term 'territorial code' to describe this detached approach to managing the periphery.

The other term – the one that has been most used since Bulpitt promoted it – is the 'dual polity'. This concept sums up the idea that there were two kinds of political systems present in the United Kingdom from 1926 to 1961. One was in the centre in London concerned with high politics; the other operated in the periphery preoccupied with the low variety. The centre's interest in pursuing high politics meant it sought to ensure the periphery was out of the limelight and was largely self-governing. This difference in interests and values was reinforced by the relatively few personal contacts that existed between the centre and periphery, which reduced their elites' knowledge of each other. The dual polity's most distinctive expression was the practice of few politicians holding elected positions as both members of parliament and councillors in local government. The duality of the system was a source of stability as both sides sought an accommodation with each other and because the centre did not have the willingness or the ability to impose uniform rules. A differentiated pattern of governance emerged, which was administered in a flexible manner based on adaptation to local circumstances. But the dual polity was also a source of instability as it fostered challenges to the system, which allowed the uneasy and messy compromises to be easily disrupted. In the end, the dual polity compounded the centre's weakness as it never had the instruments and knowledge to govern the periphery properly. When territorial crises inevitably emerged, the centre did not have the tools and capacity to deal with them.

Many of these concepts are not original to Bulpitt. The account of the dominance of the UK elites in London is a common idea in historical studies, especially the court/country distinction. The closed and court nature of the policy-making community appears as the central theme of Heclo and Wildavsky's (1974) classic work about the Treasury; the account of the consensual policy-making style dominates Richardson and Jordan's influential survey (1979). And Bulpitt cited historians who used the term 'official mind'. The tendency for the centre to want to get rid of matters of administration and to concentrate on high politics has been a well-established theme in studies of local government and its history (e.g. Hampton 1966), and the term high and low politics appears in English historical studies (e.g. Bentley and Stevenson 1983). The duality idea is newer, but comparativists had already acknowledged that some countries, such as France and Italy, do not have this quality. For example, the *cumul de mandats* in France ensures that local politicians are national players at the same time, operating so as to merge the two spheres of politics (Tarrow 1977), which is in contrast to the UK (Ashford 1977). What was new in Bulpitt is the stress on these terms as operating principles of the system and their application to the territorial politics of the whole of the UK. What Bulpitt did so brilliantly was to weave these ideas and practices into an account of statecraft, which operates over a long period. For 'statecraft' is itself another Bulpittian term, referring to the dynamic character to governance and way in which a certain kind of institutional intelligence accumulates over time, embedded in the state and in the mindset of its politicians and bureaucrats. With these reflexes and institutional memories in play, the state can constructively respond to crises. But it may also have limitations and blind spots too.

With the deployment of his conceptual system, Bulpitt re-interpreted UK politics and history in terms of the interplay of territorial interests. He integrated much that was familiar in the study of central-local relations and the history of the territories; but he set out a wider picture that described territorial management as core to the UK's statehood. Bulpitt's language allowed him to offer an original interpretation of UK history and politics. He made considerations of territory central to the development of the state, not only in its management of central-local relations, but also its stance and style on foreign policy and economic management. And it is no surprise that Bulpitt subsequently worked on UK economic and foreign policy (1988).

POLITICAL POWER AND ITS EXERCISE

Bulpitt's account of the UK's statecraft illuminates his subtle account of political power, which is of interest to political scientists more widely, not just to those working on territorial politics and the UK state. There is nothing surprising about his account of the power of the centre, which has vast constitutional resources at its disposal, such as the legal power of parliament and financial controls. Nor is it controversial to talk about the benefits of agglomeration of culture, elites, and other national institutions in London. But what is interesting is his account of the reluctance of the central elite to exercise its power directly. With all its resources at its disposal, London could have created a centralised and uniform system of administration to implement public policies and to ensure that bargaining with local elites would not be necessary. But this did not happen. The centre held back, and did not use its direct power, preferring to delegate to others in the periphery and to act to appease territorial interests. The guiding principle was the wish to offload problems, which was different to the belief in the commanding role of the central state in other nations. This accommodation was a clever strategy even if in the end it was unsustainable. Showing remarkable intelligence, the centre recognised that attempts to centralise power would be futile given the complexity of the tasks it faced in governing the periphery. Bulpitt correctly argued that formally centralised systems often lacked state power. Local elites used their resources and skills to capture the bureaucrats in the decentralised or field offices of central state and the practical discretion of local authorities and other public bodies often negated the formal allocation of powers to the central authority. In some ways the managers of the UK state were too wily to be caught up in this trap, realising the myth of the efficacy of the one and indivisible state. But the subtlety of the exercise of power also affected the stability of the administration of the periphery because the very elites the centre sought to control gradually weakened their hold on their local followers, possibly as a result of accommodation with the centre and its ambiguous policies. The centre sought to build up the legitimacy of its rule through adjustments and compromises; yet the absence of principle and the lack of concern with peripheral affairs may – in the long run – have fostered the decline of that authority and promoted challenges to it, partly because the regime lacked intellectual justification. Perfidious Albion in the end may get caught out!

It is difficult to know how Bulpitt evaluated this statecraft. The text seems to imply praise at this judicious and very British way of exercising power that wants to find pragmatic solutions rather than follow a grand design. The territorial code implies an acute sense of the limitations of government, which draws on the liberal political tradition, and again marks out the UK from France with its direct controls over the localities and its concern to impose a civil code wherever there was domestic administration, such as in Algeria. The strategic retreat may in the end be a more clever use of power and one more guaranteed to maintain the state's autonomy rather than being locked into drastic disputes. The centre recognised the sheer difficulty of delivering local services responsive to local people. Better to offload, and to manage from afar.

Bulpitt alluded to the link between the management of centre-periphery relations with the UK's other territorial strategy toward its empire. UK empire builders established strong links with local elites in Africa and India, much of the time seeking to govern indirectly and pragmatically. In the Twentieth Century central politicians, even imperialist ones, decided to retreat from empire once they had made the final calculation about the limits to its longevity – even if they had resolutely sought to hold on to these possessions in the face of nationalist rebellions. Again the contrast is with more the direct administrative approach to running other empires and their violent ends, such as with the French territories in Africa and Asia. But in Bulpitt you do not get direct praise of this approach to political management. Nor do you get much on the possible criticisms of this kind of politics, bar an aside about realism. The book informs the reader about the complicity and arrogance of the elites at the centre; their false sense of grandeur about their international role; the lack of planning; the tendency to move from to crisis to crisis; the propping up of reactionary elites in Northern Ireland; and the underlying instability of the system. But the text almost never makes judgements. This neutrality is a tribute to Bulpitt's scholarship. The book simply prompts more general thoughts about the nature of the governing system, both its good and bad points.

A SUMMARY OF THE ARGUMENT OF THE BOOK

So how does Bulpitt develop his argument? He decided that the first two chapters should be a literature review. He was determined to provide a critique of existing studies, from traditional accounts of central-local relations and federalism to Marxist approaches, which was a way of knocking out all accounts bar his own. This critique is probably less entertaining to read now than at the time it was written because – unlike Bulpitt's – many of these works have been largely forgotten. They concern debates that do not interest many academics much nowadays, though of course the term unitary state to describe the UK still dominates studies of comparative politics, and remains in need of a correction. Although the more historically-minded can easily start at chapter two or even three, these two opening chapters help the reader understand the intellectual contribution of this book. Studies of central-local relations were very institutionally-orientated at the time. They did not take into account the political and historical contexts of intergovernmental relationships and they vastly overstated the extent to which central government centralised local authorities. The internal colonialism thesis was flawed because it did not give enough attention to politics; it left out England and did not define the centre in spite of making some powerful insights into the way in which territorial identity had been maintained in modern economy. The main concepts in the federalism literature were not well adapted to the complex political geography and institutions of the UK.

Chapter two sets out the full thesis making it a good place for the reader to understand what is going on, especially the second half where he set out the term territorial politics and explained many of the other concepts. Bulpitt was a political scientist – he did not eschew theory. And these definitional sections are a model of clarity. Bulpitt was able to write with the fluency and perception of the historian, with an eye to events and their contexts; but he also set out the concepts and theory in an accessible style of writing. And his prose style is very good. He wrote with economy and precision, but also with his own voice using lively turns of phase. Then there are his humorous asides, especially in some of the footnotes.

Chapter three starts the story. Bulpitt went back to the eleventh century to explain the territorial character of English politics and its surrounding areas. It is a familiar tale, but with a spatial twist. It outlines the importance of the territorial dimension to the development of the state, which emerged without a clear strategy and vision. He developed the concepts as they described emerging practices; such as the role of parliament in maintaining links between court and country. He stressed the powerful assumptions behind the territorial management of the nations of the UK, which created a path dependency of practices and institutions. The overriding message is that the periphery largely governed itself in this period.

Chapter four is concerned with how the dual polity became established as the pre-modern political system adapted to industrialisation and economic development. Bulpitt rejected a simple modernisation hypothesis based on the homogenous spread of national political parties, the diffusion of the mass media and the rise of economic interdependence, largely because regional cultures and institutions had sustained themselves. In addition, he showed how the centre had become better organised and stronger in this period up to 1926, exercising more influence over matters in the periphery. It is a complex and fast-moving period of history, with challenges to the existing governing order, which makes it hard to identify the central elements and cohere them into one story and set of messages. Bulpitt's analytic and narrative skills keep the project on the road allowing the reader to see how political views and values were solidified in this period and were re-enforced by the particular choices elites made to deal with crises, particularly over Ireland.

Ireland takes up much space in chapter three, which deals with turbulence of its politics, the fight for independence, and how this struggle shaped UK territorial politics. Telling the story of Ireland is a hard feat to pull off given its complexity and the twists and turns to English policy, which moved from allowing authoritarian forms of rule to the inevitable periods of accommodation and compromise with its challengers. Ireland could have taken up the whole book, but Bulpitt's aim was to show how important it was in revealing the territorial code. Ireland's pre-independence history indicates how gradual were the solutions that emerged and showed the lack of planning at the centre in London. Most of all, the story illustrates one of the key causes of the asymmetry of territorial politics: the contrast in histories and political forces across the UK.

Chapter five is the core of the book, dealing with the period from 1926–1961 when the challenges to the territorial order had worked themselves out. It was the main period of stability of the dual polity. After the setting up of the Irish Free State, the rest of centre-periphery relations turned into consensual management, with a lack of detailed central invention, the weak organisation of the periphery and central accommodation with local elites, but also the under-representation of those elites in the centre. Bulpitt labelled this period the *Ancien Régime*, with relationships being mainly bureaucratic and administrative in character. He described the international and economic preoccupations of the centre, which encouraged its territorial indifference, so producing the varied kinds of institutional administration and differences in the content and quality of public services across the UK. The strategy of detached political management was successful because it produced stability, but it did enquire of a rational solution. It arguably succeeded in sustaining particularist loyalties, perhaps more than other states. The regime preserved many social institutions in the Celtic nations and allowed room for administrative autonomy, which may have prepared the ground for the assertion of peripheral political power at a later point in time. Bulpitt also discussed the political sociology of the centre. He was particularly interested in the dominance of the civil service and the small circles of personnel that occupy its highest ranks.

Chapter six is of particular interest for the contemporary reader, partly because the events are closer, but also because Bulpitt described the potential breakdown of the system, making the 21st century seem like less a radical break from the past, but more of another chapter in the long run decline of the dual polity and part of a continual search for a new territorial code. The book outlined the loss of confidence of the centre because of economic decline and the failures of international influence. The elites in the territories were no longer content to keep quiet within the framework of consensual politics, but they sought to challenge the regime in Northern Ireland and Scotland. Even rebellious local authorities sought to disrupt the code. The centre had also interfered with the periphery in ways that were not comprehensible to the dual polity, such as local government reorganisation, where both central and local government had signed up to modernisation. Bulpitt was careful not to herald the end of the system because many of the assumptions and practices carried on as before, which continued the historical narrative rather than broke off from it. He was wary of stating there was a new politics, seeing the rise of the Scottish National Party (SNP) as the only serious challenge to the old order, which he believed was fuelled by special circumstances. In the end the centre recovered its authority and confidence at the end of the 1970s.

Chapter Seven is again of interest to the contemporary reader because it discusses a period of great importance in UK politics, the period of Conservative rule in national government from 1979 under the leadership of Margaret Thatcher. Many writers regard this period as a fundamental break in the UK's political history (e.g. Gamble 1994). Particularly important was the change in the character of Conservative politics away from its belief in the importance of managing consensus towards the idea of using the power of the state to force through market-based policies. If this account were true, then it would be another death knell to the operation of traditional territorial politics, as it would imply the breakdown of the old existing code. Most of all Thatcherism implied criticism of the official mind, challenged traditional civil servants and questioned established institutions. The poll tax, formulated and introduced after Bulpitt wrote his book, would seem to represent the ultimate breakdown of the dual polity, and its early introduction in Scotland showed central contempt rather than indifference to the periphery. The tax, amongst other Conservative policies, contributed to the rise of Scottish national-ism, leading to the near electoral destruction of the Conservative Party in Scotland. The departure of the Conservatives from the territorial code could be seen as part of a series of events that led to the establishment of devolved politi-cal institutions after Labour came to power in national government in 1997.

It is no surprise that Bulpitt interpreted the Conservatives in power within his language of territorial management, but he is rather ambiguous as to whether the period was an attempt to revive the territorial code or was a signal of its break-down. He stated that the Conservatives believed their assertive strategy would rebalance central-local relations and thereby quieten the political conflict that had emerged from the expansion of the state and from the rising expectations of dependent publics and self-interested professionals. In the end economic domi-nance based on the prosperity of London and the South East of England would return and international influence would follow. The dual polity would return once more. But Bulpitt recognised the centralisation of the period as a particular and new form of statecraft, one more wedded to a formalistic interpretation of parlia-mentary sovereignty rather than a restrained version of limits to central interven-tion that had prevailed in the dual polity era. The ambiguity of the old system had allowed a more assertive form of rule to emerge without much constitutional debate. Taking away powers of local government broke no constitutional law or convention, but it did change the rules of the game. He also saw that the new regime had limitations because it was unlikely to implement its policies success-fully. Bulpitt expressed doubts, echoed by many others, that they could have real-istically achieved their centralising objective. He implied there would always be temptations to go back to the old territorial code. But it is also clear that once the state had asserted its new-found authority there was no going back to the old days.

With hindsight it is slightly frustrating to read this penultimate chapter: it con-tains what appears to be unnecessary detail on the less interesting phase of the Conservatives in power. At the time of writing, Bulpitt did not know of the miner's strike of 1984–5, the defeat of radical local government by legislation and finan-cial controls, the abolition of the GLC and the metropolitan authorities in 1986, the poll tax introduced in 1990, and the fall of Thatcher in the same year. Even his much-cited 1986 article on Thatcherism, where he summarises the mix between pragmatism and the search for a code of governance, which characterised this period of rule, only covered the first post-1979 administration. But it was only in the second and third terms that this regime experimented with radical decentralist politics to the discredit of old systems of territorial management. Overall Bulpitt was wise to conclude that it was not clear whether the territorial code would sur-vive Thatcherism, which implied he thought it was under threat. Finally, the con-clusion sums up the book rather than develops or pulls together the analysis, and the 'astrology' section feels dated now with its references to Bennism, the Alternative Economic Strategy and the Social Democratic Party.

SOME COMMON CRITICISMS

In reviewing *Territory and Power*, it would be fair to mention some of the critical thinking that this book can provoke and where appropriate to provide some counters to these lines of thought. The first criticism, which was levelled by Rhodes (1988, 31), is that the concepts are hard to define, such as centre and periphery – they are not like institutions with clear borders. If they are ambiguous, they are hard to research, which makes it difficult to operationalise Bulpitt's conceptual scheme as part of a programme of study. In its place, Rhodes offered a definition of territorial politics that was wider than intergovernmental relations, which included institutions, interests and networks, but was not as broad as Bulpitt's. In part, Bulpitt anticipated the difficulty of defining terms for, as with all good writers, he was his own best critic. But lack of ease of definition does not mean lack of importance. Some topics are harder to research than others. Researchers should not just choose the easy topics as that would bias research, possibly toward the less interesting but measurable aspects of political behaviour. What matters is whether the analysis is effective and adds explanation. In addition, it is interesting to note that Rhodes' definition of territorial politics has not taken off as the starting point for researchers, and the policy networks paradigm he championed only had only a brief, if colourful, life (Dowding 1995).

The second criticism is that Bulpitt offered a top-down perspective, with a rather dismissive account of the periphery. He may have failed to appreciate the power of the peripheral forces and how they have shaped politics of the UK. This focus was partly a consequence of concentrating on the values and actions of the elites, both at the centre but also on the elite collaborators in the periphery, which means the mass movements below the elites were not part of the analysis, bar references to peripheral dissidents. Keating (1998, 2005) is a good example of this critical view, and he has a much more detailed analysis rather than the literature review Bulpitt offered. Others consider that Scotland had an extensive civil society before devolution (Brown *et al* 1996). This kind of criticism does have some merit because *Territory and Power* lacks detail about the decentralist aspect of territorial politics. But Bulpitt quite forcefully said at the outset that his book was about the perceptions of the centre, which was a deliberate choice on his part to correct an imbalance in the literature. What Bulpitt was saying – like all researchers – is that he needed to focus on particular kinds of activity for the sake of clarity, to answer the question he has set and to make a logical argument rather than indulge in thick description. This does not mean that other approaches stressing the role of the periphery are wrong; they are probably right. But they do not invalidate Bulpitt's exercise either.

The third criticism is that he created a self-referential system of thinking that made all outcomes automatic consequences of the framework. Like the Marxists he criticised, Bulpitt may have elaborated a total intellectual framework. All action is contained within it so it can never be confirmed or refuted – each twist and turn is the inevitable part of the conceptual system. Territorial politics becomes a language that accommodates any territorial arrangement. The term 'territorial code' can be applied with infinite flexibility to any regime, whether decentralising to or interfering with the periphery. To be fair, Bulpitt was as much concerned with breakdown and change as with stability, which implies the territorial code could fade when under challenge, and which he started to describe. But it is the case that he presented no hypothesis that can be tested. And it is hard *a priori* to think what predictions the framework produces. Did it predict the crisis of the system in the 1960s, for example? There is no model of political behaviour, more an assumption of a system that moves toward equilibrium, which occasionally breaks down, but often rights itself again, which gives the book more of a hint of functionalism and thus circularity in its analysis (the reference to Shils does not dispel this suspicion!). On the other hand, what historical account produces predictions? Histories succeed to the extent they offer explanation and provide better understandings. *Territory and Power* succeeds massively on these terms.

The fourth criticism is that it is possible to offer other interpretations of the historical account than the one Bulpitt provided in *Territory and Power*. In particular, it may not be right to see the UK in such a decentralised fashion, with such a soft use of parliamentary sovereignty. The term 'dual polity' is not right because there has never been a decade when central government had not sought to restructure decentralist politics: the debacle of Poplarism in the 1920s, the nationalisations of the 1930s and 1940s, the creation of the welfare state, and the formation of the central grant regime in 1958. The financial angle is a powerful weapon of centralisation as England ended up with one of the only examples of full-needs equalisation in central grant distribution where there was no strong local tax or taxes to compensate. This helped sustain central control as did the Treasury's supervision of the finances of the territories of the UK. So when was the period of the dual polity? Does it amount to what the French call *les trentes glorieuses*, a period of economic and policy stability that occurred in a few decades after the Second World War? It is probably the case that the centre was always more interested in what happened in the periphery than Bulpitt gave credit for, but it is hard to resolve this question authoritatively either way as there are still few published histories of intergovernmental relations in the UK.

A fifth criticism is that Bulpitt provided scant direct evidence to support his claims about the intentions of the centre. He consulted no documents or official records. The text often just states what Bulpitt thought alongside his summary of the secondary literature. The book often relied on assertions. And *Territory and Power* is quite a short book for such a long period of history. But again, in an effective auto-critique, Bulpitt admitted this limitation from the start, regarding the exercise as interpretative only. The lack of research is intrinsic to the idea of a literature review; and the book is at base a conceptually-driven exercise. An account of this kind could not have used primary sources. It is really up to others, such as Bradbury (2008), to apply his framework to carry out further empirical research.

The sixth critique is that globalisation and Europeanisation have removed the issue of territorial politics as a site for management by the UK central state.

Globalisation supposedly removes or limits the role of the central state in many of its traditional activities, but this argument cannot be really taken seriously given the sustained power of contemporary states (Hirst and Thompson 1995). Moreover, Bulpitt was very interested in the way in which the UK state managers dealt with and sought to overcome economic constraints. The same argument can be placed against Europeanisation. Far from creating three levels of government, the impact of the European Union on sub-national territories has been limited to strategic bids for funds under the control of central government in London (Bache 1998). The UK state has integrated EU procedures into its existing codes and working practices (Bulmer and Burch 2005). In the end, as Bulpitt explained, the managers of the state sought international arrangements that promoted their overall project. The EU was no exception to this strategy.

The seventh is that the thesis is not relevant to the territorial politics of today. The devolution of power to Scotland, Wales and Northern Ireland would seem to contradict its central thesis. Moreover, the rise of the electoral fortunes of SNP, which held the largest number of seats in the Scottish Parliament after the elections of May 2007, allowing its leader, Alex Salmond, to assume the post of first minister, would seem to show that a particular period of territorial politics in the UK had finally concluded. The existence of fully-functioning formal democratic institutions to govern the nations of the UK would appear to show the predominance of formal rules rather than the informal code. There is now what appears to be straight-forward bargaining between leaders in one political system with those in the others, rather than the centre's incorporation of local elites of yesteryear. More generally, there appears to be a dissembling of the old centre with its self-confidence and hidden assumptions. In its place, a public media-driven culture has emerged, where all issues, including centre-peripheral ones, are up for attention. Most of all, the centre appears obsessed about the administration of public services in England: detailed regulation, target setting, monitoring, inspection, and direct intervention when public services go wrong. Civil servants are now not expected to sit in Whitehall thinking about overall policy, but to be involved in its delivery. The *Ancien Régime* is dead, so it seems.

But the whole point of Bulpitt's book was to insist on how territorial politics was both embedded in the past and subject to challenge and change. The last chapters showed the system decaying as early as the 1960s, so that the momentous events of the 2000s are part of a long-running show, particularly of Scottish nationalism, that have shaped the territorial politics of the UK. During the 1960s and 1970s, there were challenges to the negotiated order in the form of demands for more autonomy and the failure of the centre in London to ensure the cooperation of local and regional elites. How much has changed since then? Even though the appearance of these new institutions resembles the beginning of a new order, they still operate within the rules, norms and political logic of the UK. Devolution politics still involves extensive informal bargaining with a London elite that is largely disinterested in the periphery, except for short-term electoral calculation, and which moves ahead pragmatically in a series of unplanned steps. The centre continues to operate from a position of weakness rather than strength; and even the currently-configured peripheral actors tend to lack full political power and dominance. Most of all, the architects of devolution need to come to terms with the messy manner in which the new institutions were created, which derives from the lack of a systematic logic in the past – the different arrangements for the countries of the UK and the failure of the British state to create a general territorial settlement in the form of consistently applied regional or state governments. The incremental path, sustaining the variable geometry of the UK, makes the devolution settlements an extension of the politics Bulpitt described so well back in 1983. The new is not so new after all – the terminology and sets of practices remain embedded in UK political life.

Moreover, it is possible to use Bulpitt's framework to help understand the changes and their historical context by using elements of the code to describe the statecraft of late Thatcherism and of New Labour itself. Thatcherism may have been a particular expression of a need to get back to the old code or a new version of it. In Thatcherism there was a desire to re-create the detached state, presiding over economic success, with the idea that once the reform of local government had taken place, it could be left alone once again. But this political project failed, even with the radical right's persistent strategy to restructure public services and to reduce the size of state. The failure during this turbulent phase of territorial management left UK politics open again for a new attempt to manage territorial politics, perhaps in a more consensual manner. New Labour attempted a territorial accord through devolution, partially influenced by the periphery that had colonised the centre, wishing to move territorial matters off the agenda (Bradbury 2006). New Labour wanted to solve the problem of territorial discontent, and to create a new equilibrium of political forces across the UK, which involved concessions and an implied compact between the politicians in the centre and the periphery. As Bradbury argues (2008), this new settlement acknowledged the weakness of the centre and also of the peripheral elites too. Those in the north of England, for example, were unable to deliver to the centre a vote for devolution, which helped collapse this attempt at decentralisation. As with the earlier settlements, devolution may itself be unstable partly from the failure to think through the constitutional principles. As before, the role and views of central elites influenced the strategies designed to rebalance the unstable institutional framework. There are continual tensions in territorial politics in the post-devolution period, which resemble some of those of earlier years, where the periphery struggled to find the political language and the will to break from a previous system of territorial management, but where the weak centre cannot quite recreate the consensual management of the glory days of the dual polity.

Even the control over public services is asymmetric with little intervention and only a weak form of new public management reform in Scotland, Wales and Northern Ireland. In England, the central state is keen to create detached systems of management through public agencies and semi-independent regulators, rather than hands-on control, and the end of the Blair years found New Labour wanting to release central controls, partly because of the perceived costs of direct intervention in the matters of the periphery. Even the creation of central agencies since 1987 re-created the classic divisions between types of civil servant: the one in the court that sits in central Whitehall and those concerned with the messy business of delivery in the agencies in the country, a form of analysis captured in Dunleavy's (1991) bureau-shaping model.

CONCLUSIONS

Any valid intellectual project has its critics, and the ones that operate below the radar of comment usually lack value. Moreover, many of the common criticisms set out above are not entirely valid or suggest further lines of enquiry and a need to deepen the research rather than a rejection of the book's central themes. *Territory and Power* remains a satisfying read, partly because of the narrative, but mainly because of its clear conceptualisation, where its terms and concepts have subsequently entered conventional thinking in academic circles. The language that today's students of politics use to describe the United Kingdom and its messy asymmetrical structures derive in part from this book. For Bulpitt anticipates much of the current debate about path dependence and the importance of history in the new institutionalism (Bradbury 2006). The book is a statement of a particular culture and system of territorial politics that was prominent in the twentieth century at the same time as being a theoretical treatise on the UK state. It provides a backdrop to evaluate the current state of territorial and devolved politics. Most of all, it provides a set of concepts and a subtle account of the exercise of power that can apply to any governing system. The reader is likely to be much wiser from reading or re-reading this classic work.

1. I am very grateful to the series editors, Alan Ware and Vincent Hoffmann-Martinot, for inviting me to write this introduction and to June Bulpitt for giving the ECPR the permission to re-issue the book. I also thank Jonathan Bradbury for comments on a draft of the introduction, which allowed me to correct some errors in my thinking.

BIBLIOGRAPHY

Ashford, Douglas (1977), 'Are Britain and France unitary?', *Comparative Politics*, Vol. 9, No. 4, 483–499.

Bache, Ian (1998) *The Politics of European Union Regional Policy: Multi-Level Governance or Flexible Gatekeeping?,* Contemporary European Studies Series, Sheffield: UACES/Sheffield Academic Press.

Bentley, Michael, and Stevenson, John (1983), *High and Low Politics in Modern Britain: Ten Studies,* Oxford: Clarenden.

Bradbury, Jonathan (2006), 'Territory and Power revisited: theorising territorial politics in the United Kingdom after devolution', *Political Studies*, 54 (3), 559–582.

Bradbury, Jonathan (2008), *Union and Devolution: Territorial Politics in the United Kingdom*, forthcoming Palgrave

Brown, Alice, McCrone, David and Paterson, Lindsay (1996), *Politics and Society in Scotland*, Macmillan.

Bulmer, Simon and Burch, Martin (2005), 'The Europeanization of UK Government: from quiet revolution to explicit step-change?', *Public Administration*, vol. 83, no. 4, 861–90.

Bulpitt, Jim (1988), 'Rational politicians and conservative statecraft in the open polity', in Peter Byrd (ed.), *British Foreign Policy under Thatcher* (Oxford: Philip Allan, 1988), 214–256.

Dowding, Keith (1995) 'Model or Metaphor? A Critical Review of the Policy Network Approach', *Political Studies* 43: 136–58.

Dunleavy, Patrick (1991), *Democracy, Bureaucracy and Public Choice*, London: Pearson Education.

Gamble, Andrew (1994), *The Free Economy and the Strong State: The Politics of Thatcherism*, Basingtoke: Macmillan.

Grémion, Pierre (1976), *Le Pouvoir Périphérique, Bureaucrates et Notables Dans le Système Politique Français*, Paris: Le Seuil, 1976.

Hampton, W. (1966), 'The county as a political unit' *Parliamentary Affairs*, 19: 462–74.

Heclo, Hugh. and Wildavsky, Aaron (1974), *The Private Government of Public Money*, London: Macmillan.

Hirst, Paul and Thompson, Graham (1995), 'Globalization and the future of the nation-state', *Economy and Society*, 24, 3, 408–442.

Keating, Michael (1998), *The New Regionalism in Western Europe. Territorial Restructuring and Political Change*, Northampton: Edward Elgar.

Keating, Michael (2005), *The Government of Scotland: Public Policy Making After Devolution*, Edinburgh: Edinburgh University Press.

Rhodes, Rod (1988), *Beyond Westminster and Whitehall*, London: Routledge.

Richardson, Jeremey, & Jordan, Grant (1979), *Governing Under Pressure*, Oxford: Martin Robertson.

Rokkan, Stem & Unwin, Derek (1983), *Economy, Territory, Identity Politics of West European Peripheries*, London: Sage Publications.

Tarrow, Sidney (1977), *Between Center and Periphery: Grassroots Politicians in Italy and France*, Yale University Press.

Ware, A. (1987) *Citizens, Parties and the State*, Oxford: Oxford University Press.

Peter John

Institute for Political and Economic Governance, School of Social Sciences, University of Manchester

ACKNOWLEDGEMENTS

I owe a general academic debt to the members of the Political Studies Association Work Group on United Kingdom Politics. They were forced to listen to and comment critically on earlier versions of most of the chapters in this book. I owe a particular debt to Richard Rose, the founder of the Group, and the man who kept it 'rolling' and made it so productive. He encouraged me to pursue and complete this project although, like others, he disagreed with many of the views expressed. Needless to say I am solely responsible for those views and any factual errors which may be present. My thanks also go to Mrs Iris Host and Mrs Gillian Chiles, secretaries in the Department of Politics at the University of Warwick. They dealt effectively and good humouredly with my deplorable handwriting. Finally, writing books usually means that wives and children suffer in a variety of ways. Mine certainly did. To them I owe the biggest debt of all.

introduction

It would be presumption in me to do more than make a case.[1]

This is a small book on a big subject. The subject is territorial politics in the United Kingdom and the power relations associated with it over time. Territorial politics can be defined as that arena of political activity concerned with the relations between the central political institutions in the capital city and those interests, communities, political organisations and governmental bodies outside the central institutional complex, but within the accepted boundaries of the state, which possess, or are commonly perceived to possess, a significant geographical or local/regional character.

This definition of our subject matter points to a more extensive analytical scenario than usual. The aim is to examine the general relationship between national and local politics throughout the United Kingdom. In other words we are concerned with what can be labelled (in terms of the principal actors involved) Centre-periphery relations. There is no doubt that this approach faces a number of problems, the most important of which are discussed in Chapter 2 below.[2] The justification for the exercise is fourfold. First, the traditional obsession of British academics with elected local authorities and their relations with the central departments of government (commonly labelled central-local relations) has not yielded much that is useful for the social sciences.[3] Secondly, even if we wish to continue this interest in the 'foreign affairs' of local governments it is clear that these affairs can no longer be studied in isolation from the general pattern of relations between national and local politics. Thirdly, the United Kingdom is a diverse territorial estate containing four major sections, England, Scotland, Wales and Northern Ireland. The number of case studies of its separate parts has increased markedly over recent years. The United Kingdom as a unit of study, however, has been neglected.[4] Finally, it is time to see what happens to some of the accepted ideas in this field when the subject matter is opened up in the ways suggested above.

Two further points about the exercise need to be mentioned. One is that the analysis is historical or developmental: territorial politics in the United Kingdom is examined over time. The other is that the discussion adopts a perspective from the Centre. It is concerned with the development of territorial politics from the point of view of the problems faced by the authorities in London and the various ways in which these problems have been resolved. This perspective is to a large extent a forced one, since it is doubtful if any macro-study of territorial politics can be carried out without viewing the subject from the Centre. Two key questions are pursued, namely: how do we go about studying territorial politics? and, how has territorial politics in the United Kingdom developed over time? Given the nature of the subject, the present state of research, and the unfortunate divorce between history and political science in Britain, these are difficult questions to tackle and capable of producing a variety of plausible answers. Hence, what follows should be regarded as a preliminary interpretation, a 'case', a point of view and no more. If it is accepted as plausible, if it stimulates argument, then it will have served its purpose. The invitation is on the table for someone else to pursue a similar exercise more thoroughly.

The analysis proceeds as follows. The chapters in Part I deal with two topics: a critical assessment of the existing models customarily employed to describe the structure of territorial politics in the United Kingdom and the outline of an alternative framework of analysis for the subject. Part II is concerned with the development of territorial politics in the United Kingdom. Chapter 3 examines the process by which the initial territorial Union was manufactured. Chapter 4 looks at the challenges to the old territorial order which emerged in the period after 1870. Chapter 5 examines the outcome of those challenges, the very peculiar territorial regime which operated throughout the United Kingdom in the period between the mid-1920s and the early 1960s. Chapters 6 and 7 attempt to identify what has happened to that regime over the last two decades.

The principal themes which emerge from this exercise are four. First, over time, territorial politics in the United Kingdom has been characterised by a structural dichotomy between Centre and periphery. To put the point in seventeenth-century and eighteenth-century political terminology, the basic division has been between the court and the country. To begin with, the Centre meant the court. Later it came to mean the Cabinet and then a 'political-administrative community' of senior ministers and top civil servants. Whatever the precise location, a court ethos has always dominated the Centre's activities. The periphery, or country, was usually, from the Centre's viewpoint, all other places. In other words, in terms of territorial management England was a part of the periphery. Secondly, the Centre or court sought increasingly to operate a distinction between 'High Politics' and 'Low Politics'. The former involved matters which, at any one time, were regarded as primarily the responsibility of the Centre, the latter covered those residual matters which in normal circumstances could be left to governments and interests in the periphery. Thirdly, in pursuit of this High/Low politics distinction, what can be called the official mind at the Centre developed an operational code for territorial politics which emphasised the desirability of autonomy for the Centre in matters of 'High Politics' and indirect rule of the periphery by local elite collaborators. In practice, this system involved an operational separation of powers between the national institutions of government in London and a considerable amount of reciprocal autonomy for peripheral governments and interests. The apotheosis of the Centre's official mind was realised in the period roughly from 1926 to 1961. In those years a Dual Polity operated in territorial terms: both Centre and periphery achieved a relative autonomy from one another, the degree of interpretation between national and local politics was low. Finally, much of what has happened in territorial politics since the early 1960s must be seen in terms of the emergence of various challenges to that Dual Polity. Up to the present, it is argued, the most serious challenges have come not from the periphery but the Centre itself.

NOTES

1 Dicey citing Burke. See A. V. Dicey, *England's Case Against Home Rule* (London, 1887), p. 289.
2 One unfortunate consequence is the enforced employment of what many may regard as a pompous and obfuscating vocabulary.
3 See Howard A. Scarrow, 'New perspectives on British local government', *World Politics* (1973); R. A. W. Rhodes, 'Analysing intergovernmental relations', *European Journal of Political Research* (1980); John Dearlove, *The Politics of Policy in Local Government* (Cambridge, 1973); and *The Reorganisation of British Local Government* (Cambridge, 1979).
4 See J. Barry Jones, *A Register of Research Into United Kingdom Politics* (Strathclyde, Glasgow, 1978).

part one
Territory and Power

chapter one | some existing approaches assessed

Here then are three sources of vague and incorrect definitions: indistinctiveness of the object, imperfections of the organ of conception, inadequateness of the vehicle of ideas. Any one of these must produce a certain degree of obscurity.[1]

INTRODUCTION

Over time, academics and others have developed three major approaches (with associated models) to describe and compare the structure of central–local relations, or territorial politics, in the political systems of the western world. These are:
(i)   Territorial systems analysis, which classifies states as either confederations or federations, or unitary systems.
(ii) The centralisation/decentralisation dichotomy which describes governmental systems as centralised or decentralised, or subject to more or less centralisation or decentralisation.
(iii) The internal colonisation thesis which argues that *within* many societies territorial politics is structured in ways similar to imperial or colonial relations *between* states.[2]
These approaches and models have assumed a significant displacement in the literature and debate on territorial politics in the United Kingdom. Thus, traditionally, the United Kingdom was described as *either* a unitary Union, not a federation, *or* a decentralised partnership between the central and local governments, *or* as an integrated society exhibiting no signs of internal territorial exploitation. Since the early 1960s these models have retained their popularity, although significant additional changes of emphasis have occurred. For example, the debate which developed as a result of the electoral successes of Scottish and Welsh nationalism gave rise to the following rival arguments: the unitary nature of the Union should be defended at all costs; the Union should be reformed on the basis of schemes for regional devolution, which would retain, even enhance, its unitary character; the United Kingdom should adopt a federal constitution and system of government; and Scotland and Wales should be allowed to secede from the unitary Union and then adopt a confederal-type relationship with England. Again, those wishing to

achieve peacefully a united Ireland sometimes talk in terms of a federal Ireland, with perhaps a loose confederal-type link with Britain. Alternatively, the structure of central–local relations in Britain has often been described as moving away from the traditional decentralised partnership between central and local government to a more centralised system in which local authorities are increasingly treated as agents of the central departments. Finally, it has now become popular in certain quarters to argue that the United Kingdom has always exhibited many of the characteristics of an internal colonial society, that the English have exploited their 'Celtic' neighbours.

The purpose of this chapter is to assess each of these approaches in terms of their internal coherence and the extent to which they adequately relate to the process of territorial politics in the West. This will enable us to come to some initial conclusions regarding the utility of their continued employment in the specific theatre of the United Kingdom.

TERRITORIAL SYSTEMS ANALYSIS

This can be labelled the classical approach to the analysis of territorial politics. It embodies two major themes. First, states are divided into three broad types, namely confederations, federations and unitary systems. Secondly, it suggests that each of these territorial systems is associated with a distinctive set of values at birth, and, thereafter, a distinctive constitutional design, political process and political output. Federations, for example, are regarded as allowing more local and regional autonomy than unitary systems, and yet more successful in combining the demands of unity, diversity and effective government than confederations.

The discussion which follows will be concerned initially to identify and evaluate the analytical methods employed to support this threefold classification. This should enable us to assess the utility of this whole approach for the analysis of territorial politics. One preliminary observation is required. Territorial systems analysis has been dominated by people primarily interested in federalism and federations. As a result confederations and unitary systems have become residual elements in the classification, important only in so far as they help to highlight the grand designs of federal analysis. The unfortunate results of this biased perspective will be noted below. At this point it is only necessary to observe that any discussion of territorial systems must inevitably emphasise federal material. This is not wholly disadvantageous since, in many ways, the best examinations of the territorial political process we have are analyses of federal politics.

Two analytical methods have been employed to support the threefold classification – the yardstick and the essential principles methods.

The yardstick method
This differentiates territorial systems on the basis of a number of constitutional and institutional yardsticks. The following appear to be the most popular:[3]

(a) the sources of central and regional government authority;

(b) whether or not secession by the constituent states is permitted;

(c) the scope and nature of central authority;

(d) the extent to which the composition of each level of government is independent of the other;

(e) the constitutional amendment process.

When these yardsticks are applied to the three types of territorial system the following results are obtained:

Confederations

(a) The central authority is established by the previously independent constituent units.

(b) The constituent states can secede from the confederation.

(c) The functions of the central authority are limited to a few areas *delegated* to it by the states: the Centre cannot operate directly on the citizens of the constituent states, only indirectly via the state governments.

(d) The central authority is composed of delegates from the constituent states, it has no independent existence: Central action often requires unanimous or overall majority support from these delegates.

(e) The constitutional amending process is controlled by the constituent states.

Federations

(a) Both the constituent states and the central authority are established and guaranteed by the constitution.

(b) The constituent states are not permitted to secede from the federation.

(c) Both the states and the central authority receive their powers from the constitution: the Centre can act directly on the citizens of the individual states: both the Centre and the states get significant powers.

(d) Both the states and the central authority are compositionally independent of the other, in other words, the Centre is not made up of delegates from the states: unequal states are represented equally in one branch of the central legislature.

(e) Neither the states nor the central authority can unilaterally amend the constitution and a supreme court exists to referee, according to the constitution, disputes between states and central authority.

Unitary systems

(a) Local and regional governments are established by the central authority, which can abolish them at will.

(b) Local and regional governments are not permitted to secede from the polity.

(c) The powers of local governments are delegated or devolved from the Centre, which can revoke them at will, and the Centre acts directly on the citizens of the separate local governments.

(d) The central authority has an independent composition, it is not composed of delegates from local or regional governments, and the Centre can suspend the operations of local councils.

(e) Local governments play no role in the constitutional amending process and the Centre's actions towards them cannot be declared unconstitutional by any court.

Assessment

This method of differentiating territorial systems can be criticised on a number of counts. First, even if the yardsticks listed above are accepted on an individual basis they reveal no general method for distinguishing between the *three* types of territorial system. In most instances they can differentiate only one from two: and usually it is the confederation which is the singleton. This applies, for example, to the yardsticks relating to secession, the independent composition of the Centre and the direct impact of the Centre on the citizens of constituent areas, all of which are characteristics of both federations and unitary systems. Secondly, past and present territorial systems have rarely followed these yardsticks very closely in their constitutional and institutional make-up: the 1781 Articles of Confederation in the United States did not envisage secession whereas Soviet federal constitution does; the second chamber in the West German federation (the Bundesrat) is composed of delegates from the state governments; and the Italian unitary constitution guarantees the existence of certain types of local and regional governments. In fact, instances can be found which break practically every yardstick listed: as presented above, they merely reflect common, and often mistaken, assumptions about the federal and unitary constitutional settlements of the United States and the United Kingdom. Thirdly, and of special significance given the last point, this method makes no attempt to weigh the yardsticks employed in terms of their relative importance to the differentiating exercise. Hence, there is no way of assessing the impact of their presence or absence on the territorial systems concerned. Finally, this method provides us only with a set of static constitutional and institutional designs; it says nothing about the political process associated with those designs, and it is not easy to infer one either.

Criticising the yardstick method requires no great effort, its defects are obvious. However, if we want to play the territorial systems game, it is probably the best method of differentiation we have. This becomes clear when we examine the second method.

The essential principles method

Criticisms such as those detailed above have led to a decline in the popularity of the yardstick method of analysis. At worst it is regarded as positively misleading, at best as an unsophisticated technique able to point only to some consequential, and primarily institutional, attributes of territorial systems. Systems differentiation in terms of *ad hoc* criteria, it is argued, should be dropped in favour of the search for the essential principles underlying the process of government and politics in the different systems. This sort of approach has been primarily concerned to discover the basic characteristics of federalism and federations. As a result, it is best examined and assessed in terms of the three federal models it has produced, and the inferences that can be drawn from these concerning the essential principles underlying confederations and unitary systems.

(i) The dual federal model
This view of federalism emphasises the twin themes of the equality and independence of the two levels of government, central and regional: equality in terms of the absence of the formal subordination of one level to the other; independence in terms of exclusive jurisdiction granted to each by the constitution. The result is a dual system of government in which the different levels of government have relatively little to do with each other. It is this combination of intergovernmental equality, independence and duality which serves to mark off federations from confederations and unitary systems.

The best illustration of this model in the academic literature is K. C. Wheare's *Federal Government.*[4] To put it another way: Wheare's concept of federalism can only be understood in terms of the dual federal model. Briefly, Wheare was concerned to isolate for purposes of comparative analysis the basic federal principle, a principle which, in his view, had to faithfully reflect the dominant characteristics of territorial government in the United States, his paradigm case of a federal polity. On this basis Wheare concluded the federal principle was 'the method of dividing power so the general and regional governments are each, within a sphere, coordinate and independent'. By 'coordinate' Wheare meant 'of equal status' and by 'independent', as it later transpired, he meant the 'autonomy' of each level of government in those policy spheres allocated it by the constitution. This principle enabled territorial systems to be assessed and labelled 'federal' according to the extent to which it was embodied 'predominantly' in both their constitutions and practical operation of government.

The results of this analytical scheme were interesting, if somewhat exclusive. Three systems, the United States, Australia and Switzerland, were found to be predominantly federal in both the senses mentioned above. Wheare, however, regarded the operation of government (or the practice of the constitution) as a more reliable test for federalism than the formal law of the constitution. As a result, Canada qualified for inclusion in his list of federations. Its formal constitutional provisions were assessed as only *quasi-federal*, but, Wheare argued, in terms of the actual operation of government (determined in large part by the Quebec problem), Canada could be regarded as predominantly federal. This co-ordinate and independent federal principle was also employed by Wheare to suggest the essential principles underlying confederations and unitary systems. Thus he defined confederations in terms of the subordination and dependence of the central government on the regional governments, and unitary systems in terms of the subordination and dependence of the regional (or local) governments on the Centre. Wheare, then, produced a federal principle which pointed to the dual federal model, and, in turn, this led him to a very convenient method of differentiating between the three kinds of territorial system.

(ii) The co-operative federal model

This is an attempt to up-date federal analysis. It accepts, as one commentator has put it, that: 'Under the heat and pressure generated by social and economic changes in the twentieth century, the distinct strata of the older federalism have begun to melt and flow into one another'.[5] Thus the dual federal model promoted by Wheare (and many before him) is discarded, not only because it has been destroyed (so it is suggested) by the growth of 'big government', but also as a result of the perceived *political* interpenetration between the two levels of government. Thus, federations are now distinguished not by governmental duality, but by intergovernmental *co-operation*. This co-operative model of federalism is now the academic orthodoxy on the subject. Significantly, it was later accepted by Wheare. Once again, the main themes associated with this model can be most conveniently, if briefly, illustrated if we look at one example of its employment, in this case M. J. C. Vile's *The Structure of American Federalism*.[6]

Vile's analysis of United States federalism led him to conclude that its operation could only be understood in terms of a series of complex relationships between the federal constitutional structure, the 'federal attitude' (or the 'mental approach' towards governmental problems), political forces such as parties and pressure groups, and the supreme court – relationships which interpenetrated and affected government and politics at both the national and state levels. In short, for Vile, any definition of federations (and other territorial systems) had to be securely rooted in contemporary political practice. It was this perspective which suggested that concepts such as 'co-ordinate' and 'independent' had only a limited meaning outside the sphere of constitutional law. Independence floundered when faced with the mass of contacts and co-operative devices which marked intergovernmental relations in the twentieth century. Similarly, co-ordinate (or equal) status was difficult to sustain when the states had varying relationships with different elements of the federal government in different policy areas, relationships which often ended with defeat (and therefore subordination) for one or other level of government. Nevertheless, Vile, like most co-operative federalism theorists, was not prepared to jettison the independent and co-ordinate concepts altogether. As he put it, if in any system the co-ordinate and independent status of the two levels of government were completely lost, then the resulting situation would be 'not characteristic', even a 'denial' of the federal spirit.

All this led Vile to conclude that the essence of modern federalism (and much nineteenth-century experience as well) was found in the mutual political *interdependence* – a balance of power – between the two levels of government, national and state. This contrasted with unitary systems where 'the regional governments are dependent upon the central government, but the later is independent of them', and with confederations where 'the central government is dependent upon the regions, but they are independent of it'. Federations, in fact, represent a *via media* between the two extremes, in other words, 'a system of government in which neither level of government is wholly dependent upon the other, nor wholly independent of the other. There is in fact a mutual interdependence...'.

(iii) The organic federal model
This is the latest model to emerge. It has been defined in the following terms:

> Organic federalism is federalism in which the Centre has such extensive pow-
> ers and gives such a strong lead to Regions in the most important areas of their
> individual as well as co-operative activities that the political taxonomist may
> hesitate to describe the result as federal at all...the organic stage begins to
> develop as the Regions lose any substantial bargaining capacity in relation to
> the Centre.[7]

This view of federalism has surfaced primarily as a result of post-war developments in certain European federations, such as Austria and West Germany, developments which revolve round the supposed lack of support given by the public to
the federal units, the wide range of important functions given to the central authorities, and the increasing tendency to use the constituent states as administrative
agencies for central policies. All this, of course, is in marked contrast to the federalism pictured by both the dual and co-operative models. Some commentators
have argued that both the United States and Australia have or are acquiring the
characteristics of this model. For example, Michael Reagan's *The New Federalism*
argues that as a result of successive supreme court interpretations of the constitution, the rapid development of central grants-in-aid to the states, and the increasing contacts between the federal and local governments (thus bypassing the
states), the twin ideas of divided sovereignty and equal status as the basis of federalism have ceased to have any meaning in the United States.[8] According to
Reagan 'no sphere of life is beyond the reach of national government'. Forty years
of increasing centralisation has meant that the only features of the traditional federal structure remaining are the existence of the states within their traditional
boundaries and their continued equal representation in the senate. The result, in
this instance, is labelled 'permissive federalism' (which approximates in meaning
to 'organic'), a situation where the main lines of policy are laid down by the
Centre.

   Clearly, if this model of federalism is accepted then the distinction between a
federation and a unitary system becomes blurred and the stage is set for the demise
of the threefold classification and the construction, perhaps, of a simple twofold
typology of confederations and unitary/federal states.

Assessment
As indicated, the essential principles method is today the most popular approach
to territorial systems analysis. Despite this popularity it can be criticised on a number of counts.[9] To begin with, there is what many would regard as an undue
reliance on vague and ambiguous terms. This, of course, is a common defect in the
social sciences, but it appears to characterise this particular method more than most.
Words such as 'independent', 'coordinate', 'co-operative', 'interdependent', 'organic', as presently employed, hardly lend themselves to systematic, *comparative*

analysis. Whatever meaning they have will be determined either by the particular perspective of the writer, who, inevitably, will tend to operate within his own range of 'more or less', or 'predominantly', or by the specific characteristics of territorial politics in individual countries. For an approach which lays so much emphasis on its comparative utility this is a very real drawback.

Secondly, this whole approach is vitiated by an obsession with federalism and federations and a cavalier attitude towards confederations and unitary systems. These are rarely examined in any detail; their key features are merely inferred, often in a simple-minded way, from what are taken to be the essential character-istics of federations. The result, as one commentator has pointed out, is that 'imag-ined theories' of confederations and unitary systems have dominated the litera-ture.[10] Not only has this inevitably produced poor federal models, it has also meant that confederations and, particularly, unitary systems, have been credited with characteristics which, in practice, they have rarely possessed. Indeed, 'unitary' appears to be a label which, traditionally, has been devoid of any real comparative meaning.

Thirdly, the conventional threefold classification of territorial systems has found it difficult to incorporate many recent (and some not so recent) develop-ments in this field. For example, the three federal models outlined above describe three very different kinds of federal 'situations'. Are all three to be regarded as valid expressions of the federal principle? Or, does the appearance of the organic model (or, perhaps, even the co-operative alternative) suggest that the federal idea has been stretched too far to provide continued employment for the traditional concept and the threefold typology? One unfortunate result is that students are now faced with a 'terminological jungle' in which the 'federal' has to be constant-ly prefixed by a variety of adjectives in order to catch the flavour of the numerous types of federalism now said to be operating. Even the idea of confederation, never very clear, is challenged by the appearance on the scene of institutions such as the European Community, an organisation which, the late Mr Crosland once declared, made the confederal/federal distinction 'irrelevant and unreal'.

But of more immediate relevance in the present context is the impact on the unitary model of recent experiments (or proposed experiments) in regional *devo-lution* in countries such as Italy, Spain, Belgium and the United Kingdom. The Royal Commission on the Constitution defined devolution as 'the delegation of central government powers without the relinquishment of sovereignty'.[11] In addi-tion, it emphasised that although different kinds of powers could be delegated to institutions with varying sources of authority, the most advanced form of devolu-tion possible – the delegation of legislative powers to elected regional authorities, legislative devolution – was still a form of territorial government firmly within the unitary category. It was *not* federalism, since the latter involved a constitutional sharing of powers. The problem here is that although constitutional lawyers often find no difficulty in accepting this distinction, other people, more interested in the operation of territorial politics than its constitutional forms, find such exercises in systems differentiation increasingly hard to accept.

This leads us to the final and most serious criticism which can be made of this particular approach to territorial systems analysis – its inability to produce principles which are meaningful in terms other than constitutional. This point can be further clarified if we examine, briefly, the development of ideas concerning the federal political *process* in relation to the three models detailed above. Despite their differences in terms of the outcome of this process, the three models share important assumptions regarding the structure of federal politics. These can be listed as follows:

(a) Federalism was viewed primarily in terms of formal intergovernmental relations. In other words, federalism was about the constitutional division of governmental powers and, above all, about the autonomy or sovereignty of the regional governments in the exercise of 'their' powers.

(b) Other aspects of the 'federal situation' – local and regional interests, courts, parties, pressure groups, bureaucracies and finance – were regarded as important only in terms of their impact on intergovernmental relations and, in particular, the autonomy of regional governments.

(c) The location of decision-making was regarded as an all-important determinant of the nature of decisions. Hence, the movement of decision-making to the capital city represented an automatic encroachment on the autonomy of regional governments and, consequently, an attack on local and regional interests.

In recent years these shared assumptions about the federal political process have been subjected to attack from three directions. Some commentators, for example, have argued that the essence of federalism is to be found not in the provisions of the constitution, or the relations between governmental levels, but in the nature of the societies underlying these and, in particular, the strength and concentration of territorial interests. Federalism, then, is a product of societies which have marked territorial cleavages and a political culture to match that societal make-up. A variation on this theme is to argue that federalism can be societal or constitutional, or both.[12] Alternatively, it has been suggested that federalism is sustained not by constitutional provisions, or even by the nature of society, but rather by the character of the party system. In other words, if the structure of power within the parties is decentralised, then the process of politics will be federal, since at all levels of government the parties will operate to protect and promote local and regional interests and governments.[13] The final attack on the traditional view of the federal political process has come from those who have emphasised the importance of capital city bargaining for local and regional interests; a bargaining process in which these interests are protected and promoted by the nature of society, its political culture, and, above all, the degree to which they can penetrate and influence central political institutions and personnel.[14]

The conclusions to be drawn from this recent work on the political process in federations are important, not only in terms of systems differentiation, but in terms of the general analysis of territorial politics. First, for the most part this research is not concerned, primarily, to fix labels on territorial systems, and then justify the choice of confederal, federal or unitary. Although associated with systems usually labelled 'federal', this label is regarded as of far less importance than understanding and describing the process of territorial politics; a process which involves a spectrum of political structures ranging from the highly centralised to the highly decentralised, and which cannot be adequately described by the labels associated with the conventional threefold classification of territorial systems. Secondly, the lack of interest in systems-labelling stems largely from an awareness that the constitutional division of powers and the whole dreary question of domestic sovereignty have played a less important role in the development of territorial politics than is customarily assigned to them, and what role they have played has varied both over time and between countries. Moreover, functions have rarely been neatly and separately divided between levels of government. The cake has been a 'marble cake' not a 'layer' one, one where most levels of government are responsible for some aspects of some functions.[15] In this situation, to argue that intergovernmental functions, jurisdictions and relations are the basis of territorial politics and, specifically, territorial systems differentiation, is highly suspect. It is not governments, in a vacuum, that we should be solely concerned with, but interests as well, and the former do not always faithfully reflect the latter. Thirdly, to adopt this view does not mean that constitutional provisions and institutional designs are of no importance whatsoever. It is merely that they are one part of the total scenario of territorial politics, and their importance must be assessed in conjunction with many other, and more 'political', factors. Finally, the emphasis on the capital city bargaining dimension of territorial politics points to the importance of this aspect of the subject and has awkward implications for those who see the central location of decisions as an indicator of increasing centralisation.

Territorial systems: a summary

The classical approach to the analysis of territorial politics was concerned to bestow the labels confederal, federal and unitary on states and then to infer that these labels reflected differences in the structures and values of territorial politics. The argument here is that outside the limited confines of constitutional law this exercise, by whatever method it is pursued, is not particularly useful. Once political factors are introduced it becomes increasingly difficult to differentiate between the three kinds of territorial systems. Perhaps more important, the labels themselves obstruct research; they have contributed to the neglect of unitary systems and in particular the varying structures of territorial politics which operate under that label. It is hard not to conclude that for social scientists at least the terms confederation, federation and unitary system should be pensioned off and left to the second oldest profession, the lawyers, to play with.

THE CENTRALISATION/DECENTRALISATION DICHOTOMY

If territorial systems analysis is the classical approach to the understanding of territorial politics, the centralisation/decentralisation dichotomy is today the most pervasive. These concepts are generally regarded as applicable to all countries and, in addition, play an important part in discussions based on the other two broad approaches examined here. Thus, what follows can be regarded as an amplification and clarification of some of the points raised in the previous section.

Our discussion of the usefulness of this popular dichotomy will concentrate on centralisation, for three reasons. First, as indicated, our main concern is with the problems of central management and centralisation is commonly perceived to be an instrument or result of that management. Secondly, centralisation is the condition against which, it is said, many people are reacting throughout the western world. Centralisation has increased, is increasing and ought to be diminished, is the motto of those who subscribe to this particular language of analysis. Thirdly, centralisation is the residual part of the dichotomy. As de Tocqueville pointed out over a century ago, 'Centralisation has become a word of general and daily use, without any precise meaning being attached to it'.[16] This is still the case today. Centralisation has rarely received serious attention. Its place in life has been to act as a 'fall guy' for the far more popular idea of decentralisation. Hence, it is interesting to see what happens when centralisation (as commonly perceived) is subjected to critical review.

The centralisation paradigm

Where territorial politics is concerned, centralisation is customarily defined in terms of the location of key decision-making functions in the capital city. Associated with this definition are two important assumptions. The first is that it is easy to identify (and measure) both the process and condition of centralisation. The second is that centralisation is bad because it has obviously bad consequences. Together, this definition and its two associated assumptions can be said to make up the centralisation paradigm. For the moment the definition can be allowed to stand. The assumptions, however, require some amplification.

A major reason for the belief that centralisation can be easily identified is the existence of a number of indicators (or, once again, yardsticks) which, if shown to be present in a political system, are accepted as suggesting some degree of centralisation. These indicators cover a variety of points but the most popular can be conveniently summarised under three headings relating to the intergovernmental distribution of functions, intergovernmental financial relations and the possession by the central authorities of a number of instruments for controlling the activities of elected local governments.

Where functions are concerned centralisation is customarily said to be indicated when their distribution between the central and local governments is unfavourable to the latter. This can take two forms: either all or most of the 'important' functions are, or are becoming, the direct responsibility of the central government; or the execution of these important functions is increasingly given to governmental units at the local and regional levels which are not elected, for example field agencies of the central departments, or *ad hoc* governmental agencies with a territorial structure. Moreover, it is often argued that centralisation (or decentralisation) can be inferred from the degree of uniformity in the standards of elected local government service provision. If, for example, it is found that these standards exhibit little variation throughout the country, then, it is usually suggested that the system is centralised. Similarly, a distribution of financial resources between the central government and elected local governments, such that the latter have few effective autonomous sources of revenue and are thereby forced to rely to a large extent on central grants-in-aid, is also felt to indicate a centralised intergovernmental relationship. Finally, centralisation is said to be present in those situations when the central authorities possess a large number of controls over the operations of local government. These controls can be of a financial, judicial, administrative or legislative character and, if used, result in considerable restrictions on the autonomy of local authorities as regards the election or nomination of its personnel, its decision-making process and the nature of its policy output. In the literature, particular significance is often given to the centralising activities of central bureaucrats working in the field (above all to prefects), whose task is seen as ensuring that local governments within their jurisdictions do not behave in a manner detrimental to the interests of the central authorities.

At this stage two preliminary observations need to be made about these centralisation indicators. First, they all operate within a framework of analysis which is essentially intergovernmental. Hence, if at any time the scope of governmental operations increases, there is a built-in tendency to regard this as something which is bound to affect territorial relations. In short, on this view, 'big government' is, inevitably, a major force for change in territorial politics. Secondly, these indicators rest on a model of power which is essentially coercive. They are associated with situations in which the Centre not only can, but does force local governments to behave in ways which, left to themselves, they would not follow.

The consequences of centralisation are assumed to be obvious, automatic and bad. Centralisation, the paradigm suggests, leads to remote government, and remote government is inefficient, impersonal and unimaginative, following policies which have little to do with local needs. In addition, so the argument runs, centralisation is undemocratic on two counts: it involves, on the one hand, the promotion of the central government's interests (or some centrally perceived national interest) at the expense of legitimate local interests; and, on the other hand, by attacking the external autonomy of elected local governments, it affects disadvantageously their internal vitality and responsibility, thereby interfering with the very basis of democracy, local democracy. At the very least this promotes *incivism*, at the worst, political instability, even revolutions. It will be noted that this whole assumption is derived from particular points of view concerning the impact of *location* on the *nature* of decision-making, the worthwhileness of local democracy as a political goal, and the acceptance of elected local governments as the main instruments to achieve that goal.

The paradigm assessed
The paradigm outlined above is the dominant view of centralisation and its consequences, in the sense that it is accepted (if not always acted on) by most people with

an active interest in politics in western liberal democracies. This general acceptance is surprising, however, given that all the major items of the paradigm – its faith in the traditional indicators, its missionary zeal in emphasising the bad consequences of centralisation and its simplistic attitude towards the implications of its own definition – are open to question. The position may become clearer if four specific criticisms which can be levelled at their analysis are briefly discussed.

1. First, the general and, above all, automatic link between some of the principal indicators and centralisation is difficult to sustain on both theoretical and empirical grounds. The general point here is that centralisation is more difficult to identify than the paradigm suggests, simply because territorial politics is a more complex, ambiguous and less isolated process than it is prepared to accept.

To begin with, the idea that the formal distribution of intergovernmental functions provides an accurate picture of the relative displacement of local interests in the overall system is suspect on a number of counts. In its simplest form the paradigm merely argues that if the central government gains functions formerly held by local governments then (as in twentieth-century Britain) this is proof enough of increasing centralisation. This, of course, is a zero sum view of intergovernmental relations – what one level gains must mean a loss for the other level. In fact, both levels of government may gain functions and this appears to be what has happened in most parts of the Western world in the twentieth century. Some local governments may have lost functions to other (generally larger) local governments, but that is merely a redistribution of functions within the local government world. This argument is often countered with the assertion that although local governments have gained new functions, they have lost functions to the Centre which are *local* in character. The problem here is that there is no agreement as to what a local function is. Nor is there any agreement amongst the local citizenry, as distinct from local councillors, that some functions regarded by the latter as obviously local in character, for example education in Britain, should remain within the ambit of local authorities. It could also be argued that elected local governments, like other institutions, can suffer from functional overload in the sense that the more they have to do, the less likely they are to have the time and energy to cause trouble for the Centre. Local authorities can be effectively depoliticised by swamping them with tasks, a managerial principle well known to any competent schoolteacher.

Equally important, this particular view of the relevance of intergovernmental functions distribution needs to be qualified in two further ways. On the one hand it assumes that bundles of functions are distributed wholly to one or other level of government. In practice, however, the position is rarely so simple. As was noted in the discussion of federalism, some commentators have emphasised that the distribution of functions is more likely to resemble a 'marble' rather than 'layer' cake: one in which no level of government is responsible for all aspects of their administration. The point is not that this is necessarily a decentralising factor, merely that the paradigm fails to take account of this phenomenon. On the other hand, even if a function is controlled completely by the Centre it does not automatically mean that local interests have no influence on how it is run. If they don't, that tells us something about the wider workings of the political system, a topic ignored by the paradigm and one to which we shall return below.

Secondly, the paradigm's perceptions of an automatic link between centralisation and the prefectorial system of field administration are also suspect. This, of course, is merely one aspect of its more general hostility to non-elected government agencies at the local and regional levels. On this point it must be said that supporters of the paradigm have been plain idle. There is no doubt that at various times and in various places, prefects, as central government officials, have curtailed the activities of elected local governments and more generally interfered in the local political process. But this unsavoury role has been associated, in almost all instances, with two kinds of situations: political management prior to the advent of modern mass electorates; or, later periods during which the central authorities felt more than normally insecure (for example, Italy and France after 1945). In short, when prefects have behaved in ways the paradigm suggests they always behave, this has merely reflected the general character of the political process. The attack on local autonomy is not something inherent in the institution. In fact, most recent research on prefectorial operations in modern pluralist systems points to the ineffectiveness of the prefect as an instrument of central control.[17] As a generalist administrator he has lost prestige in face of the continued demand for specialised skills in administration: a fancy uniform and generous entertainments allowance may not always serve to cover up such deficiencies. Moreover, and more important, the emphasis now placed on the prefect's role as a conciliator of local interests means that he often becomes an articulator of such interests in the capital city bureaucracy. Far from pushing the interests of the Centre, many prefects are 'colonised' by local factions, particularly those with powerful friends in the central legislature. Neither of these two pictures give much support for an automatic link between prefects and centralisation.

This sort of argument can be generalised to cover the whole issue of non-elected governments at the local and regional levels. They may act as positive instruments of central control and central policy preferences. But, just as likely, they may be divorced from the local (and national) political process, they may operate in a political vacuum. Alternatively, despite their non-elected character, they may be colonised by local political groups. How they operate will be determined in large part by the general structure of territorial politics. The whole subject of non-elected agencies still requires considerable investigation, and nowhere is that more true than in the United Kingdom.

There remains the problem of intergovernmental finance, specifically the utility of central financial aid to local governments as an indicator of centralisation. The basis of the paradigm's view on this matter is the maxim, 'He who pays the piper calls the tune'. In other words, the greater the percentage of local finance supplied by central grants, the greater the degree of central control. Local democracy, so the argument runs, is best protected by locally raised tax revenues. For a number of reasons this would appear to be an over-simplified picture.[18]

To begin with, this argument is rarely put in absolute terms: all grants are bad and dangerous because they lead to central controls. Usually the argument is couched in relative terms; beyond a certain point, or percentage of total local income, central grants lead to an illegitimate increase in control over local governments. Just what this percentage is, just when the line is crossed between beneficent and dangerous grant levels, is not clear. Moreover, there is little empirical evidence to support this sort of argument. The degree of central control over local and regional governments does not appear to be related either to the overall levels of grant aid or to the specific sums going to individual local authorities. This seems to be the case for both specific and general grants. Equally, this obsession with the dangers of centrally determined grants appears to be a peculiarly British characteristic: other countries spend less time worrying about this issue.

Sometimes the direction of the argument is shifted. It is not so much that grants lead to controls, rather that they obscure the accountability of local councils to their electorate. Alternatively, it is sometimes suggested that central grants create a cultural climate in which local politicians are persuaded that if they spend the national taxpayers' money they ought to be controlled. On the first point, it is not clear that this accountability theme is related to control and centralisation, since these are concerned with the external relations of local governments, not their internal bad habits. In any case it has been argued that a high percentage of grants relative to locally raised revenues actually increases public accountability, because the smaller the proportion of local taxes the greater the political impact of any increase in the rate of that taxation, the so-called 'gearing effect'.[19] Evidence to support the culture point is difficult to find and even if such cultural predispositions to servility were discovered, it would seem plausible to regard them as part of a political culture wider in scope than that concerning intergovernmental relations.

If we adopt a central perspective on grants then the position becomes even more confused. Apart from the fact that the central authorities may not wish to employ grants as a means to financial control, they may not possess the administrative resources or political strength to do so effectively. In addition, for the Centre, a vital distinction has to be drawn between the macro- and micro- dimensions of such control. Macro-control means that the Centre can only bring its influence to bear via the determination of the total amount of grant fixed to go to all local governments. Micro-control extends that control to the separate budgets and policy decisions of individual local authorities. The latter is much the most effective method of supervision, yet it is rare in the Anglo-American context and requires considerable administrative resources in the field to operate effectively. Of course, the two methods are not mutually exclusive: the macro-method can lead to threats or sanctions against individual local authorities. But in the nature of things such threats will be both *ad hoc* and *post hoc*; since they are not part of the normal *tutelle* they will be difficult to justify and, in most cases, sanctions will only be applied after the event. Paradoxically, micro-financial control is usually found in those systems (such as Italy) with a relatively low percentage of central grants to local revenue incomes.

One final point on this matter needs to be noted. The paradigm views central grants-in-aid as a potential danger to local autonomy and a victory for the Centre over the traditional spirit of local independence. But the reverse seems equally plausible. Central grants may represent a political victory for local interests: a victory in the sense that local governments or local interest groups have been able to 'screw' subsidies from the Centre for local policies and yet, at the same time, have reduced local tax bills, or a victory in the sense that the only way the Centre can get local agreement to its desired policies is to sweeten the pill with a heavy coating of financial aid. Either way, local citizens may regard a possible increase in controls over their local governments as less important than the services consequently provided and the lower local tax bills. At this point, a potential divorce emerges between the interests of corporate bodies called local governments and the interests of local citizens as taxpayers and service consumers. The paradigm regards these interests as synonymous, but this need not necessarily be the case. This point will be considered in more detail below.

Thus the case supporting a positive relationship between grants and controls is weak. But it would be dangerous to take the reverse argument too seriously, that there is no relationship between grants and control. The only plausible position is that no general and automatic conclusions regarding the overall character of territorial politics can be drawn from examining, in isolation, the amount and nature of financial cash flows from one level of government to another. It is not the flows or transfers themselves that matter, but the degree of political 'clout' possessed by all those concerned in determining the amount, distribution and operation of such grants.

2. The second major criticism which can be levelled at the paradigm concerns its lackadaisical approach to the concept of power. It is, of course, well known that this concept is one of the most complex in the social sciences. Hence, any approach which fails to note this can be regarded at the outset as highly suspect. The paradigm's approach to this matter is defective on three grounds: its prime actors in the process of centralisation – central and local government – are highly abstract terms which conceal rather than illustrate the reality of this particular power game; it overrates the resources available to central governments and hence exaggerates their power potential; and it confuses central intentions in crisis situations with the routine of intergovernmental relations. These points require some brief discussion.

First, the abstract nature of the terms central and local government: for the paradigm these mean, in practice, the central administrative departments in the capital city and elected local authorities. Even within the restricted ambit of intergovernmental relations this is too simple a scenario. Where the central government is concerned it omits the central political executive (the Cabinet in the United Kingdom), the national legislature and the judiciary: each of these may play an important role, and all are capable of representing a different interest field. Moreover, the administrative departments at the Centre are customarily treated as a homogeneous unit, whereas, in practice, considerable differences may exist in terms of their attitudes and operations towards local authorities.

The term 'local government' also poses problems. Clearly, it is wrong to make this synonymous with elected local authorities: 'government' at the local level also includes field agencies of the central departments, the mass of *ad hoc* agencies with some form of territorial organisation and even local branches of the judiciary. All these have an impact on the citizen. Even if the term is confined to elected local authorities problems still remain. Some kinds of local authority are more important than others and particular local authorities may be politically more important and awkward than others. In short, what has been called the asymmetry of intergovernmental relations may make generalisations difficult. But two further dimensions of local authority operations need to be noted: on the external front they are often combined into competitive 'peak' associations, which handle many of their negotiations with the Centre; on the internal front they may often divide into sets of warring committees, departments and political/bureaucratic factions, which rarely present a united front to the Centre. Once again, generalisations about 'local government' become difficult. Intergovernmental relations, then, are more complicated than the paradigm suggests and it is not hard to see why perceptions of those relations amongst those involved often differ considerably.

This brings us to the paradigm's attitude to central resources. Here the paradigm assumes that central dominance of local government is easy: the Centre can continuously and closely supervise the operations of local authorities and, moreover, is constantly willing to use coercion, or threats of coercion, to ensure that its will is done. Is central dominance so easy? The analysis so far suggests otherwise: local government covers more disparate and complex institutions than traditionally emphasised, and the Centre is less easy to unite and its control instruments more ambiguous in impact than commonly supposed. Moreover, although it may be relatively easy to stop particular actions of local governments, it may be much harder to positively force them to adopt policies they dislike. There is, however, a more important general point. To be effective, controls rest on knowledge, knowledge of what is happening in political and administrative activity at the local level. And knowledge, in turn, can only come from continuous and detailed supervision by 'observers' wholly in tune with central government aims. On this basis it is clear that even if such supervision is confined to the operations of elected local governments, then to be effective such supervision would represent a formidable task for the Centre, involving the committal of considerable resources of time, personnel and money, and this assumes that such supervision is generally acceptable to the personnel of local government, that the issues involved have not been politicised.

The final point is concerned with the problem of central intentions. What do most central authorities in western pluralist democracies want from life in the sphere of territorial politics? Do they desire such continuous, general and close supervision of elected local governments? Are they always willing to use coercion to achieve their ends? Do they need to use coercion to achieve their ends? The difficulty here is that, once posed, these questions reveal a gap in academic research efforts. We know very little about central intentions. Nevertheless, on *a priori* grounds, it would seem reasonable to suggest that the paradigm's view of this matter is too simple.

One possible alternative code for the Centre which requires discussion runs as follows. The most important policy areas for governments today cover such matters as control of the national economy, the general provision of social welfare, security from external threats and internal law and order. Territorial management will be regarded as important only in so far as it becomes associated with the achievement of the Centre's aims in these policy areas. In a busy and dangerous world these issues are, from a central perspective, matters of 'High Politics'; all else, as the saying goes, is 'embellishment and detail', 'Low Politics'. Hence the control of territory is not an end in itself (in times of normalcy) but an instrument to achieve objectives in major policy areas, in matters of 'High Politics'. The lives of governments and the existence of regimes do not normally turn (in the west at least) on the continuous and close supervision by the Centre of elected local governments. On this basis it seems plausible to suggest that most central governments, most of the time, will settle, in an awkward world, for a quiet life. In general they will seek to control only at the margin; to negate illegalities rather than continuously promote and impose their policies on elected local governments. In these circumstances it is a mistake to equate potential power with actual power. Coercive *restraint* in search of co-operative compliance may well be the operational code of most central authorities on most occasions.

It seems reasonable to suggest that the above represents a plausible general picture of the *routine* of intergovernmental relations. The Centre's aims will be limited and reasonable; local compliance will be sought via methods other than costly continuous supervision or disruptive threats to employ coercion. Routine will be complex in operation and highly ambiguous in terms of results, and few of the actors involved may wish to clarify the relationship. As well as *ad hoc* co-operation and hostility, there will be partial friendships and enmities in both camps. Moreover, in a busy world there may well be a considerable amount of indifference between actors (friendship and hostility cost time and resources).

Thus, intergovernmental power relations will be complex and ambiguous and will differ between political systems not so much in terms of their routine, but over the extent and the ease with which this routine can be broken and the consequent necessity, from the Centre's viewpoint, to increase its control over local government and local politicians in order to retain its successful management of 'High Politics'. The routine of intergovernmental relations may decline or collapse for a variety of reasons. When this occurs the central authorities will attempt to rebuild it and this may involve the employment of force and sanctions: the paradigm's view of a power-grabbing assertive Centre will be operationalised. But such circumstances, in twentieth-century western pluralist democracies, have been exceptional: they represent a failure to perpetuate the norm of routinised, depoliticised local government. For the most part, territorial politics is 'Low Politics'. The paradigm's determination to promote this game to a permanent spot on the agenda of 'High Politics' is a mistake.

3. Many of the weaknesses of the centralisation paradigm discussed so far stem from a too narrow framework of analysis, a framework primarily concerned with inter-governmental relations, relations between the central government and local govern-ments. It is not true to say that the paradigm has completely ignored extra-govern-mental factors. It has always suggested that the consequences of centralisation are system-wide in their impact. Moreover, periodically, attempts have been made to allow for the influences of party systems, political cultures and the concentration of commercial and industrial activity on the process of centralisation. Nevertheless, it is probably fair to add that these new aspects have always been looked at in relation to the old subject – intergovernmental centralisation. The paradigm assumes that this is what centralisation is all about, that intergovernmental relations affect political, economic and cultural relations and, if these become affected by centralisation, then this can be cured by intergovernmental decentralisation.

All this, of course, has a curiously old-fashioned air. To confine analysis with-in such a narrow framework goes against all the tendencies of modern political science. Its intellectual base is old-style 'pub admin'. The results are both curious and unfortunate. In Britain, for example, in the 1960s, a well-orchestrated chorus of complaints developed about increasing centralisation, the outcome, so it was said, of a decline in the autonomy of local authorities. Yet, at the same time, in another arena of political activity of at least equal importance, namely industrial relations, observers were constantly decrying the awkward consequences of local workshop, and particularly shop stewards', power. The respective literatures and moaners, however, remained completely separate. This would not matter so much if the claims made by the paradigm were as restrictive as its analytical framework. But this is not so. From a very narrow base the paradigms draw ambitious gener-al conclusions concerning centralisation in the overall political system. This little 'trick' needs to be noted. In fact, the centralisation paradigm, like territorial sys-tems analysis, can only be understood in terms of formal intergovernmental rela-tions. Once it moves beyond that framework it loses its coherence. In short, it is not designed to take account of the *political* process within which intergovern-mental relations must operate.

4. A major reason why the paradigm has this obsession with intergovernmental relations is its rosy view of the workings of, and benefits obtained from local democracy, and what it sees as the principal instrument to achieve that goal, name-ly, elected local governments. It is at this point we encounter the problem of the bad consequences of centralisation. As already indicated, the idea that these are obvious, automatic and inevitably bad is a major assumption of the paradigm.

Given the importance attached to this matter it is, perhaps, surprising that the paradigm's treatment of this whole topic is so woefully weak. Of course, this is partly because the very nature of the supposed bad consequences – inefficiency, red tape and an unfeeling attitude towards local interests – is such that they are very difficult to subject to vigorous and value-free analysis. One man's red tape may be another man's concern to follow the prescribed rules and regulations. However, there is also the little problem of relating these drawbacks *directly* to the state of territorial politics, to centralisation. As Austin pointed out in the nineteenth century, these bad consequences may well be primarily the result of 'extrinsic causes', having only a marginal connection with the nature of central-local relations.[20] In short, they may be a result of 'big government' rather than centralisation and the two are not necessarily related, even less synonymous. At all events, the point to be emphasised is that given the nature of the problem, any automatic and direct link between the bad consequences and centralisation will be difficult to make, and in practice few attempts have been made. Even in those circumstances when the problem might have been pursued, such as the inquiries of British Royal Commissions, the matter has been avoided and refuge taken in the repetition of aphorisms, crude historical generalisations, a priori banalities, or the bleatings of interested witnesses.[21]

There appear to be two major reasons why the paradigm has not thought it necessary to provide empirical backing for this assumption. The first relates to the inference it draws from its definition of centralisation. As we have seen, this is couched in terms of the location of key decision-making functions in the capital city. By itself, of course, this definition is neutral. It only becomes 'alive' when the paradigm builds into it a major assumption, that the *location* of decision-making affects, in this case disadvantageously, the *nature* of decision-making. But once again, above all in these days of high-technology communications and state economic and welfare management, there is very little empirical backing for this. It is plausible only if it is assumed that the central political and administrative structures in the capital city are completely divorced from local and regional knowledge and pressures, in other words, that centralisation from above can and does operate in a vacuum. Such situations may exist, but when they do the bad consequences will be less the result of location than of the peculiar structure of territorial politics in operation.

Hence, if the paradigm's view of location is not backed by empirical data it must be backed by something else. And the argument here is that such backing is provided by a piece of ideology – a belief in the virtues of local democracy and a concern to emphasise that the main instrument to achieve this is an autonomous system of local self-government. Now in certain circumstances local democracy may be a good thing, it may be better than democracy at the national level, and it may even be a necessary basis for democracy overall. But to make this into a general and automatic rule of political life is a piece of special doctrinal pleading. So too with elected local governments: once again, these may be eminently desirable institutions, but to suggest that in developed political systems they are the only instruments, even the best, to defend and promote local interests is to go too far. Local interests, even local democracy, may well be defended in a variety of places and by a variety of instruments.[22] Traditionally, for example, they were defended by local representatives in the capital city. Only the relatively late arrival of elected local government in the nineteenth century pushed this particular technique to one side (at least in academic theory). The point is that no one method is intrinsically more effective or more democratic than another, it depends on the specific territorial circumstances. Considerations such as these indicate that the paradigm's automatic assumption about the bad consequences of centralisation need to be treated with a considerable degree of caution.

The centralisation paradigm: a summary
The prevailing centralisation paradigm has been criticised on a number of counts: the weakness of some of the popular indicators of centralisation; its simplistic attitude towards the analysis of power; a too narrow framework of analysis; and finally, an inability to establish a direct link between centralisation and its supposed bad consequences. A major result of these defects is an unfortunate propensity to constantly overrate both the resources of the Centre and its urge to control or dominate territorial communities. At the very least this means that arguments about centralisation, especially those which suggest it is increasing, should be treated with a considerable degree of caution. The theoretical and empirical weakness of the paradigm is such that it is hard not to conclude that its continued popularity is the result either of idleness on the part of social scientists, or their unwillingness to accept that its continued employment is really rooted in its ideological attractions. All this does not mean that as a concept centralisation should be expunged from the armoury of the social sciences – there are too few effective weapons in there to be able to afford to do that. Centralisation needs to be repaired, not written off. A more plausible and fruitful definition would help and its incestuous relationship with elected local governments should be ended. The concept also needs to be unpacked. In other words, the different dimensions of centralisation need to be identified. Above all, the different models of central management require discussion. These points will be discussed in the next chapter.

THE INTERNAL COLONIALISM THESIS

This is the third and most recent attempt to explain the general condition and operation of territorial politics.[23] Whereas territorial systems analysis is concerned primarily with the constitutional division of powers between levels of government and the centralisation/decentralisation dichotomy with the degree of central control or local autonomy, the principal themes of the internal colonialism thesis are three – dependency, domination and exploitation. As the label suggests for this approach the structure of territorial politics *within* states is perceived as operating in a manner similar to colonial or imperial relations between states. In both instances, it is argued, economically and culturally advanced areas colonise less favoured areas, such that relations between them present an overall picture of dependency, domination, and exploitation. These preliminary observations require some amplification.

First, the internal colonialism thesis must be understood not simply in terms of describing a structure of territorial politics, but, in addition, as an attack on a more general theory of social and political development. This theory suggests that with the advent of industrialisation, urbanisation, mass communications and mass education and the vast expansion of governmental activities, local and regional community loyalties, culture and behaviour, will be gradually and finally replaced by integrated, nationalised, homogeneous societies, in which the main divisions of interest will be economic and not territorial. Both territorial systems and centralisation analysis have been prone to accept the main themes of this theory of social and political development. The internal colonialism thesis rejects it.

Secondly, within this general perspective the internal colonialism thesis has been associated with attempts to describe and explain a variety of territorial situations. The most important of these have been the following:[24]

(a) Discussions concerned with the pattern of territorial politics within *separate* developing countries. Analysis has concentrated primarily on Latin American states in the nineteenth and twentieth centuries, but some consideration has been given to circumstances in the United States and Italy in the nineteenth century.

(b) Analysis of the subordinate position of certain territorially concentrated minority groups in contemporary North America and South Africa. For example, the blacks and chicanos in the United States, French-speaking Canadians in Quebec and the Bantu in the tribal lands of South Africa.

(c) Studies concerned to relate the present pattern of territorial politics within the former colonies of the Third World with the continuing dominance of the western capitalist and imperialist system.

(d) Research seeking to explain the revival of peripheral nationalism in the established, industrialised states of Western Europe. For example, the thesis can be applied to explain recent developments in the Basque and Catalan provinces of Spain, Corsica and Brittany in France, the Flemish areas of Belgium and even Greenland's relations with Denmark.

Thirdly, despite the diversity of origins and usage, a number of specific common themes are associated with the thesis. To begin with, the analytical framework adopted to examine internal colonial situations employs the terminology of the Centre/periphery distinction, and within that framework a key theme concerns the consequences of uneven economic development. Because, it is argued, some areas (the Centres, or cores, or metropolitan areas) industrialise earlier and more successfully than others (the peripheries), then this sets up a continuing syndrome of inequalities and dependency between the two. In turn, this inequality and dependency produces a set of territorial relations characterised by the domination and exploitation of the peripheries by the Centres. This exploitation is basically of an economic nature, but associated with this are other forms of exploitation, such as political centralisation and cultural subordination. Combined, these various exploitation dimensions produce the condition or situation of internal colonialism. Again, in the relations between Centre and periphery particular emphasis is placed on the mediating roles of peripheral elite groups, who act as the agents of the

Centre's policies and benefit from that agency status. Inherent in the thesis there is also the assumption that, in the end, internal colonialism produces a reaction by the peripheries against the dominant and exploiting Centres, a reaction which takes the form of demands for economic and cultural equality, more political autonomy or even secession from the internal colonial state. Hence the internal colonial thesis can be used not only to describe a structure of territorial politics but to explain the advent and actions of peripheral protest movements as well.

Fourthly, although this thesis holds increasing attractions for many people (not least because it appears to inject a breath of radical fresh air into a subject dominated by academic and political conservatism), there is no doubt that it is ambiguous on a number of points. For example, the range of internal colonialism is not clear. Does it apply, as is sometimes suggested, to all states, or only to some of them? Again, a major difference of opinion seems to exist between those writers who regard internal colonialism as part and parcel of a world-wide 'chain' of capitalist exploitation – 'It is capitalism itself' – and those who see it as the product of particular conditions in specific countries and as more of a cultural than an economic phenomenon. Moreover, within states, is there just one dominant Centre and one subordinate periphery, or is the position more complex? Is the economically dominant Centre the political capital city and its hinterland (something it would be difficult to argue where the United States, West Germany, Italy and Spain are concerned), or does a distinction have to be made between economic, cultural and political Centres, and, if so, what happens to the *general* syndrome of dependency and exploitation? Further, the mechanics of dependency, domination and exploitation are often neglected and, as a result, the direct and automatic relationship between the three tends to be asserted and not argued. As one commentator on the literature has put it: 'everything is connected to everything else, but how and why, often remains obscure'. Does dependency automatically lead to dominance and exploitation as the thesis suggests? Do Centres always have the intentions and resources to effectively exploit peripheries? Up to the present, the general literature on internal colonialism has failed to deal with such questions in an adequate fashion.

A reasonable conclusion from this discussion would be that although the internal colonialism thesis exhibits attractive potential, it is still at a painfully preliminary stage of formulation. In the words of one writer on the topic: 'Understanding the facts of internal colonialism remains sporadic'.[25] Given this, plus the general lack of interest shown by British academics in the development of the thesis, it is perhaps surprising, though certainly convenient, that one of the most important and seminal studies of territorial politics in the United Kingdom – Michael Hechter's *Internal Colonialism* – represents an explicit attempt to apply the concept to an industrialised country.[26] Hechter's book, therefore, merits some brief attention.

Michael Hechter's *Internal Colonialism*
The principal arguments contained in *Internal Colonialism* appear to be as follows:

(i) Hechter's preliminary concern is with the survival, 'to a large extent mysterious', of separate ethnic and national identities in outlying regions of advanced industrialised states. As an analytical framework within which this phenomenon can be discussed Hechter identifies two broad models of national development, which he labels the *diffusion* and the *internal colonial* models. Both these assume two territorially concentrated 'collectivities'; a core or dominant cultural group 'which occupies territory extending from the political centre of the society (e.g., the locus of the central government)' and a periphery, or peripheral cultural group which is subordinate to the core group and occupies territory on the geographical fringe of the society.

(ii) The diffusion model of national development (which aggregates a number of somewhat different views) represents for Hechter the academic orthodoxy. Its principal message runs as follows:

> The kernel of the diffusion perspective concerns the consequences of industrialisation and the concomitant increase in core-periphery interaction. As a rule the diffusionist holds that from *interaction will come commonality*. The type of social structure found in the developing core regions will, after some time, diffuse into the periphery. (Italics Hechter's)[27]

This model admits that initially industrialisation 'may heighten the sense of cultural separateness in the periphery'. But, as Hechter notes, in the long run the model suggests that 'the economic, cultural and political foundations for separate ethnic identification disappear' to produce a fully integrated society; one where regional wealth differences are minimal, where cultural differences assume no real importance and where the political process will be based on national class differences, not regional cultural cleavages.

(iii) The other model of national development, the internal colonial, presents a totally different scenario. According to Hechter there are four general themes. First, the 'spatially uneven wave of modernisation over state territory creates relatively advanced and less advanced groups'. Secondly, the more advanced group, or core, 'seeks to stabilise and monopolise its advantages through policies aiming at the institutionalisation of the existing stratification system'. Thirdly, the result of this is that the core 'is seen to dominate the periphery politically and to exploit it materially'. Fourthly, this domination and exploitation are counter-productive. Peripheral cultures survive in spite of such conditions and, eventually, there is a reaction against core dominance,

(iv) For Hechter core dominance and exploitation in relation to the periphery has three broad dimensions:

(a) Economic

In general terms economic development in the periphery is dependent on, and complementary to, that in the core. It is designed to serve the interests of the latter. The result of this economic dependence is that wealth in the periphery 'lags behind the core'. More specifically, peripheral economic activity is dominated by core personnel; is highly specialised (often with a concentration in the agricultural and mineral sectors); and decisions with major impact are taken in the core area, such that a 'branch line' economy is created, subject to constant threats of closures, and with high unemployment and low living standards. Constant emigration from the periphery is an important consequence of this kind of economic dependency.

(b) Cultural

The dominant culture belongs to the core group and this dominance is protected by what Hechter calls 'a cultural division of labour', a situation where societal roles and rewards are distributed on the basis of a system 'institutionalised' to favour members of the dominant core culture, or those in the periphery willing to accept that culture. In short, culture becomes an instrument to protect and promote the core's general dominance over the periphery.

(c) Political

In the political process the periphery's position is 'feeble'; it is 'resource poor' relative to the core group. As a result legislative representation, at all levels, is a mere formality, a cover for core numerical and political dominance. Whether discrimination against the periphery is formal and overt, or informal and covert (using, for example, the selective co-optation of peripheral élite groups), the central state machine is always used to reinforce core advantage.

(v) Hechter assesses the relative merits of these two models in the context of the development of territorial politics in the British Isles and United Kingdom over the four hundred year period 1536 to 1966. In his view the Centre or core is represented by England and the periphery by the 'celtic fringe' of Northern Ireland, Scotland and Wales.

(vi) Of the four cultural groups occupying the British Isles, one, the English, began with a number of advantages, in particular geography and climate favoured them. To these initial (and ultimately economic) advantages were later added those of numbers and a more efficient governmental machine. Hence England's attitude towards the periphery was always and inevitably predatory and imperial. The political incorporation of the periphery (the Unions of 1536, 1707 and 1800) was pushed through during critical periods of English politics and to further English interests; primarily to protect England's territorial integrity in the face of external threats and, secondarily, to guarantee food supplies. The result was that: 'the Celtic periphery was swallowed whole into a state system in which it became economically and demographically only an insignificant part'.[28] Union was also followed by the attempted promotion of English cultural values in the periphery and the suppression of the traditional celtic cultures.

(vii) Industrialisation and democraticisation in the nineteenth century did not alter this structure of territorial politics. In the century following 1850 the periphery remained distinctive and, at the same time, its economic, cultural and political exploitation by the core, England, continued. It is worth quoting Hechter at some length on this exploitation point. Not only does this enable us to cash his complex arguments as briefly as possible, but it also gives the 'flavour' of Hechter's analysis better than any summary could ever manage.

Industrialisation *per se* did not, therefore, serve to eliminate the relative economic disadvantages of the Celtic periphery. The *per capita* income of Celtic counties has been consistently lower than that of English counties. Regional economic inequality persists even after the level of industrialisation is eliminated as a source of variation between regions. Rather, the situation of the Celtic fringe in the British Isles is analogous in several respects to that of the less developed countries in the world system. Development occurred in a largely dependent mode and created dualistic structures within the Celtic periphery. As a consequence the spatial diffusion of industrialisation in the Celtic lands was considerably restricted. Further, production in Wales, Scotland, and Ireland was excessively specialised, whereas England alone developed a diversified industrial economy. Finally, it is suggested that the persistence of these systematic disadvantages may partially result from the institutionalisation of policies which have the effect of discriminating against the Celtic periphery in a manner similar to that which has been described as institutionalised racism. The perception of a certain Celtic cultural distinctiveness on the part of significant English institutions may serve to discourage prospects for development in these regions.[29]

(viii) Democratisation did not create a politically integrated United Kingdom. Hechter argues that after the franchise extensions of the 1880s the periphery continued to exhibit a high degree of political distinctiveness; its voting patterns never reflected the class politics of England. In particular, it never supported the Conservative Party, the party of Union, as much as its social structural composition would suggest and, apart from Ulster, it never succumbed to the attractions of imperialism to the extent that England did.

(ix) This persistence of political sectionalism in the periphery allied to its economic and cultural exploitation leads Hechter to pose three questions:

(a) Why was Southern Ireland the only territorial section to secede from the United Kingdom following nineteenth-century industrialisation and democratisation?

(b) Why was Scottish and Welsh nationalism so politically quiescent in the period from the mid-1920s to the mid-1960s?

(c) What explains the rise of political nationalism in Wales and Scotland since the mid-1960s?

The answer to the first question is couched in terms of 'the particular mode of dependent development which emerged in Ireland during the period 1846–1921'. More specifically, because the bulk of Ireland failed to industrialise there were no 'enclaves' of modernisation which could act as bases to support the political penetration of core political institutions, e.g. political parties and trade unions. Hence Irish nationalism as a political movement had no serious rivals. The answer to the second question follows from this. Industrialisation in Scotland and Wales was sufficient to create 'enclaves' which could be penetrated by core political institutions, in the beginning by the Liberal Party and then, most notably, by the Labour Party and wider labour movement.

In effect then the Labour Party contributed to the continued incorporation of Wales and Scotland while simultaneously campaigning on a platform of regional devolution. In this sense Labour served to 'negatively integrate' the British Isles.[30]

Finally, the resurgence of celtic nationalism since the mid-1960s is explained in terms of the 'profound shift in the legitimate rationale for regional autonomy', a shift caused, in large part, by the realisation in Scotland and Wales that neither of the two national parties, even Labour, was sufficiently committed to peripheral interests to bring about radical change – 'They are in essence English parties for the English electorate'.

(x) Hechter draws three general conclusions. First, whilst the pattern of territorial development in England approximates to the dictates of the diffusion model, that of the celtic fringe is closer to the internal colonial model. Secondly, since the process of state building in the United Kingdom was 'not, by any means, idiosyncratic' in comparative western European terms, then further research might well establish internal colonialism as 'the modal form' of national development in industrial societies. And, finally, despite a history of dependency, domination and exploitation the prospects for achieving equality between core and periphery in the United Kingdom 'seem relatively good', given the impact of the peripheral nationalist resurgence on governmental and 'status-conferring' institutions in the core.

The internal colonialism thesis: an assessment

We began this section by detailing the general origins and themes of the internal colonialism thesis. We concluded that its attractive potential had not been fulfilled in practice. Does Hechter's book force us to change this assessment? Does it provide a plausible account of the development of territorial politics in the United Kingdom? Does it advance the general study of internal colonialism? The answer to these questions is, unfortunately, a negative. But this requires an immediate qualification. Criticising Hechter, and by inference the internal colonialism thesis in general, shows all the signs of becoming an academic growth industry. The two most popular criticisms are that the book is methodologically suspect, and that it is just plain wrong in attempting to push United Kingdom development within the confines of this thesis.[31] In passing, it should be emphasised that many of the book's specific arguments, particularly those regarding the tradition of 'indirect rule' and the twentieth-century impact of the Labour Party, are both interesting and plausible. Moreover, Hechter is well aware of the methodological problems surrounding his arguments and some popular perceptions of United Kingdom development are very close to his principal themes. In the present context, however, these are not the most relevant criticisms which can be levelled at the book. For the key to understanding Hechter is not how, but *why* he fails, in other words, why he doesn't provide a plausible account of United Kingdom development and why he fails to advance the general study of internal colonialism.

In terms of his United Kingdom case study, Hechter's arguments lack plausibility not because he pursues the internal colonialism thesis 'against the facts', but because he adopts a framework of analysis which doesn't allow him to score very highly in terms of the thesis itself.

To begin with, his periodisation of United Kingdom development doesn't help. Although the book was published in 1975, Hechter says very little about events occurring after 1966, and before that date he is concerned only with the pre- and post-industrial structure of territorial politics. As a result he fails to say much (though what he does say is interesting) about the vital period from the end of the First World War to the mid-1960s. Again, in important respects, Hechter's analysis lacks any systematic external dimension. His internal colonial state is divorced from the outside world. It is true that his analysis of the Union process takes some account of external forces and, of course, a whole chapter is devoted to the impact of nineteenth-century imperialism. But in neither case does he pause to consider what these particular instances suggest concerning the power of the centre. More generally on this point, Hechter appears to believe that the English state is typical of west European development: many would argue the opposite; it is, and has always been, *sui generis*.[32] At all events the point deserves more supporting data than it receives.

Hechter's internal colonial state is also presented in a domestic vacuum. Its hegemony is merely inferred from his analysis of economic dependency. This failure to discuss, in any detail, the nature of the colonial state structure and its operations is surprising given Hechter's insistence on the important role played by the state in economic development and his conclusion that not much is known about the mechanisms of state control. It seems reasonable to argue that if you want to play the internal colonialism game you should pay attention to the colonisers and their state machine. This neglect of the political process and the mechanisms of central exploitation leads us to the final weakness in Hechter's analysis – his free and easy attitude to the location of the Centre. He does admit that the United Kingdom periphery may need more sophisticated formulation than the general label 'the Celtic fringe'. But he never considers that his Centre may require similar reformulation, that it is not just England as a unit, but something else, that England itself may be a part of the periphery. At this stage the point to be made is simply that Hechter never considers these possible criticisms concerning the location of his Centre and periphery.

Given the weakness of his United Kingdom case study we can see why Hechter does not advance the general study of internal colonialism. It is not so much that Hechter emphasises the cultural division of labour and neglects the external dimension (both of which makes him a peculiar internal colonial theorist, but rather that his book is not really about internal colonialism at all. That concept has only a residual role in his scenario. His real concern is to attack the diffusion theory of national development via the presentation of data which points to the persistence of peripheral sectionalism. With this general thesis (although not all the details) it is hard to disagree. But it is not an internal colonialism thesis.

The internal colonialism: a summary

We must conclude that the explanatory and predictive value of the internal colonialism thesis has still to be cashed. This is not only because, as generally presented, it is often conceptually ambiguous and empirically weak but because, unlike territorial systems and centralisation/decentralisation analysis, it has never been formulated and applied in a systematic way. Hechter's book does not change this. As a general study of territorial development in the United Kingdom it is excellent. As an attempt to test the internal colonialism thesis it is a missed opportunity.

CONCLUSIONS

Three existing approaches to the study of territorial politics have been examined. Each has been criticised and found wanting on a variety of counts. Given that each of these approaches has been associated with structural models which have assumed considerable displacement in United Kingdom debate on this subject we are faced with a dilemma. Within what analytical framework can this particular aspect of United Kingdom politics be usefully examined? This question will be tackled in the following chapter.

NOTES

1   James Madison, *The Federalist*, no. 37 (London, 1961), p. 180.
2   These, of course, are not the only approaches in this field. But they are the most relevant to any United Kingdom case study.
3   See Ivo D. Duchacek, *Comparative Federalism* (New York, 1970).
4   K. C. Wheare, *Federal Government* (London, 1946), Chapters 1 and 2.
5   J. A. Corry, 'Constitutional trends and federalism', in A. R. Lower *et al.*, *Evolving Canadian Federalism* (Durham, North Carolina, 1958), p. 122.
6   M. J. C. Vile, *The Structure of American Federalism* (Oxford, 1961), Chapter 10.
7   G. F. Sawer, *Modern Federalism* (London, 1976), p. 104.
8   Michael D. Reagan, *The New Federalism* (New York, 1972).
9   The best general assessment is found in S. Rufus Davis, *The Federal Principle* (London, 1976).
10   Christopher Hughes, *Confederacies* (Leicester, 1963), p. 3.
11   Royal Commission on the Constitution, *Majority Report* (Cmnd 5460, 1973), para. 543.
12   William S. Livingston, 'A note on the nature of federalism', *Political Science Quarterly* (1952); and Aaron Wildavsky, 'Party discipline under federalism: implications of Australian experience', in A. Wildavsky (ed.), *American Federalism in Perspective* (Boston, Mass., 1967).
13   William H. Riker, *Federalism: Origin, Operation, Significance* (Boston, Mass., 1964), pp. 91–101 and p. 136; and Morton Grodzins, *American System* (Chicago, 1966), especially Chapter 10.
14   R. J. May, *Federalism and Fiscal Adjustment* (Oxford, 1969); D. J. Elazar, *The American*

System: A View from the States (New York, 1972); Grodzins, op. cit.

15 Grodzins, op. cit., Chapters 1 and 3.

16 Alexis de Tocqueville, *Democracy in America* (World's Classics, London, 1961), p. 69. See also James Fesler, 'Centralisation and decentralisation', *The International Encyclopedia of the Social Sciences*, II (New York, 1968).

17 H. Machin, *The Prefect in French Public Administration* (London, 1977); R. C. Fried, *The Italian Prefects* (New Haven, 1963); Jean-Pierre Worms, 'Le préfet et ses notables', *Sociologie du travail* (1966); J. Milch, 'Influence as power: French local government reconsidered', *British Journal of Political Science* (1974).

18 Opinions differ on this point. The Layfield Committee accepted the traditional argument that central grants-in-aid do lead, 'in the end' to greater central controls. See *Local Government Finance: Report of the Committee of Enquiry* (Cmnd. 6453, London, 1976), p. 67. For opposing views see Douglas Ashford, 'The effects of central finance on British local government', *British Journal of Political Science*, (1974), and Royal Commission on the Constitution, *Majority Report*, para. 662. On the general question of what factors influence local government policies see L. J. Sharpe, *Does Politics Matter? A Summary* (ECPR Conference Paper, 1980).

19 Layfield Report, p. 40, paras. 6 and 7.

20 John Austin, 'Centralisation', *Edinburgh Review* (1847).

21 The worst example was the Royal Commission on the Constitution; op. cit., Chapters 8 and 9.

22 J. G. Bulpitt, 'Participation and local government: territorial democracy', in Geraint Parry (ed.), *Participation in Politics* (Manchester, 1972); John Dearlove, *The Reorganisation of British Local Government* (Cambridge, 1979).

23 It is not clear who used the term internal colonialism first. One candidate is C. Wright Mills. See his 1959 lecture, 'Remarks on the problems of industrial development', reprinted as 'The problem of industrial development', in Irving L. Horowitz (ed.), *Power, Politics and People: The Collected Essays of C. Wright Mills* (New York 1963).

24 Examples of this literature are: Pablo Gonzales Casanova, 'Internal colonialism and national development', *Studies in Comparative International Development* (1965); Robert Blauner, 'Internal colonialism and ghetto revolt', *Social Problems* (1968/9); Harold Wolpe, 'The theory of internal colonialism: the South African case', in I. Oxaal *et al.*, *Beyond the Sociology of Development* (London, 1975); Andre Gunder Frank, *Capitalism and Underdevelopment in Latin America* (London, 1967).

25 Casanova, op. cit.

26 Michael Hechter, *Internal Colonialism: The Celtic Fringe in British National Development*, 1536–1966 (London, 1975).

27 *Ibid.*, p. 7.

28 *Ibid.*, p. 45.

29 *Ibid.*, p. 130.

30 *Ibid.*, p. 292.

31 The most important methodological criticisms are in Edward Page, 'Michael Hechter's internal colonialism thesis', *European Journal of Political Research* (1978). For specific criticisms relating to the United Kingdom see A. H. Birch, *Political Integration and Disintegration in the British Isles* (London, 1977), pp. 33–4.

32 Perry Anderson, 'The origins of the present crisis' in P. Anderson and R. Blackburn (eds.), *Towards Socialism* (London, 1965); and Tom Nairn, *The Breakup of Britain* (London, 1977), Chapter 1.

chapter two | an alternative prospectus[1]

Once the traditional confines of the subject have been breached a variety of leads can be followed.[2]

One must start with the assumption that power relationships are not naturally compatible, before studying the means by which conflict has been resolved in modern society.[3]

INTRODUCTION

This chapter is concerned with three interrelated topics: a summary of the principal general criticisms which can be levelled at the existing approaches in this field, the selection of four analytical perspectives on the structure of central-local relations in the United Kingdom and an exercise in concept repair. Combined, these topics represent something much less than a new coherent framework of analysis. What follows is merely an alternative study prospectus: a list of things we should avoid doing or saying, identifying some methods of approaching the subject and specific aspects requiring consideration, and a discussion of some of the advantages and disadvantages inherent in the scheme. The justification for such a conservative approach will be outlined below.

THE EXISTING APPROACHES: A CRITICAL SUMMARY

Chapter 1 identified and assessed three major approaches to our subject. These share certain common weaknesses. The principal ones are as follows.

(a) All three approaches are guilty of a considerable degree of 'concept stretching'. In other words, concepts such as federal, unitary, centralisation, and internal colonialism, have been used to describe too many different things. Thus, 'unitary' appears to be a word devoid of any real meaning and is applied in a casual manner to too many different structures. 'Centralisation' is in a similar position, apart from simple attempts to draw a distinction between 'over-centralisation' and what can presumably be labelled 'normal' or 'acceptable centralisation'. 'Internal colonialism' is also a concept which has been applied to a variety of situations and it carries the inference, on some occasions, that all western societies suffer from this particular brand of exploitation. But perhaps the best example is federal analysis, which has produced three principal models – dual, co-operative and organic (plus a variety of sub-models) – each of which is very different in form and operation.

To sum up; there may be different types of unitary, centralised and internal colonial states in the western world. Alternatively, where federalism is concerned, there are now so many types that the concept has lost any meaning.

(b) Common to all three languages is a general ideological 'gang up' regarding the supposed virtues of local democracy, and what amounts to an obsession with elected local government as the instrument to achieve that goal. Yet the arguments supporting these views are often theoretically weak or ambiguous and lack empirical support. More specifically, the general mobilisation of bias in favour of that 'holy trinity' – decentralisation, local democracy and local self-government – has exacted a double analytical penalty in terms of central-local relations research. On the one hand, the interests of local communities have been too often and too easily equated with those of elected local councils, and, on the other hand, there has been a reluctance to admit that, in certain circumstances, local regional interests may be satisfactorily promoted and accommodated within the confines of capital city politics. In other words, much of the literature takes on a simple nineteenth-century 'states rights' approach to this problem: only autonomous elected local governments can represent, defend and promote the interests of local communities. Significantly, Calhoun and other political theorists of the Old South were eventually forced to reject this as too simple a programme of territorial defence.[4]

(c) An unfortunate consequence of (b) above is an unwillingness, common to all three approaches, to examine sympathetically and in detail the resources, intentions and operations of the central authorities. This is most marked in discussions of centralisation and internal colonialism, where it is legitimate to expect that the sources of centralisation and colonialism would receive the attention commensurate with their role in the total analytical scenario. It is, however, a criticism which can be levelled reasonably at territorial systems analysis, at least in so far as it has failed to pursue seriously the concept and workings of unitary states, precisely the system in which the central government is supposed to be dominant. The consensus is that central governments are constantly engaged in a search for more power over local communities and government, have the resources to back up that search, and that it is always a bad thing when they seek to do so. Again, the empirical evidence to support this series of assertions is often weak.

(d) All three approaches to the subject operate within a framework of analysis which fails to sufficiently emphasise the *political process* of central-local relations. They are only plausible when they neglect that process. Territorial systems analysis, for example, is primarily a language of static constitutional designs; the centralisation/decentralisation dichotomy is expressed in terms of the formal powers and functions of intergovernmental relations, whilst the internal colonialism thesis is concerned primarily with economic and cultural factors. The argument here, it should be emphasised, is *not* that these factors are unimportant; merely that the time has come to see what happens when more overtly political matters, such as interests, parties, elite codes and conventions, are given due weight and attention in the analysis of central-local relations.

(e) Finally, one of the reasons for the neglect of the political process should be noted, since it is of general importance. The apolitical nature of these three languages stems in part from the problems they encounter when they try to relate to the complexities and all-embracing nature of mid-twentieth-century politics in the West. In a very real sense these are nineteenth-century theories rooted in nineteenth-century political values and the nineteenth-century political process. Central-local relations has developed little theory for the twentieth century. Perhaps the eighteenth century, as in other spheres, may be a more appropriate century in which to search for clues to construct such theory.

SOME DIFFERENT PERSPECTIVES

There are three possible reactions to the criticisms detailed above: they can be ignored, used as a justification for adopting an entirely new framework of analysis, or employed as the basis of a less radical alternative.

They can be ignored on the grounds that such criticisms are unfair; most, if not all, are well known and many students of the subject have produced work avoiding such weaknesses. This is certainly true. It seems reasonable to suggest, however, that given the range of criticisms which can be levelled at the existing approaches, some formal break with the past is required. On the other hand, those attempts to examine the subject within an entirely new analytical framework, based either on an alternative ideology (for example, Marxism) or on the concepts and techniques of other disciplines (for example, the sociology of organisation) have not been very successful so far, at least in terms of practical application.[5] Moreover, this sort of reaction not only threatens to impose a new analytical orthodoxy but puts at risk those advances which have been made. It is true that the study of central-local relations has been 'a kind of methodological Cinderella after midnight'.[6] But the principal reason for this is not that no useful work has been done in this field, rather it is that those interested in the subject have failed to combine their ideas.[7] We are faced with what Fesler has called 'the distinctiveness of the several literatures'.[8] In other words, the subject has produced no coherent academic community. The present situation, to use a poker analogy, is that the three existing approaches have all produced studies contributing something worthwhile to the 'pot'. The problem is to draw these together into a useful and coherent whole. In these circumstances there seems no point in political scientists running off to other disciplines to find a completely new methodology and set of concepts.[9] The existing corpus of knowledge needs to be repaired, not forgotten. This said, the principal alternative perspectives on the subject are as follows.

Territorial politics

Two criticisms levelled at the existing approaches were their obsession with elected local governments and their general neglect of the political process within which central-local relations operate. One way to emphasise that we ought to be concerned with broader, more political matters is to give the subject a new label. 'Territorial politics' appears to fit the bill in terms of both approach and contemporary academic dialogue.[10] It is defined here as that arena of political activity concerned with the relations between the central political institutions in the capital city and those interests, communities, political organisations and governmental bodies outside the central institutional complex, but within the accepted boundaries of the state, which possess, or are commonly *perceived* to possess, a significant geographical or local/regional character.

A number of points concerning this definition need to be noted. First, the traditional concentration on intergovernmental relations, and even more on central departments and local authorities, is avoided. And, in so far as this aspect of the subject is taken into account, the scope of 'government' at both levels, national and local/regional, is expanded. The central government means not just the civil service departments but the political executive, the legislature and the judiciary as well. At the local level, government means field agencies and *ad hoc* administrative structures as well as elected local authorities. Secondly, instead of an emphasis on governments, we have a subject concerned with the variety of politically oriented *linkages* between local and national theatres.[11] Thirdly, by inference at least, this definition accepts that the relations and specific linkages concerned involve *power* struggles which, in certain circumstances, may be non-bargainable. Finally, the definition points to intra-state relations. But, as will be noted below, once this wider domestic framework is adopted it becomes difficult to omit completely the possibility that external forces may play a part in the process and outcome of territorial politics.

Thus, a general arena of political activity on which research should be focused has been identified; the analytical scenario has been extended, the subject opened up. It must be admitted, however, that a number of very real problems of analysis arise (or, better, cease to be obscured) once this territorial perspective is adopted. Three principal difficulties can be briefly noted.[12]

One is suggested by the use of the word 'perceived' in the above definition of territorial politics. Societal cleavage patterns are usually classified in one of two ways. Either a threefold typology of class, status and territorial cleavages is employed, or, alternatively, a simple dichotomy of functional and territorial is utilised. Whatever the method, and there is considerable confusion on the matter, the important point in the present context is that social scientists are unable to differentiate territorial attributes from non-territorial ones in any systematic way. We may talk of territorial communities, interests, political organisations and governments, but these things are often not easily identified and isolated.[13] Moreover, in practice, many political conflicts will draw on strains from all three (or two) societal attributes. Even more confusing, some political issues may be fought out *across* territory but may not be, at root, about territory.[14] 'Territory', then is a highly ambiguous concept in which to deal; it provides no obvious unit of study, and perceptions of its existence and importance may be as important as objective analysis.

Even if this little difficulty is disregarded there exists another problem. Thus far we have dealt with the static structural characteristics of territorial politics. If, however, we consider how these 'statics' are politicised, how and why they enter the political arena, it becomes clear we are faced with a considerable research task. The potential range of territorial politics is considerable: demands from territorial governments and political organisations; territorial doctrines and values which may hinder or support those demands; electoral support for parties of 'territorial defence'; the extent to which other interests and political organisations use, or pick up, territorial issues as a resource in the general game of politics; and the continuing issue how, and to what extent, the central authorities manage their territorial 'estate'.

There remains what is perhaps the most difficult problem. The more the analytical framework is extended, the less easy it becomes to separate central-local relations from the wider workings of the political system. Everything will appear to be connected, and the whole subject will become ragged at the edges. Very often the distinctiveness of the territorial political arena will be obscured.

Combined, these problems represent a real dilemma. It is true that problems of differentiation, range and boundaries, are not exactly rare occurrences in the social sciences. It is also true that the safe restricted frameworks of the traditional languages of analysis have not yielded many benefits to political science. But the problems remain, and the awkward consequences resulting from this choice of perspective need to be noted.

Territorial development

It seems reasonable to argue that any study of territorial politics (as defined) should possess some form of historical perspective. The principal reasons for this are as follows:

(a) Even if the point of the exercise is a detailed examination of the contemporary structure of territorial politics, a base point, a view of that structure in the immediate past, is required. Without this, discussions of the present will take place in a time vacuum, and, as a consequence, it will be difficult to sort out cause and effect, or provide any meaningful assessment of the range of new developments and their relative intensity.

(b) The past, history, will often be a major item in contemporary debates about territorial politics. It is a resource which can be used by the various actors. In so far as political scientists may wish to assess such debates then it is necessary to go back in time to test their interpretations of past events and processes.

(c) Over the last fifteen years or so, political scientists have recognised a need to 'return to history'. As one practitioner has put it, 'History is too important to be left just to historians'.[15] One reason for this is the belated recognition that many of the general questions in political science, particularly in the field of comparative politics, can only be tackled via a study of past politics. Another is the realisation that relatively little is known about the European experience of state and nation building. Hence, if the study of central-local relations is to be linked with the wider interests of political science the demands of this new development need to be recognised.

(d) Other than general histories of local government (and even that is not a popular subject these days), British political scientists have not developed a serious historical perspective. There appear to be two reasons for this research gap: a cultural hostility on the part of liberal social scientists towards the state, its development and mechanisms; and the influence of the dominant paradigm of British historians, which is highly critical of historical overviews and looking at the past with the present in mind.[16]

Territorial development can be studied in two ways. It can involve a detailed account of the *Ancien Régime*, the period immediately prior to the 'present', or, it can attempt an historical overview of the development of territorial politics. For example, it can try to identify the various regimes (structures persisting over time) which have existed in the past, examine the outcome, in territorial terms, of certain 'critical junctures' or 'option points' in the past, and attempt to isolate any factors which are associated with periods of territorial political instability. Clearly, the latter exercise is the more difficult. Much relevant data will be either missing or contested, and the historians will be hostile, criticising the results as 'synthetic history', a gross abridgement of a complex process. Nevertheless, the general point stands: in the study of territorial politics some form of historical perspective is a necessity.

Centre and periphery

The study of territorial politics may be facilitated if we accept the framework and some of the ideas of the centre/periphery school of analysis. These terms were first employed by Shils in the early 1960s, to point to a general and primary cleavage in society between 'the central value system', its institutions and élite supporters, and subordinate peripheral value systems and their non-élite supporters.[17] Although Shils emphasised that his dichotomy referred to the distribution of authoritative values in society, Finer has pointed out that 'because the formulation in this essay is imprecise, a generation of sociologists and political scientists have fastened on the phrase (it sounds good) and used it not in Shils' sense, but to refer to spatial or functional centrality etc., both. This makes it very handy'.[18]

In territorial terms the centre-periphery framework has been employed in two main ways: as a set of convenient shorthand terms to denote the general actors in the arena; or as the basis for a number of theories purporting to describe the structure of territorial politics, either now or in the past.[19]

The latter approach has produced three principal theories: centre-periphery as one of the great historical cleavages in society, destined to decline as society modernises; general theories of territorial dependency (for example, internal colonialism) in which an economically dominant centre exploits its periphery; or, as the basis of studies emphasising the importance of administrative and political 'brokerage' in central-local relations.[20] In addition to this interesting difference between its original conceptualisation and the variety of territorial formulations which have followed, it should be noted that centre-periphery analysis presently suffers from several specific analytical 'loose ends'. For example, despite increasingly common usage, exact definitions of these terms vary. Stein Rokkan, for example, employed them to cover central and local governments, central and peripheral regions, and urban and rural areas.[21] Moreover, as noted earlier, it is never very clear whether centre-periphery theorists are suggesting that this particular structure of territorial politics is present in all countries, or just some of them. Again, the theories sometimes assume a static one centre/one periphery framework, whereas in practice there may be a multiplicity of centres and peripheries, and some centres, for example, may be external to the polity under discussion.

Nevertheless, despite these ambiguities (or, as Finer suggests, because of them) the language of centre and periphery has provoked considerable discussion and some useful research. The terms are generally accepted as convenient descriptions of the major territorial actors; they have become 'a useful vantage point' from which to mount analysis of central-local relations. In addition, the existence of such a broad operational structure is open to testing.[22] For those interested in the United Kingdom they are of particular importance since, as will be argued below, territorial politics in this country has always been biased towards a centre-periphery structure, or, to put the point in seventeenth- and eighteenth-century English political terminology, a court/country distinction.

A Centre perspective

A major criticism of the existing approaches in this field was their willingness to examine seriously the resources, intentions and operations of the central authorities. Thus it seems reasonable, in the present context, to argue that the examination of United Kingdom centre-periphery relations should concentrate on the former, that the analysis should adopt a Centre perspective. Hence, a key question to pursue is: how has the Centre managed its periphery over time? And, following that: in what circumstances has effective central management been threatened?

In addition to filling a gap in academic research, a Centre perspective has two further advantages. It is, perhaps, the only way to provide a macro-development study of territorial politics. Peripheral perspectives can provide only partial territorial discussions, or face insuperable difficulties in attempting generalisations. The second advantage is that this perspective does do something to reduce the territoriality problem mentioned earlier. Territorial interests, actors and problems can be defined in terms of the Centre's perceptions; they emerge in so far as their politicisation, the so-called 'politicisation of the periphery', is perceived to pose problems for effective central management. Unfortunately, the very neglect of the Centre in the academic literature means that any such perspective faces a number of very real problems. One of these, the general problems surrounding the concept of centralisation, will be tackled in the next section. At this point some more specific difficulties require brief discussion.

The first, and most obvious, is that analysis on these lines requires careful attention to the location and nature of the Centre. This may change over time (as may the periphery), and location will determine to some extent the resources and intentions of the Centre. Secondly, the Centre's operational code towards territorial politics may be difficult to isolate.[23] Not only is there the well-known problem of secrecy, but what does one do with an inarticulate or silent Centre, which rarely makes public its code of practice in the territorial sphere? The temptation is to emphasise 'presumptuous empiricism' or conspiracy theories. Alternatively, the code may be 'read' from political practice, a classic case of circular argument. Again, in many places, for most of the time, territorial politics or peripheral management may not be regarded by the Centre as a matter of 'High Politics'. Hence, serious things may be said in non-serious ways. Of course, this is a general problem in political science, but it is often encountered in a more intense way in this particular area of study.

Thirdly, a distinction is commonly drawn between two different types of central management, direct and indirect rule. In the second part of this book the importance of the English tradition of indirect rule will be constantly emphasised. Yet, in practice, this distinction is often difficult to establish, since *all* Centres have to rely on indirect rule techniques to some extent.[24] In short, the ubiquity and ambiguity of indirect rule is a real problem. The classic sense of the term refers to the reliance by the Centre on local notables to manage the periphery in the Centre's interests. But since the end of the nineteenth century all sorts of people have behaved as the local representatives of the Centre; local councillors and officials, local party organisations and their elites and pressure group leaders. On the other hand, centrally appointed officials may escape direct control and supervision from the Centre, be 'colonised' by local interests and behave as quasi-autonomous local notables. Thus a Centre perspective emphasises, once again, the importance for territorial politics of those institutions, groups and individuals which can, if they choose, act as links between periphery and Centre.

Finally, such a perspective means that much of the detail of peripheral politics must be omitted. If it doesn't directly concern the problems and nature of central management then it falls outside the scope of analysis. On the other hand, adoption of this perspective means that many matters not normally regarded as territorial in character may be pulled into the analytical framework. For example, in the United Kingdom in the years after the early 1960s, race relations, industrial relations, economic development and local party organisation all became matters which, it could be argued, were relevant to the Centre's management of the periphery. This again emphasises the problem of abstracting territorial politics from political activity in other arenas. The point is of specific importance where the Centre's policies towards external affairs are concerned, since this supposedly non-territorial aspect of politics has been, it will be argued below, of very real relevance to the Centre's management of the periphery in the United Kingdom. This requires some brief discussion.

The link between centre/periphery relations and external affairs must be approached with some caution.[25] However, on *a priori* grounds, it seems reasonable to argue that there may be a link between the two (omitting in the present context the extremes of the completely closed system and military occupation). Accepting this does not involve accepting Otto Hintze's general declaration in 1902 'that in the life of peoples external events and conditions exercise a decisive influence upon the internal constitution'.[26] On the other hand, academic study until recently went to the other extreme: the analysis of external affairs, foreign policies and international relations was largely divorced from domestic politics. The problem is to find a *via media* between these two positions.

One possible solution is to hypothesise that in terms of a Centre's management of its domestic environment it will attempt to construct what can be labelled an *external support system*, that is to say it will attempt to minimise the impact of external forces on domestic politics, or ensure that these forces are favourable to the maintenance of domestic tranquillity. Of course the relevant items of the support system will tend to vary over time and place. What may be regarded as an external force with an integrative domestic impact in one place may have a disruptive impact elsewhere (for example, compare the varying domestic impacts of the cold war and the EEC on the United Kingdom and Italy). Nevertheless the general point is clear, if banal: few Centres will knowingly pursue foreign policies or join external organisations which will have a direct unfavourable impact on domestic politics. Most will attempt to construct an external support system which will assist internal management. Some may even spend so much time on the maintenance of this system that it becomes an end in itself. Eventually, its very maintenance becomes disadvantageous in terms of effective internal management. Hence, if at any time a Centre's external support declines or collapses, this may adversely affect domestic politics, and in this context, its management of the periphery. The link may not be immediate since, for a variety of reasons, many of the actors on the territorial stage may not perceive a decline. Nevertheless, when perceptions and reality combine, peripheral communities may be politicised and doubts may even arise concerning the necessity of maintaining a link with the Centre. 'Exit' may become a viable option for nationalist or secessionist movements.

CONCEPT REPAIR: CENTRALISATION

A concern for the Centre and central management leads back inevitably to the concept of centralisation, one of the most important in this field and, yet, as customarily employed, subject to all the criticisms listed in the first section of this chapter. In Chapter 1 it was argued that the prevailing centralisation paradigm has three themes: a locational definition, territorial policy is made by the central authorities in the capital city; and two assumptions, centralisation is obvious (it is easy to identify) and centralisation is automatically a bad thing. A minor theme, common to both assumptions, is that centralisation involves the use of, or threat to use, coercive power by the Centre. As a concept, centralisation is ripe for repair. This may be achieved if we pose, and attempt some illustrative answers to, the following questions.

What is the Centre?
The location of the Centre may vary over time, and, as noted, location will determine in part its resources, goals and operational code. The paradigm's approach to this question equates territorial centrality, governmental authority and political power. Hence, its Centre is the central government, above all the central bureaucratic departments, in the capital city. Assuming there is a single Centre, this is certainly one sort of Centre situation. However, there are other possibilities: the national legislature, a core region, a central value system, a dominant mass party, a political elite (or 'establishment'), a ruling class, or some external force or forces. Clearly, if we seek the locus of actual political power rather than the source of formal governmental authority, then the question becomes more difficult and the range of possible answers is expanded, especially if the real power holders do not have a significant territorial connection.

What are the major dimensions of peripheral management?
Or, what options are available to the Centre in terms of the instruments of peripheral management? The following would appear to be one plausible shopping list.
(a) Central penetration
This refers to the Centre's control over its own 'real estate': to the presence of the central authorities throughout the state territory. Essentially, it covers an ability to impose internal law and order, raise taxes and ensure a basic military capability. At best it refers to a continuous effective presence of civil and military officials owing allegiance to the Centre; at worst, the kind of presence or penetration which results from *ad hoc* punitive expeditions to problem areas of the country. Between these two extremes there will be a whole range of possibilities. This is the most basic dimension of centralisation. Until some minimal form of penetration is achieved, the central authorities are not really in business.
(b) Local elite assimilation
This refers to what traditionally has been called 'indirect rule'. Here the Centre succeeds in gaining support for its authority and general policy aims from local social leaders, such as feudal magnates, landowners, tribal or clan chiefs, religious, bureaucratic, educational and political leaders. Such support may be gained by threats, patronage or ideological influence. The benefits of this particular method of central management are fairly obvious: it enables a reasonable degree of continuous penetration to be achieved at minimum cost. Nevertheless, local elites are often administratively ineffective, they stand between the ordinary citizen and the central authorities, and since they have their own interests to defend, there may be certain policies of the Centre which they will refuse to execute. Few local elites, even the most servile, are completely assimilated to the Centre's norms. Above all, their effectiveness depends on the degree to which they can control their followers; if this declines then the Centre will face problems.

(c) Central control of local governments
The classic dimension of centralisation, the control of territorial governments, especially elected local authorities. Two points need to be noted about this dimension. First, it assumes less significance in so far as local elites have been assimilated to central norms. Secondly, control can be negative or positive in character; the ability to stop local governments breaking the law, or the capacity to impose a broad range of policy objectives on territorial governments. Of the two, the former is easier to achieve.

(d) Organisation mobilisation
The ability of the Centre to establish, control and deploy in its own interests the resources of local political organisations such as parties and trade unions.

(e) Citizen mobilisation
The capacity to mobilise the citizens of territorial communities to give continuous active support and assistance to the full range of the Centre's policy objectives. Presumably, this is the ultimate dimension of centralisation and probably rarely achieved in pluralist polities, except perhaps, in times of war.

The above list is by no means comprehensive. Its prime purpose is to illustrate the range of peripheral processes which an aspiring dominant Centre can aim to control. It suggests that when we talk of central control of the periphery the task, if taken seriously, is a considerable one. It also suggests that when we say a country is centralised we need to identify how many of these dimensions are covered by that statement.

What can a Centre aim for in terms of its overall peripheral strategy?
This question is concerned with the Centre's intentions. One possible answer was provided by Griffith, whose analysis of the relationship between central departments and local authorities in England and Wales led him to conclude that departmental intentions could be classified as promotional, regulatory, or *laissez-faire*.[27] Clearly, this typology could also be applied to the broader context of territorial politics. But the problem, as Griffith noted, was that different sections of the same department often possessed different intentions and that there was always scope for these to change over time. Moreover, the Centre may adopt different strategies in different peripheries, and the intentions as listed may be designed to produce different results. Promotional intentions, for example, could lead to territorial justice or exploitation. Again, the strategy adopted may depend on the number of peripheral actors the Centre can influence, and what sort of influence it is. There may be no point in attempting a promotional strategy when all you can influence are the members of the local elite. The Centre does have, however, some sort of choice. There is a considerable difference, in terms of peripheral impact, in going for a promotional, regulatory, or *laissez-faire* strategy. And only the first resembles in any way the leviathan Centre so popular in the literature.

What resources must an aspiring dominant Centre possess?

Let us assume that the Centre is aiming for maximum possible control of the periphery, in terms of both peripheral actors and its overall strategy. In these circumstances it will need to possess most (just how many is not clear) of the following resources:

(a) An hegemonic 'Unionist' culture, influencing peripheral bureaucrats, political leaders and citizens.

(b) A constitution which either obstructs, or does not positively assist the articulation of peripheral interests.

(c) An effective central bureaucratic machine with an extensive presence in the periphery.

(d) A mass party system controlled by politicians at the Centre, which, as a result, can be used as an instrument to colonise peripheral politics in the Centre's interests.

(e) The resources and abilities to manage the overall economy such that peripheral communities rarely perceive any intense degree of economic deprivation.

(f) Sufficient time to devote to peripheral politics. In other words, the Centre should not be preoccupied with the problems of other political arenas, for example foreign affairs, or, in the terminology set out above, a difficult or fragile external support system.

Once again, the object of the exercise has been to *illustrate* the range of resources required by the Centre if it wishes to continuously and effectively control most aspects of peripheral politics. It should be noted that this list assumes a reasonably homogeneous territorial society. Control will be that much more difficult if the Centre is faced with a difficult geography (including the awkward siting of scarce mineral resources) and/or unintegrated and distinctive territorially concentrated cultural groups capable of mounting plausible peripheral nationalist demands. This provisional resource register suggests that central dominance in pluralist polities is much more difficult than the literature customarily suggests.

What general power models of centralisation are possible?

We have seen that traditional analysis emphasised a *coercive power model*: the Centre achieved its aims by the use of, or threats to use, coercion against peripheral interests, communities and governments. Hopefully, enough has been said to suggest that coercion on the scale required may be neither the intention nor within the capabilities of most Centres in pluralist polities in the age of mass suffrage. A more plausible model is the *central authority model*: the Centre achieves its aims because peripheral citizens, politicians and officials accept that it has a legitimate right to demand their co-operation and acquiescence. In such situations peripheral politicians will act as unofficial field agents of the Centre. In terms of the locational definition of centralisation two other models are possible, though each in turn casts doubts on the utility of that definition. These are the *capital city bargaining* and the *central autonomy models*. The former suggests a structure of territorial politics in which peripheral groups and governments articulate, defend and satisfy their interests within the institutional complex of the Centre, especially the legislature and executive. In terms of the traditional definition this has to be labelled a centralised structure, and yet in this sort of polity the penetration of the Centre by the periphery may be such that the result is at least cooperation between the two, and, at most, the colonisation of the Centre in those areas of high concern to the periphery. The latter model, that of central autonomy, is, however, the most interesting since it postulates a Centre seeking and gaining autonomy from peripheral forces to concentrate on what it regards as 'High Politics'.

The literature of territorial politics talks obsessively about local autonomy from the Centre's interference. There seems no reason, however, why the Centre should not seek a similar autonomy from local or peripheral interference in those matters which it regards as important. In such circumstances the Centre will act like a garrison state, seeking to insulate itself from peripheral interests by restricting the extent to which they can penetrate its fortress. Presumably, the conditions allowing such a model to operate will be rare, since, to be successful, it will require correspondingly weak or servile peripheral forces unable or unwilling to penetrate the institutional complex at the Centre. Nevertheless, such a model is a possibility. It will produce a structure of territorial politics in which the Centre is prepared to allow considerable operational autonomy to peripheral governments and political organisations, so long as they do not challenge its autonomy in matters of 'High Politics'. The consequent political duality between Centre and periphery is not something which fits easily with prevailing ideas of centralisation, or for that matter decentralisation.

To sum up, there are a variety of central power models, not all of them are based on coercion, and some cast doubt on the utility of the locational definition and the bad-consequences assumption of the prevailing centralisation paradigm.

How should centralisation be defined?
The analysis above suggests that as a concept centralisation would be more useful if defined differently. In place of the old locational definition and bad-consequences assumption a definition in terms of the process of territorial politics should be sought and assumptions about the consequences avoided. In this sense the following definition is suggested: 'A centralised structure of territorial politics is one in which the displacement of peripheral interests is low'. Admittedly words such as 'displacement' and 'interests' are vague, and thus identifying a centralised polity is made more difficult. Nevertheless, this sort of definition does capture the political flavour and style of what we mean by centralisation in ways which the traditional definition cannot. It concentrates on the thing itself rather than its causes or effects, it allows for the phenomenon of capital city bargaining, and testing it requires the student to widen his framework of analysis. Moreover, since it carries no fixed message regarding the causes of this state of affairs, it forces the analyst to accept, at the outset, that centralisation may result from effective central management, a politically weak periphery, or both. Finally, it carries neutral implications regarding the consequences of such a condition.

SUMMARY

This chapter has merely emphasised the obvious: it is easier to criticise existing approaches than provide plausible alternatives. Hopefully, two general points have emerged from this very conservative prospectus. The subject is more difficult and complex, yet more subtle and interesting than the traditional approaches suggest, and central dominance/exploitation of the periphery involves many things, may not be a popular aim of many Centres, and requires more resources than traditionally supposed. Part II of this book is an exercise within the broad framework suggested by this perspective.

NOTES

1   This chapter is an amended version of a paper written for the SSRC. Central-Local Relations Research Committee in March 1980, entitled *Territorial Politics in the United Kingdom: An Analytical Prospectus*.

2   R. A. W. Rhodes, 'Analysing intergovernmental relations', *European Journal of Political Research* (1980).

3   Keith Middlemas, *The Politics of Industrial Society* (London, 1979), p. 13.

4   Jesse T. Carpenter, *The South as a Conscious Minority, 1789–1861* (Gloucester, Mass., 1963).

5   See R. A. W. Rhodes, 'Research into central-local relations in Britain: a framework for analysis' in *SSRC Central-Local Government Relationships* (London, 1979), Appendix 1; and Michael Harloe (ed.), *Captive Cities* (London, 1977). See also A. Lee Fritschler and Morley Segal, 'Intergovernmental relations and contemporary political science: developing an integrative typology', *Publius* (1972); Richard J. Samuels 'Extra local linkages and the comparative study of local politics', *Comparative Urban Research* (1975); Stanley L. Elkin, 'Comparative urban politics and interorganisation behaviour', in Ken Young (ed.), *Essays on the Study of Urban Politics* (London, 1975); Cynthia Cockburn, *The Local State* (London, 1977); Patrick Dunleavy, *Urban Political Analysis* (London, 1980).

6   A. Lee Fritschler and Morley Segal, *op. cit.*

7   One reason for this is the inordinate amount of time and energy spent on community power studies, a subject which has produced little of benefit for central-local relations research.

8   J. W. Fesler 'Centralisation and decentralisation', *International Enclyclopaedia of the Social Sciences*, II (New York, 1968).

9   Especially when interested sections of the public and politicians continue to perceive central-local relations in terms of the traditional models and concepts.

10 For example, Sidney Tarrow *et al.*, *Territorial Politics in Industrial Nations* (New York, 1978). The alternatives, 'spatial' and 'areal' are less appealing.

11 Richard J. Samuels, *op. cit.* and L. J. Sharpe (ed.), *Decentralist Trends in Western Democracies* (London, 1979).

12 See the criticisms of 'the systems approach' in R. A. W. Rhodes, 'Analysing intergovernmental relations', *European Journal of Political Research* (1980).

13 Richard Rose and Derek Urwin, *Regional Differentiation and Political Unity in Western Nations* (London, 1975); Peter Saunders, *Urban Politics* (London, 1980), Chapter 1.

14 Tarrow, *op. cit.*, p. 1.

15 D. A. Rustow, 'Transitions to Democracy', *Comparative Politics* (1969/70).

16 Herbert Butterfield, *The Whig Interpretation of History* (London, 1973). Note the reluctant enthusiasm towards this sort of analysis exhibited in Keith Thomas' 'The United Kingdom' in R. Grew (ed.), *Crises of Political Development in Europe and the United States* (Princeton, 1978). On the state, see Kenneth Dyson, *The State Tradition in Western Europe* (Oxford, 1980).

17 The most convenient entry into this analysis is now Edward Shils, *Centre and Periphery: Essays in Macro Sociology* (Chicago, 1975).

18 S. E. Finer, 'State building, state boundaries and border control', *Social Science Information*, XIII, 415.

19 See, for example, S. Tarrow, *Between Centre and Periphery* (New Haven, 1977); and S. M. Lipset and S. Rokkan, 'Cleavage structures, party systems and voter alignments: an introduction', in their *Party Systems and Voter Alignments* (Glencoe, 1967).

20 For example, research on political clientelism. See Steffen W. Schmidt *et al. Friends, Followers and Factions: A Reader in Political Clientelism* (Berkeley, 1977).

21 S. Langholm, 'On the concept of Centre and periphery', *Journal of Peace Research* (1971).

22 Rajni Kothari, 'Variations and uniformities in nation-building', *International Social Science Journal* (1971).

23 For the operational code concept see Alexander C. George 'The operational code: a neglected approach to the study of political leaders and decision-making', *International Studies Quarterly* (1969). A code is something less than a philosophy of government and yet more than a collection of specific policies. It relates to the accepted rules of 'statecraft' as employed over time by political elites.

24 Even the great historic centralised empires of the pre-modern world. On the Roman empire see Fergus Miller, *The Emperor in the Roman World* (London, 1977). On the Inca empire see G. Balandier, *Political Anthropology* (London, 1972) pp. 139–40.

25 For a general discussion of the literature in this field see Peter Byrd, *The International Environment for Territorial Politics in the United Kingdom* (University of Strathclyde, Centre for the Study of Public Policy, 1981).

26 Otto Hintze, 'The formation of states and constitutional development' (1902), reprinted in Felix Gilbert (ed.), *The Historical Essays of Otto Hintze* (New York, 1975).

27 J. A. G. Griffith, *Central Departments and Local Authorities* (London 1966).

part two

The United Kingdom

chapter three | the making of the United Kingdom: the anatomy of English imperialism[1]

The silent nations undistinguished fall,
And Englishman's the common name for all,
Fate jumbled them together,
God knows how;
What'er they were, they're true born English now.[2]

...the force of the imperial power is to be measured not only or even primarily by the overt acts of political control but by the degree to which the values, attitudes and institutions of the expansionist nation infiltrate and overcome those of the recipient one. In this process native collaborator or sepoy is indispensable.[3]

INTRODUCTION

It seems appropriate to begin at the beginning, or at least what can be plausibly argued, in the present context, to represent the beginning. Hence, this chapter poses and attempts to answer two principal questions – what were the conditions which led to the creation of the political Union known as the United Kingdom of Great Britain and Ireland? and what were the principal characteristics of the structure of territorial politics in the largely pre-industrial and pre-democratic state which followed that Union? In short, this is a chapter which seeks to generalise about the process which led to, and the initial operation of, that peculiar piece of political real estate, the United Kingdom.

Clearly, this sort of exercise faces a number of problems. Few general accounts of the early history of the British Isles exist and the usefulness of much of the case study literature is often vitiated by disputes between historians. Equally important, there is no easy answer to those (principally British historians) who argue that the making of the United Kingdom was the result of a series of separate events about which no meaningful generalisations can be made. How can anything serious or interesting be said about a project in which William of Normandy, William of Orange and William Pitt all played some part? Moreover, the process of Union took different forms: the Anglo-Welsh Union (1536) resulted from a *diktat* by a court-dominated English parliament; the Anglo-Scottish Union (1707) from a treaty negotiated by representatives of both parties and then ratified by their respective legislatures; and the Anglo-Irish Union (1800) from a deal struck between the executives of both countries, which was then accepted by the parliaments concerned. These points provoke three possible replies. First, the problem is not so much that data are scarce and disputed, rather that what data exist have rarely been drawn into an overall perspective. Secondly, objections to the propriety of the whole exercise are based on the dominant analytical paradigm of British historians. There is no reason, however, why social scientists should follow these particular rules of the game. Finally, general explanations of the Union process and its results do exist, though more often in terms of political rhetoric than academic analysis. In short, this aspect of the United Kingdom's past is an item in contemporary debates regarding territorial power and reform and on this ground alone the subject deserves some attention and assessment.

THE UNION: THE EXISTING LANGUAGES

At this point it is useful to identify, and examine critically, the principal existing languages of analysis regarding the making of the United Kingdom. These can be conveniently, if roughly, categorised under three labels, the Whig, the peripheral nationalist and the internal colonial views.

The Whig language
Until recently this was the dominant, or exoteric view of the Union. It has three major themes. The first is that while the territorial sections concerned may have agreed to Union for different reasons, the creation of the United Kingdom was inevitable.[4] This inevitability was seen to be the result of a variety of factors: geographical proximity, England's predominance, a common language, the accession to the English throne of the 'Welsh' Tudors and the 'Scotch' Stuarts, England's security problems and economic attractions, and the pressing need to integrate the Catholic Irish into a wider and less divisive community. The second theme concerns the absence of anything which could be described as federalism from the post-Union structure of government – the United Kingdom was created as a unitary state, provincial legislative jurisdictions were abolished.[5] The third and final theme emphasises the beneficial effect resulting from the Union for all, or almost all, concerned. As the Royal Commission on the Constitution put it – 'The story of the United Kingdom has thus been, at least in the larger island, a success story'.[6]

The peripheral nationalist language
This is the traditional language of political and academic dissent regarding the creation of the United Kingdom. It accepts the inevitability and unitary arguments of the Whig view, but draws different conclusions from them as regards both the nature of the Union process and the benefits of the subsequent English 'connection'

for Wales, Scotland and Ireland. Supporters of this language regard the Unions as the successful completion of an age-old English plot to subjugate the celtic periphery. Moreover, so the argument runs, in each case Union was pushed through largely as a result of English coercion, coercion involving either the use of, or threat to use, military force, or the employment of patronage or bribery, or both.[7] Thus the Union was imposed on the periphery to suit England's interests (its quest to dominate and its security fears), and any benefits which resulted went overwhelmingly to England as well. On this perspective the Unions were essentially illegitimate and, as a consequence, could, indeed should, be repudiated when circumstances allowed.

The language of internal colonialism
The internal colonialism thesis, and Michael Hechter's particular application of that thesis to the United Kingdom, were described and assessed in Chapter 1. In the present context, Hechter's specific arguments regarding what he calls 'the expansion of the English state' and its political consequences require some further comment since, although they bear some resemblance to the previous language, they are significantly different in a number of important respects.

Hechter's principal points on this subject appear to be the following:

(a) Within the British Isles, geography, in particular the distribution of the highland and lowland zones, favoured English economic development and not the economies of the celtic periphery. In addition to these natural advantages England also benefited economically and politically from the impact of the Roman and Norman conquests and the Reformation. The British Isles, then, developed very early a naturally dominant core society, England, and three naturally subordinate peripheral societies, Wales, Scotland and Ireland (though the degree of subordination varied).

(b) In political terms, England's relations with this celtic periphery were inherently imperial in character. Hence, when Union came it was carried out in each case for reasons largely specific to England's interests and on England's terms. As Hechter puts it

> ...each of the Celtic regions became politically incorporated at a critical juncture in English history. Largely out of *raisons d'etat* England desired to insure its territorial integrity at all costs, rather than suffer the threat of invasion by hostile Continental neighbours (p. 69).

(c) 'The net effect of all three of these unions was to deny to each Celtic territory the exclusive right to determine the policies which would govern it. . . there is no question that the unification of the British Isles represented a loss of Celtic sovereignty' (p. 68). This loss of political sovereignty made the economic and cultural dependency of the periphery 'inevitable'. More positively: 'In common with colonialism overseas, the English state attempted to rule the Celtic lands for instrumental ends' (p. 342).

(d) These, however, were the broad consequences of Union. In terms of the techniques of government, Hechter emphasises (somewhat paradoxically) the traditions of local elite rule, extensive local authority autonomy, and the absence of direct state intervention in England. These traditions, he argues, were extended to the periphery after unification. As a result he concludes:

> incorporation did not, in any real way, result in the effective political integration of the Celtic periphery into the United Kingdom. The British political structure on the eve of industrialisation continued, in significant respects, to resemble that of a decentralized patrimonial state. (p. 123)

AN ALTERNATIVE APPROACH

The three languages of Union examined above differ in fairly obvious ways. The important point, however, is that they all share a common analytical base, they all accept (or do not dissent from) the twin ideas that the United Kingdom was inevitable and that the post Union structure of territorial government is most aptly described as unitary or resulted in increased central control, even exploitation, of the celtic periphery.[8] Their differences stem from the varying inferences they draw from these two themes and these inferences relate ultimately to their views regarding English attitudes towards the desirability of Union and English methods of territorial management in the post Union period. All this points to the obvious. If we want to understand the making of the United Kingdom, we have to pay considerable attention to England and the English, or, as Pocock has put it, 'The history of an increasing English domination is remarkably difficult to write in other than English terms'.[9] Unfortunately, where academic analysis is concerned, with the partial exception of Hechter, general surveys of the Union process have neglected the English. Hence, our first task must be to examine the nature of the English Union and the development of English ideas regarding territorial management. This may cast some light on whether England desired to dominate the celtic periphery and what sort of arrangements it would make to sustain that dominance.

If the necessity for an English perspective is accepted, then another necessary dimension to our analysis emerges. England's seemingly predominant position in the early history of the British Isles, its perceived success in bringing about the effective completion of Union, against considerable opposition where Scotland and Ireland are concerned, and general talk of English dominance in post-Union arrangements, all these themes raise the spectre of imperialism, or a set of imperial type relations. As we have seen, Hechter's analysis explicitly accepts this, and so too, though often less directly, does the peripheral nationalist language. On the other hand, the Whig view may well be at fault in blandly seeking to expunge power and conflict from the whole process and avoiding the whole issue. In fact, there seems no harm in admitting at the outset that the making of the United Kingdom may have involved an imperial situation. Accepting this reaps two advantages. First, as Hechter has pointed out, nation building 'in its early states might be better thought of as empire building'. Put negatively; given the complex inanities of much of the political science literature on state and nation building, old fashioned imperialism might be as good an analytical perspective as any. Secondly, although in general terms, 'the whole subject of imperialism is terrifyingly complicated', one strand of the literature, namely the work of Robinson and Gallagher on nineteenth-century British imperial expansion, may be capable of yielding useful insights on the earlier English process in the British Isles. As one observer of their work has put it – 'Their insights can be applied to various regions and different eras'.[10]

Robinson and Gallagher have managed to throw new and interesting (though much disputed) light on the motives, causes and methods of British imperial expansion in the nineteenth century, largely as a result of their concern to relate that expansion to domestic, political and administrative elite perceptions and calculations, and to the structure of politics in those societies at the receiving end of British interest and rule. This concern with the politics of imperialism has obvious utility for the present exercise. Their most relevant themes are as follows:

(i) The distinction they draw between potential and actual power: they emphasise that throughout the nineteenth century most of the European powers had the capacity to take over Africa, or parts of it, but it was not until the 1870s that the scramble for Africa began. In other words, formal primacy and predominance may not automatically lead to a desire to annex weaker polities. Is this a distinction we should bear in mind where the British Isles is concerned?

(ii) They reject 'the fearful symmetry of old theories of imperialism which confounded the politics of empire with the economics of capitalism'. In other words, economic advantage was not a primary force behind the annexation by Europeans of vast tracts of Africa. Businessmen were not interested, governments had other motives and, in any case, where tropical Africa was concerned there were no economic gains to be had. As they put it: 'the imperialists were merely scraping the bottom of the barrel'. Can economic forces be similarly downgraded for England and the British Isles? Had England scraped the barrel before 1870?

(iii) The distinction they draw between informal and formal Empire, the former characterised by indirect external influences, the latter by annexation and direct rule. The nineteenth century, they argue, exhibited continuous British pressures for expansion, but discontinuity regarding methods of influence. The British preferred the indirect 'sway' of informal Empire to direct rule. Annexations were to be avoided if possible. Power was extended in its subtler forms...' Only when indirect methods of influence failed would the British move towards formal Empire; hence the difference between informal and formal Empire was often one of degree only. Colonial rule was essentially a 'reconstruction' of as much of informal Empire as could be retained. Did the English exhibit similar preferences for informal Empire at 'home'? Can the Union be seen as an earlier 'reconstruction'?

(iv) The perceived differences between motives and causes: motives are derived from the traditional notions and common calculations of elites. To have an impact they need to be activated by 'causes' or 'triggers'. They argue that British motives for going into Africa were primarily strategic (specifically to protect India), but the causes were nationalist revolts against British influence in Egypt and South Africa. As a result their theories have been labelled 'peripheral' or 'eccentric', since they emphasise that imperialism cannot be explained in a Eurocentric way. Did similar motives and causes influence England in terms of the making of the United Kingdom?

(v) Throughout their work Robinson and Gallagher (especially the former) emphasise the importance of political factors in determining the scope of British expansion and the imperial rule. In particular, they stress three themes: the vital role of the British 'official mind', the elite's operational code regarding expansion, its shortsighted, parsimonious nature and its obsession with security; the imperialism of the Centre's agents, the ability of settler politicians and imperial officials in the field to determine the Centre's policies; and the essential role, in determining the nature of British rule, of indigenous, native 'collaborators'.[11] What was the English 'official mind' regarding territorial politics in the United Kingdom? To what extent did agents and collaborators play a significant role in the management of the domestic Empire?

From this discussion of the main themes of Robinson and Gallagher's work it seems plausible to conclude that they provide us with some interesting questions to pose and some useful concepts to employ in our analysis of the making of the United Kingdom. These themes then, plus the English perspective, form the basis of the present exercise. We are concerned with the forces behind the creation of the United Kingdom and the anatomy of the subsequent structure of territorial politics. The analysis proceeds as follows. First, England's position is examined in terms of the development of its 'official mind' regarding the desired structure of territorial politics. Secondly, the nature of the informal Empire – the pre-Union stage – is analysed. Thirdly, the principal forces behind the move from informal to formal Empire – the Union process – are identified. Finally, the structure of territorial politics after the Unions – the formal Empire – is examined.

England: territorial development and the 'official mind'
The development of the early English state, in particular the attitude of its political elite regarding the desired structure of territorial politics, is of crucial importance for an understanding of the making of the United Kingdom. More specifically, because, in comparative perspective, English territorial development was peculiar and the English 'official mind' idiosyncratic, then the forces which led to, and the eventual structure of, the United Kingdom were more complex than commonly supposed. Cashing this argument, however, is a difficult task. The early history of the English state is a jungle of conceptual contortions, scarce data and differing interpretations.[12] This said, the following brief points are relevant.

To begin with, and in the beginning, ecology favoured the English. If our point of reference is France (as a geographical expression) then England in the early Middle Ages was a small, poor, sparsely populated, relatively homogeneous and easily penetrable society. It possessed about one-third the acreage of France and about one-fifth its population. As Hintze put it, 'such an area could be organised'.[13] Moreover, England had few awkward physical features, no 'frontier' to conquer or settle (as, did Spain or Prussia), no powerful neighbours with adjacent land borders and, with one exception, fewer awkward regional particularisms. More positively, the traditional core lowland area of Wessex, Mercia and East Anglia was economically culturally predominant and its capital, London, had no urban rival throughout the country. God, however, had not smiled throughout its creation. Apart from wool, England possessed few commercial resources and its rulers and ruled always believed themselves to be poor. High tax rates were always difficult to fix if not to collect. Again, if the Centre could penetrate the periphery relatively easily, the reverse could also happen. Perhaps more importantly, the whole country was easily penetrable from the sea: invasions and coastal raids by hostile maritime powers (such as the Scandinavians in the tenth and eleventh centuries) were always perceived to be a potential threat. Finally, there was the ever-present problem of the 'the north parts', which on a maximum definition included all the land north of the Trent. The north was both ruder and poorer than the rest of the country. It was also strategically important because it shared a border with Scotland. As an armed fortress the north could look two ways towards the old enemy, Scotland, or towards interfering peace-seeking governments in London.

Most commentators support the argument that for most of the medieval period there was a direct link between the positive aspects of English ecology and its governmental system. The academic consensus appears to be that the English feudal community was one of the most highly integrated and effective in Europe.[14] Unification under one monarch was achieved in the tenth century, and although the Anglo-Saxon regime soon declined, it bequeathed to both Danes and Normans in the eleventh century a proto-state structure of considerable organisational capacity, in terms of both central penetrative and extractive abilities. The Norman conquest only served to increase that capacity. In eliminating one elite and substituting another, William of Normandy was able to fashion a feudal polity more favourable to the Centre's interests than elsewhere. In comparison the French monarchy at this time administered a petty statelet. By the fourteenth century, military successes and empire in France and the beginnings of a diffused sense of national identity had served to reinforce England's traditional political integration.[15] Thus the medieval English polity was characterised by a relatively effective central authority, no secession movements or sentiments, and a society which, although by no means law-abiding, possessed no powerful tradition of political outlawry or social banditry. In builders' parlance, Robin Hood was a one-off, northern job.

However, this precociously integrated English feudal polity rested, as elsewhere, on a complex and essentially fragile system of bargaining between the Crown and the great landed magnates. A combination of weak kings, defeats by external enemies and an increase in magnate cohesion and resources, could seriously weaken central authority. In England such a combination of circumstances occurred in the fifteenth century, initiated by the successful northern-inspired coup against Richard II in 1399. Despite its initial success, the ultimate result of this peripheral coup against the Centre was that series of armed skirmishes and period of political turbulence dignified by the label 'The Wars of the Roses' (in which the northern barons played important roles on both sides). It was not until the advent of the Tudors that England appeared to return to its traditional territorial pattern of an effective Centre faced by weak peripheral forces.

The territorial achievement of the Tudors was threefold.[16] First, they reimposed domestic peace and tranquillity. This was done by reducing the military power of the landed magnates and their retainers. The Crown finally achieved a monopoly of violence. An important part of this process was the demilitarisation and more complete political integration of the north.[17] Though it took more time and energy than sometimes suggested, magnate power (the basis of organised peripheral protest during the feudal era) was eventually broken by the last decades of the sixteenth century. Secondly, all medieval polities contained a mass of quasi-autonomous areas not subject to direct central administration and justice. England, especially in the Welsh Marches and the northern counties, was no exception. Henry VIII and Thomas Cromwell abolished these separate jurisdictions by the Franchise Act, 1536. Henceforth, 'for the first time the whole realm without qualification became subject to government from Westminster'.[18] Thirdly, the power of the Centre was both illustrated and increased by the Reformation settlement. Anglicanism was imposed on the periphery by the court via an important intermediary, parliament. This broke the link with Rome and thereby established the English state's sovereignty in terms of the last remaining formal external constraint. At the same time, Protestantism provided the state with a distinctive popular national and nationalising ideology. The closure of the monasteries also provided the funds and land which enabled the Centre to build up a new class of client gentry collaborators in the periphery.

Thus far (that is, up to the early seventeenth century), the development of territorial politics in England can be represented as a highly successful exercise in state and nation building. The Centre had achieved sufficient control over its own real estate, local elites had been militarily neutered and assimilated to central norms, a single parliament existed to legitimise policies and a strong sense of Protestant nationalism had developed. Yet from the middle of the sixteenth century there were signs of a decline in the Centre's power, at least in a comparative Western European sense. On the one hand, it can be argued that many of the economic and cultural developments which had helped create a more nationally integrated society – the change from script to print, the increasing commercial significance of London, the importance of law, lawyers and the Inns of Courts – all these could also help those opposed to the Centre's policies or assist in the rise of a more distinctive set of local community loyalties. In short, the early seventeenth century saw an increase in the sense of both national and local identities, and the latter were probably stronger. On the other hand, it has been argued that the English monarchy failed to remodernise its structure to take account of the changed conditions of government at the end of the medieval period.[19] In particular, although it tried to follow more positive policies it failed to develop strong and autonomous bureaucratic, financial and military resources. The process of state building continued, but without a state machine. The result was to politicise the periphery without the means of controlling it. Given the increasingly close links between Parliament and local communities, and the displacement the House of Commons had achieved in the legislative and fiscal process, all this only served to compound the Centre's difficulties. The resulting division between court and country – the post-feudal structure of English territorial politics – was as dangerous to the Centre as the Crown/magnate division in the feudal period.[20]

The decades of revolution between 1640 and 1688 have been taken by many to represent the triumph of peripheral forces over an absolutist-inclined Centre, and the operation of territorial politics after 1688 as further proof of this view. In other words, the seventeenth century witnessed, in terms of territorial politics, a great reversal: a highly integrated society with a strong Centre and relatively weak periphery was transformed into one where the Centre was far weaker and peripheral forces far stronger than elsewhere in Europe. A plausible case can be mounted to suggest that this is altogether too simple a picture of seventeenth-century events. In fact, neither the Centre nor the periphery won an outright victory. Much of the old Tory view of territorial politics survived and much of the new Whig ideology represented a continuity rather than a break with the past. The political settlement, so painfully worked out in the years following 1688 was a highly ambiguous one.[21]

First, three times in the seventeenth century, in the 1630s, 1650s and 1680s, the court, or Centre, attempted to move closer to the absolute government model and a consequent increase in both the scope and intensity of its control over local interests. It is true that on each occasion these moves were defeated. More important, however, is the degree to which English local interests were prepared to accept such moves. It was not so much the strength of country opposition which defeated the Centre, as the intrusion of external forces (Scotland and Holland) to bolster weak and failing English opposition.[22]

Secondly, if we identify, or attempt to identify, what appear to be the main features of the English 'official mind' (or élite operational code) regarding the desired structure of territorial politics after 1688, it is difficult not to conclude that it differed very little from moderate opinion before the revolutionary decades. This code had four articles which, when combined, produced a very subtle set of ideas concerning how to manage and structure a difficult territorial situation.

(a) The desired aim was the peace, order and tranquillity of the realm. Management was preferred to government, and conflict within the periphery, and between it and the Centre, was to be avoided as far as possible. Territorial management should be depoliticised.

(b) Although the Centre lacked a state machine it regarded the personnel of government at the local level as, in the last resort, its field agents, or collaborators, in the grand design of 'self-government at the King's command'.[23] Thus, institutions of local government (or, as Blackstone called them, the subordinate governments of the realm) were regarded as instruments of central administration and control. Ecclesiastical structures were viewed in much the same light. The Centre preferred this system of indirect rule because it was cheap and, in English conditions, reasonably effective. So long as local elites accepted the ultimate authority of the Crown, they could be allowed considerable autonomy in supervising the boring details of local administration.

(c) Members of parliament had three roles. They advised the court or executive on occasional key issues of national policy; they legitimised executive policies (to do so they had full powers of attorney, they were on these occasions not merely delegates; and they pressed, defended and settled the interests of their constituencies. The latter was their continuous task, the others were *ad hoc*. In England, then, the important issues and conflicts of local communities were to be settled in the capital city: local politics was to be located in parliament, not local government.

(d) A distinction was made, or attempted, between 'High' and 'Low' politics. The former were regarded as essentially matters for the executive or court, and to be settled, as far as possible, independently of outside, particularly territorial, interests. The latter were seen as part of the wider game of political management and could properly be settled by bargaining between the executive and interests involved. What counted as a matter of 'High Politics' varied, but defence, foreign affairs and taxation were obvious candidates for attempted permanent inclusion. The separate procedures for private bill legislation (the bulk of legislative activity in this period) were designed to facilitate the process of 'Low Politics'.

Thirdly, in the conditions of post-1688 English politics this code was difficult to operationalise effectively over any length of time. The Duke of Newcastle, for example, despite his office, can hardly be described as a man able to devote his life to 'High Politics'. Nevertheless, he (and others like him) were forced to interfere in local politics in order to preserve some semblance of autonomy for the executive.[24] Moreover, the court/country distinction, the basis of much of the code, appears to have had general cultural support, especially among that important group, the independent country gentlemen. In other words, the code was important because, though often broken, most politicians assessed problems and designed solutions to them with its dictates in mind. Finally, it must be emphasised that this English code accepted implicitly two things supposedly absent from English constitutional development – an operational federalism between Centre and periphery and a separation of powers between court and parliament. Parliament, in fact, was the linchpin of the whole structure. It was the essential intermediary between court and country and it was on its brokerage and socialisation capacities that the whole operation depended.

In comparative perspective the development of the early English state was highly idiosyncratic. In no other comparable western European polity did the Centre achieve so much power and authority so early and lose so much after the mid-sixteenth century. The response of the English 'official mind' to the changing circumstances of territorial politics was complex, subtle and, on the whole, effective. There was always sufficient connection between the dictates of the 'official mind' – tranquillity, indirect rule, parliament and 'High/Low Politics' – and the practice of territorial politics, for the resulting settlement to hold considerable attractions when confronted with related problems outside England. In short, if territorial politics in the heartland of the British Isles was peculiar, the chances were that any United Kingdom-wide Union settlement would also be peculiar.

The informal Empire

What, then, was the structure of England's informal Empire – the pre-Union English connection with the celtic periphery of the 'Atlantic archipelago', Wales, Scotland and Ireland? To what extent did this structure reflect the preferences of the English 'official mind' outlined above? What inferences can be drawn from this analysis concerning the forces behind the transformation from informal to formal Empire in the British Isles?

Of course, any attempt to answer these questions, to generalise about the structure of the informal Empire, faces problems. To begin with, it is not always easy to say when this particular phase began. The periods considered here are those most likely to gain general acceptance: namely, for Wales from 1284 (Edwardian conquest and Statute of Rhuddlan) to 1536; for Scotland 1603 to 1707 (that is, the regal Union); and for Ireland from 1603 (the end of the Tudor conquest) to 1800. One point does become clear from such periodisation: if Union was inevitable then this took a long time to dawn on those involved. In addition, there were important constitutional and political differences in the separate structures of the informal Empire. Thus, Wales and Ireland, unlike Scotland, were never united under one native monarchy. Wales never had a parliament of its own; Scotland and Ireland did. Scotland did not have to suffer Poynings' Law, the Declaratory Act, or the formal apparatus of castle government; Ireland did.[25] Wales and Ireland were both conquered by force of English arms; Scotland, apart from the Cromwellian episode, was not. Ireland was a plantation or settler polity; Scotland, and to a lesser extent Wales, were not. Again, the informal Empire was never a tidy structure. The English parliament had claimed the right to legislate for Ireland as far back as the thirteenth century and Wales sent representatives to Westminster on odd occasions before 1536. What this means is that very often those most involved in working the informal Empire had little idea what the rules of the game were supposed to be. Nevertheless, it can be argued that in terms of English attitudes and practices significant similarities did surface over time. Several points need to be made here.

First, within the British Isles England possessed certain initial, and over time increasing, natural advantages. By the beginning of the sixteenth century England was superior to her celtic neighbours in terms of population, tax capacity, agricultural production, trading resources and per capita income: England for example, had five times the population of Ireland and Scotland and one observer has estimated that in 1706 her comparative advantage over Scotland in terms of land tax revenue was 41:1 and the general wealth ratio was 36:1 in her favour.[26] By inference these advantages could easily be translated into military superiority as well. Moreover, all the celtic lands were traditionally much less integrated and more faction-ridden politically than England. As Defoe said regarding Scotland: 'There is entire harmony in this country, consisting in universal discords'.[27] In part, of course, these political divisions were simply the result of England's presence: those vanquished in the political battles of Scotland, Wales and Ireland could always appeal to the English court for support and so keep the conflicts alive. Alternatively, as in the case of the Irish plantations, the English could deliberately follow a policy of divide and rule. Nevertheless, England's presence does not completely explain the deep divisions between north and south Wales, the Highlands and Lowlands of Scotland, or the constant petty feuding of the indigenous Irish princes. On the basis of these arguments England was a model political economy surrounded by a bunch of 'banana republics'. England, then, was the obvious source of imperialism in the British Isles: her 'potential power' led automatically to the 'actual power' of annexation.

England's primacy may be one part of the story, but it is certainly not the whole story. On another geopolitical perspective England could be regarded as a frontier outpost of European 'civility', forced to share the British Isles with a number of awkward, antagonistic, less developed societies which, combined, produced what Seeley called the 'British problem'. In other words, it is not England's natural hegemony in relation to its neighbours which should be emphasised, but its continuing political fragility. Domestically, for example, the celtic periphery may have been less politically integrated than England, but Anglophobia was always a potentially powerful unifying force, and England's military resources and skills (especially after the medieval period) were never so superior that invasion or occupation policies could be undertaken lightly. Moreover, there was the ever-present danger that in their dealings with England the celtic polities would find allies in continental Europe, or, even worse, be used as bases by those allies to invade England. The Auld Alliance is one obvious example. But the popular saying regarding Ireland illustrates the underlying English fear – 'He that will England win, Must first with Ireland begin'. Again, England's domestic politics were sometimes affected by the celtic presence. Wales played an important role during the Wars of the Roses, whilst Scottish and Irish politics were important during the English Civil War. As one commentator has put:- 'Though the Civil War is often known as "The English Revolution" it was not the English who started it but the Scots and the Irish who gave them their opportunity'.[28] The Scottish army played an important role at the Restoration of 1660 and Ireland acted as a base for the attempt by James II to regain his kingdom in 1690. Clearly, then, the line between potential power and actual power was not an easy one to draw.

Thirdly, despite its problems, informal Empire suited the English. It enabled them to reap the maximum advantage with a minimum of commitment. After 1284 and 1603 the celtic connection was always a narrow one. In each case it was based on the Crown. Scotland, of course, after 1603 was the paradigm case, but in a real sense both Wales and Ireland during the period of informal Empire can be described as bastard regal Unions. And apart from the policy of 'Thorough' pursued in the 1630s, the English Crown or court made little attempt to intervene directly in Welsh, Scottish and Irish affairs. There were few attempts from London to pursue anglicisation, even Anglicanism. Indeed, the only 'imperial' religion was Scottish Presbyterianism.[29] In practice, what policies the Crown had towards the celtic periphery in these periods were mediated and operated by its collaborators within the peripheral elites. In Scotland these were primarily members of the Committee of Articles, the body which effectively controlled the Scottish parliament before 1689. In Wales, from the fifteenth century, they were increasingly the native squirearchy who monopolised, in both the Principality and the 140-odd Marches lordships, the lower and middle ranges of the administration machine, and often, because of English absenteeism, the upper ranges as well. In Ireland, before 1767, the non-resident viceroy made deals with the principal Irish borough holders, the 'undertakers', granting patronage in return for promises to expedite policy. In short, during the informal Empire, the periphery administered itself.[30] This undoubtedly put very real restrictions on the sort of policies the Crown could pursue. On the other hand, indirect rule was cheap (despite the patronage involved), kept the affairs and people of the celtic dependencies away from London, and was reasonably effective in satisfying England's security interests. Its principal drawbacks were greed, corruption and internal feuding amongst the collaborative elites involved, and the inability, or unwillingness, of the English court to support its peripheral agents during periods of trouble or follow consistent policy over time.

Finally, moves towards closer Union lacked popular English support. Such proposals came from the celtic dependencies themselves or, on occasions, the English court; they were rarely supported by the English periphery and its 'voice', parliament. Apart from racial prejudice, allied, where Ireland was concerned to a virulent anti-Catholicism, Union appeared to involve two principles regarded with great disfavour by most members of the English political class – celtic representation at Westminster and celtic penetration of the increasingly protected English and colonial markets; and the more important parliament became in English politics, the more significance these views assumed. Nor did Union offer any positive attractions in terms of economic opportunities in Wales, Ireland and Scotland. English mercantile capitalism had no wish to scrape 'the bottom of the barrel' in unprofitable commercial ventures in the dark corners of the British Isles. Its economic imperialism was essentially protectionist.

Thus, in the period of informal Empire England was a satisfied imperialist. For the majority of the English the celtic dependencies represented a dangerous nuisance: their economic attractions were derisory, their inhabitants disliked or feared, and in general they represented a constant threat to the peace and good order of the realm. The imperial exercise, such that it was in these periods, was undertaken for essentially defensive reasons. The structure of the informal Empire followed the English 'official mind' regarding territorial politics: indirect rule, parsimony, autonomy of court politics from peripheral interference and sufficient control at the margin. It is a fundamental error to perceive some grand English strategy favouring Union. A highly critical situation would have to occur before the English gave up the benefits of informal Empire.

From informal to formal empire

If it is a mistake to regard the creation of the United Kingdom as inevitable, if there were so many forces throughout the British Isles against it, what then explains the Unions of 1536, 1707 and 1800?[31] On the basis of the analysis so far the following preliminary observations can be made.

First, it seems clear that analysis must concentrate, once again, on the English. They were the primary force involved in all the Unions and it was their political elite which had to be persuaded to abandon the perceived advantages of informal Empire. It is true, of course, that many interests in Scotland, Ireland and even Wales had to be persuaded to accept Union. But these laboured under a fundamental disadvantage: they had no plausible alternatives to Union or informal Empire. Secondly, from the discussion above it seems reasonable to conclude that the English political elite would only accept change under extreme pressure. Union would be accepted only at a general critical juncture in English politics, one which threatened the Centre's authority, caused problems for its relations with the celtic periphery as a whole, and which forced it to act positively towards the most troublesome or weakest link. Thirdly, it follows from this that explanations of the Union process which emphasise just one causal factor – a peripheral revolt or external security problems – are likely to be defective, on the grounds that as single problems these could probably be absorbed by the English without resort to annexation or incorporation.

This said, we can hypothesise that the Unions, the change from informal to formal Empire, can be plausibly explained (no more) in terms of the appearance on the political scene, at broadly the same time, of the following three conditions:-

1. The growth of political instability in England in terms of the decline of traditional political certainties and/or the growth of a popular or elite reform syndrome, plus a decline in elite consensus.
2. A marked decline in the effectiveness of collaborative arrangements in Wales, Scotland and Ireland.
3. A perceived or threatened decline in the autonomy of the English state from external forces.[32]

Because they are so diffuse it must be admitted that the explanatory power of these conditions is not very great. However, they are not meant to explain the specific reasons why, on three separate occasions, Union policies were pursued successfully. Rather, they highlight the general circumstances in which politicians in England were forced to accept that Union was the only solution to their problems. The application of this approach yields the following results.

The Anglo-Welsh Union
This took place in the midst of the Henrican Reformation and what Professor Elton believes to have been a revolution in English government. At all events, the 1530s was obviously a decade of reform and political uncertainty, and witnessed a decline in the level of elite consensus. An important theme of these years was the determined attempt to bring about the territorial consolidation of the English state. Attempts to reduce political power of the landed magnates, increased Crown interference in borough elections, the development of the office of Lord Lieutenant in the counties, and the Franchise Act of 1536 which abolished the separate jurisdictions still existing, are all examples of this policy. More generally, central penetration of society was increased in order to police the establishment of the new religion throughout England.

On the external front the 1530s saw the break with Rome and the forceful assertion of the autonomy of the English state from external influences. However, in the short run these policies weakened England's international position to a point where invasion by one of the Catholic powers in Europe was constantly expected. These events had their impact on the celtic periphery. Although the Irish parliament accepted the Reformation, a serious rebellion broke out in 1534, the revolt of the Kildares, the prime Irish collaborators with the English. Its defeat was important, since temporarily, at least, the English dropped their indirect rule philosophy and were forced to intervene directly in Irish affairs.[33]

At this stage the weak point in the system, certainly the one with most potential for trouble, was Wales.[34] The Edwardian settlement had broken up in the fifteenth century and Wales had become an area of extreme lawlessness. A major reason for this was divided responsibility. The Crown directly controlled only northeast, south and south-west Wales, the border areas were governed by the Marcher lordships. Most of these were in decline by the 1530s, but they still posed a threat to law and order, not only in Wales but in the border English counties. The old trust between the Tudors and the Welsh elite had suffered a blow with the arrest and execution for treason of Rhys ap Griffith in 1531 and there were fears that Wales would be influenced by the Irish revolt. Above all, the Reformation settlement required a new constitution for Wales. The 1534 Act of Settlement had made the English king head of the Church of England. However, although Wales was under the ecclesiastical jurisdiction of Canterbury, it was not part of the legal jurisdiction of parliament. Hence, if the Reformation was to have legal effect in Wales, parliamentary statutes would have to apply there, thus the necessity for a parliamentary Union and much closer control over Welsh administration by the Crown. As a preliminary, the Council of the Marches was revitalised by the appointment in 1534 of Bishop Rowland Lee, who pursued a forceful law and order policy on the borders for the next nine years. Then in 1535, the Lord Chancellor was empowered to appoint justices of the peace in all parts of Wales. Finally, the following year came the Act of Union incorporating Wales into the English parliamentary system and abolishing the Marcher lordships.

The Anglo-Scottish Union

Here the crucial period is 1689 to 1707. In England the events of 1688 hardly represented the settlement so emphasised in later years by Whig historians. In these years the English were forced to work out a new constitutional settlement by a series of *ad hoc* measures, at a time when divisions over constitutional issues went deep and the structure of politics was extremely fragile, largely because the executive was temporarily in a very weak position. Problems on the domestic front were compounded by those on the external. The arrival of William of Orange increased English participation in Europe, and war, and the threats from war were a constant feature of the political scene. Queen Anne was forced to sign the Scottish Act of Security, a significant step in the breakdown of the collaborative arrangements, precisely because the English army appeared, at the time, to be 'marching to its doom down the Danube valley' (the victory of Blenheim became known several days later).

This period also saw a major change in the collaborative arrangements in Ireland. The 1690s saw the final downfall of the 'Old Irish', the nearest source of indigenous collaboration, and the rise of the Protestant ascendancy, a plantation polity which was later to show all the drawbacks of settler collaboration. But this was for the future. With Wales relatively quiet, the weak point in the system was Scotland.

The problem was that neither the English nor the Scots had been able to digest the vague constitutional settlement of 1690 which, by effectively removing or weakening English instruments of control, created a situation in which conflict between the two could occur more easily, and all this at a time when Scottish politics and parliament became much more representative and active than ever before. The specific problems of the regal Union under William, Glencoe and the Darien fiasco, are well known. But in the early years of the eighteenth century the situation worsened as a result of the royal succession problem, English military weakness abroad and, above all, divisions within the Scottish political elite, divisions which were reflected, and came to the fore, in the unpredictable parliament of 1703. As Riley had argued, it was not that the parliament was anti-English, merely that it lacked a workable majority and effective leadership.[35] Faced with difficulties at home and abroad, and lacking an effective collaborative class in Scotland, the English government gave up and pushed, successfully this time, for what they had spent years rejecting, an 'ever closer Union' with their northern neighbour.

The Anglo-Irish Union

For this the relevant period is roughly 1770 to 1800. Within England these years are marked by social changes consequent on industrialisation, the economical and parliamentary reform movements and, in general, the breakdown of the mid-eighteenth-century political consensus. On the external front they were prefaced by defensive and pessimistic attitudes following the realisation of the greatly enlarged responsibilities which had resulted from the settlement of the Seven

Years War in 1763, a climate in which people feared that the fate of seventeenth-century Spain would overtake England – 'pulled down by weight of international commitments'. These feelings of a declining autonomy in relation to external forces were supported by the successful revolt of the American colonies, a revolt which showed a dangerous diplomatic isolation. Then, in the 1790s, there came the threat from revolutionary France.

The American war, the debate it caused in Britain and the nature of London's rejected peace offers in 1778, had a considerable impact on the celtic periphery.[36] In Ireland there had been signs of change since 1767, when the Crown had been forced to drop the classic indirect rule of the 'undertakers' and employ for the first time a continuously resident viceroy and chief secretary. But the growth of Protestant nationalism, the nationalism of the collaborative class, together with the weakness of the metropolitan power during the American crisis, enabled the Irish parliament to demand and get a considerable increase in its autonomy in the early 1780s. As one historian has put it: 'By 1783 Ireland had achieved a degree of constitutional independence within the Empire with no equal until 1931'.[37] The parliamentary reform movement, American independence and Irish autonomy had some effect on Scotland as well. The assimilaterist tendencies of the mid-eighteenth century were to some extent checked. Just as important, many contemporary English observers believed that Scotland would take advantage of England's weaknesses. In 1782, for example, Horace Walpole declared: 'I shall not be surprised if our whole trinity is dissolved, and if Scotland should demand a dissolution of the Union. Strange if she alone does not profit from our distress'.[38] Even Wales stirred. The first political pamphlets (discussing the American issue) were published in this period.

Yet after 1783 most events, including the Irish Union legislation of 1800, seem an anticlimax. Grattan's parliament with legislative independence, the end of the Declaratory Act and freedom to trade with the empire (though not Britain) began with a bang. But the contradictions inherent in an autonomous parliament of settler collaborators, with no control of the executive and few intentions of allowing the mass of Catholics to join the elite (though in 1793 they got the vote), were soon apparent, especially after the arrival in Ireland of a rival ideology to Protestant nationalism, the republican radicalism of France.

Significantly, the English, at the outset, were prepared to accept this 1780s 'revolution' in Anglo-Irish relations. The Protestant ascendancy was loyal to the Crown, supported a useful standing army and appeared to govern effectively. In addition, the displacement of Irish affairs at Westminster could be reduced. What Pitt and others did not realise was that the Protestant nation had run out of steam: it had no viable view of the future, was divided amongst itself and, as the 1798 rebellion showed, could no longer be trusted to keep reasonable security in time of war. Once again, at yet another critical juncture, for want of any other solution, Union was forced on the English.

The three conditions outlined at the beginning of this section appear to provide a plausible general explanation of the change from informal to formal Empire. In passing it might be added that they can also be employed to explain another critical juncture and another (temporary) Union process, the Cromwellian Union of 1653 to 1660. The return to normalcy in 1660, despite the mild popularity of that experiment in Scotland, illustrates the attractions of informal Empire for the English political elite. One final point on this subject needs to be made. The three conditions operated over time, but that does not mean that they were equally important throughout the periods involved. The argument is merely that they were present on the scene at some point during the critical juncture period and to that extent operated in combination.

The anatomy of formal Empire

What were the results of these moves from informal to formal Empire in the British Isles? What was the structure or anatomy of territorial politics under the early post-Union regimes?

We have seen that most commentators have emphasised the unitary or 'fully incorporating' nature of the Union settlements. Others have gone further and argued in terms of an English dominated and exploited United Kingdom estate. It is clear that the three Unions did share a number of features which, on the surface, give support to such views. These are:

(a) Each Union involved the abolition of the major quasi-independent legislative bodies on the celtic periphery: the Marcher lordships in Wales and the Scottish and Irish parliaments. In return, Wales, Scotland and Ireland were granted, on the whole, reasonably fair representation at Westminster.[39] On this basis a unitary parliament was constructed to act as the keystone of a wider unitary political structure.

(b) Each Union involved the creation of an established Protestant church: the Anglican Churches of Wales and Ireland and the Presbyterian Church of Scotland. In this sense it could be argued that a common dominant culture existed to buttress the unitary political structure.

(c) Each Union assisted greater economic integration. An ever closer economic community evolved with a common fiscal system and external tariffs plus free trade in goods, capital and labour throughout the British Isles. Once again it could be argued that all this was the necessary basis for an English take-over of the weaker celtic economies.

Of course, since each Union followed the incoherent stage of informal Empire not all of these integrative features were entirely new. Nevertheless, at the very least they represented a considerable formalisation of past practices and the establishment of a unitary Parliament was certainly a major innovation. Celtic representation at Westminster, however, could be regarded as more than a constitutional innovation. It could also act as a major instrument of English political control. As an under-secretary put it to Pitt in 1799: 'By giving the Irish one hundred members in an assembly of 650 they will be rendered impotent to operate in that assembly, but it will be invested with Irish assent to its authority'.[40] If this was the major English strategy behind the whole exercise they were certainly assisted by the post-Union willingness on the part of many members of the Welsh and Scottish gentry and nobility to accept not only Union, but English speech and culture.[41] In addition, although the Unions were unpopular in many circles in Wales, Scotland and Ireland, no effectively organised opposition with a plausible anti-regime programme appeared on the scene before the latter half of the nineteenth century.

However, these integration features of formal Empire must be placed once again in the context of the wider nature and workings of its society and political structure. When this is done the post-Union polity assumes a somewhat different character. The following are the principal points which need to be considered. We can start with a very general point. The United Kingdom was manufactured in the period 1536 to 1800. In many respects it can be argued that in terms of the evolution of an integrated Union this historical timing was both too soon and too late. It was perhaps too late for the celtic territories, above all Scotland and Ireland, to be regarded, and more importantly to regard themselves, as natural and inevitable associates of England. On the other hand, it was too early for societal and political forces to give practical support to constitutional provisions for a unitary state; too early for political theory to provide any alternative method for accommodating celtic interests other than by a unitary parliament; and too early for the Unions to reap the positive integrative ideological and economic benefits which resulted from later European bourgeois nationalist movements. All this is to emphasise the obvious: at the beginning the United Kingdom was a pre-industrial, pre-democratic and pre-nationalist Union; an elite affair in which the masses were markedly absent and which relied for integration impetus on elite parliamentary accommodation, a shared monarch and a common religion. Hence, in the first instance, a unitary constitution could not be supported by appropriate societal, cultural and political forces.

It is important to note that the unitary provisions of the Union settlements did not extend very far. Apart from its parliamentary dimension, formal Empire did not establish a single constitutional corset. It is well known that the Anglo-Scottish Union maintained the distinctive Scottish legal and local government system, confirmed Presbyterianism and the Church of Scotland as, respectively, the established religion and church, and, as a result, allowed separate educational and poor-law systems to continue. In addition, the numerous municipal and aristocratic regalities were maintained until after 1745. Scotland may have lost a parliament but her governmental system remained distinctive. Similarly, the Irish Union produced yet another constitution. The old Dublin Castle executive machine, involving a separate bureaucracy, viceroy and chief secretary, continued to operate after 1800 as an early example of administrative devolution. Moreover, Ireland was governed almost continuously by Coercion Acts and, as a consequence, the military assumed a greater displacement in Irish affairs than in Britain. Westminster's legislation on Irish civil matters was also distinctive in terms of timing and content. Even in Wales, the Council of Wales and the Marches continued to exist until 1689 and the largely autonomous judicial administration of the Courts of Great Sessions remained until 1830. Hence, the three Union settlements differed considerably: in terms of governmental structure there were few unitary characteristics.

Whilst there is no denying that the Union did affect economic development throughout the kingdom, the extent to which the English were interested in, and *positively* sought to dominate the economies of Wales, Scotland and Ireland is open to question. Clearly, England's market attractions exerted considerable influence over areas like Ulster and this in turn was one factor determining later attitudes towards the Union. Moreover, there is some substance in Hechter's argument that where industrialisation was absent, support for the Union was weak. Nevertheless, arguments favouring a positive drive by the English towards economic control seem flimsy. Until the mid-twentieth century most economic activity throughout the United Kingdom was still locally controlled and financed. More important, England was not an inward-looking domestically orientated economy. The repeal of the Corn Laws in 1846 illustrates this. English capitalism, especially finance capital, had world-wide interests and did not stand or fall on the degree to which it could colonise the economies of the celtic periphery. There were better markets for goods, capital and labour elsewhere.

The degree of operational political integration achieved under formal Empire depended, ultimately, on the English. They were the only territorial community possessing, in theory, the physical and cultural resources to impose a strong, coherent pattern of government on the Union. Against this must be set three points. First, on each occasion Union had been undertaken reluctantly by the English Centre and with no great support from its periphery. Secondly, despite all the integrative forces mentioned above, each Union stage created a more heterogeneous and potentially politically troublesome polity. Any incipient moves towards greater centralisation in England were probably stifled by the birth of the United Kingdom. Thirdly, as described above, over time the English had managed to develop and sustain a very peculiar structure of territorial politics, one characterised by a high degree of constitutional ambiguity and an unwillingness on the part of the central authorities to interfere directly in the affairs of local communities. In other words, all the traditions and precepts of the English 'official mind' were against the construction of a highly integrated positive Union.

On the basis of these points it seems plausible to argue that, in political terms, formal Empire was not 'the start of something big', but rather a *reconstruction* of as much of the political style and content of informal Empire as was possible within the changed constitutional framework. For want of a viable alternative the English had saddled themselves with a series of fully incorporating legislative Unions. But they were not prepared to introduce any innovations in the making of the United Kingdom. For obvious reasons such attitudes had the support of the dominant political groups in the celtic periphery as well. Thus the domestic imperialism of the English was a peculiar thing. This, of course, should not be regarded as surprising. The whole history of English expansion overseas – the external Empire – was marked by a reluctance to move away from a governmental paradigm first laid down to manage the boroughs, shires and local gentry of Devon, Warwickshire and Yorkshire.[42]

Successively, Wales, Scotland and Ireland were managed on the English 'system': a Centre seeking relative autonomy from, and 'quiet subordination' on its periphery, via indirect rule by collaborative local elites and the appeasement of local interests at Westminster. Indeed, until the second half of the nineteenth century the system worked better for the Centre in its celtic than in its English periphery. English MPs were more politicised, more organised, more independent and more likely to interfere in the Centre's 'High Politics' concerns for their counterparts from Wales, Scotland and Ireland. For the most part the Centre was successful in 'hiving off' its celtic responsibilities to the Welsh gentry, Scottish 'managers' such as Dundas, and that other 'Indian administration', Dublin Castle.[43] Back at the ranch, at Westminster, the representatives from these territories could usually be relied on to stay away or provide useful lobby fodder for governments in trouble.

Despite its obvious weaknesses this system was sufficiently effective to survive the Napoleonic wars, the early stages of industrialisation and the political reforms of the 1830s. The system worked in the 1860s pretty much as it had fifty or a hundred years earlier.[44] And over time the Union, even in Ireland, lost much of its original imperial character: it existed, it worked, it brought economic benefits to many, it suffocated domestic divisions, and no serious alternative had appeared on the scene. But it remained an essentially contractual Union: a deal between celtic elites and the central authorities in London, in which both had rights and duties, and towards which the English periphery played the role of arrogant, yet uncomprehending, bystander. The contractual nature of the union was most marked in terms of the Irish Protestant ascendancy.[45] But a similar sort of contract existed for the Scots and even the Welsh political elites, no matter how deferential they were in the day-to-day management of the Union.

CONCLUSION

This chapter has surveyed the extended and complex process which led to the making of the United Kingdom. It suggests that providing sufficient account is taken of English attitudes and practices regarding territorial politics, then plausible generalisations can be made regarding the nature of both the pre- and post-Union political structure in the British Isles, as well as the three Union processes which created the state known as the United Kingdom. Within that framework the specific arguments are as follows:-

(i)   From the sixteenth century to the early eighteenth century a series of developments took place in which the English Centre and periphery (or court and country) achieved an effective, if ambiguous, equilibrium. This equilibrium produced a structure of territorial politics marked by an operational federalism and separation of powers allied to an autonomy-seeking (if not always achieving) Centre, which exhibited a strong preference for the indirect rule of local communities and the settlement of major territorial conflicts at Westminster.

(ii) In its relations with the celtic periphery prior to the Unions, England was a relatively satisfied, if somewhat fragile, imperialist. Annexation was the solution of the last resort

(iii) The three Unions were pushed through largely as a result of critical junctures in English politics. On each occasion these junctures exhibited three features: the growth of English political instability, a decline in the autonomy of the English state from external forces, and a marked decline in the effectiveness of her celtic peripheral collaborative arrangements.

(iv) The post-Union political settlements are best seen as a series of reconstructions of as much of the old indirect management of the celtic periphery as could be achieved in the changed circumstances. Each Union settlement took the form of a contract between the Centre and relevant celtic elites.

(v) Given the above arguments, the creation of the United Kingdom was not inevitable, nor was the post-Union structure of government unitary (in so far as that term has any meaning).

(vi) If England was the imperialist territorial section, then this imperialism closely resembled the imperial designs described by Robinson and Gallagher and detailed earlier. One major qualification must be made to their analysis: for the United Kingdom the impetus to the imperial process was governed by events in England as much as 'abroad'. The 'eccentric' explanation cannot stand on its own.

(vii) It seems plausible to argue that future territorial developments in the United Kingdom would be highly influenced by the English 'official mind' and its territorial code as described above.

NOTES

1   This chapter is an expanded version of an article published by the author in *Parliamentary Affairs* (Spring 1978), entitled 'The making of the United Kingdom: aspects of English imperialism'. I am grateful to the editor and publishers of that journal for allowing me to make use of material in that article.

2   Daniel Defoe, 'The true-born Englishman: a satire', *De Foe's Works, V* (Bohn's Standard Literary Edition, 1901) p. 442.

3   Richard Graham, 'Sepoys and imperialists: techniques of British power in nineteenth-century Brazil', *Inter-American Economic Affairs* (1969).

4   G. M. Trevelyan, *History of England* (London, 1947), p. 200; Anthony H. Birch, *Political Integration and Disintegration in the British Isles* (London, 1977), pp. 19–20 and 24.

5   C. F. Strong, *Modern Political Constitutions* (London, revised edition, 1972), Chapter 4; A. V. Dicey, *Law of the Constitution* (London, 1920 edition), Chapter 1.

6   Cmnd. 5460 (October 1973), I, para. 62. See also Tevelyan *op. cit.*, pp. 359, 481, 588.

7   W. Ferguson, 'The making of the Treaty of Union, 1707', *Scottish Historical Review* (1964); W. E. H. Lecky, *A History of Ireland in the eighteenth century* (London, abridged edition, 1972), pp. 445–6.

8   This is an inexact but convenient label and will be employed henceforth as the generic term
    for Wales, Scotland and Ireland.

9   J. G. Pocock, 'British history: a plea for a new subject', *Journal of Modern History* (1975).

10 William Roger Louis (ed.), *Imperialism: The Robinson and Gallagher Controversy*
    (London, 1976), p. 37. Robinson and Gallagher have developed their ideas over time.
    Nevertheless, they have produced a coherent analytical framework and founded a 'school',
    the Cambridge 'brahmans'. Their principal publications are: John Gallagher and Ronald
    Robinson, 'The imperialism of free trade', *Economic History Review* (1953); R. Robinson
    and J. Gallagher, *Africa and the Victorians: the Official Mind of Imperialism* (London,
    1961); R. Robinson and J. Gallagher, 'The partition of Africa', *New Cambridge Modern
    History*, XI, Chapter 22; R. Robinson, 'Non-European foundations of European imperialism:
    sketch for a theory of collaboration' in E. R. J. Owen and R. B. Sutcliffe (eds.), *Studies in
    the Theory of Imperialism* (London, 1972).

11 'Collaborator' and 'collaboration' are words generally used in pejorative sense. As Marty
    Feldman once put it, collaboration involves 'things you do with the Germans during the war
    and get shot for it in the third reel'. Robinson and Gallagher employ these words in a neu-
    tral sense: collaborators are local people willing to manage their localities broadly in the
    interests of the central authorities.

12 See the introduction and chapter on England in Orest Ranum (ed.), *National Consciousness,
    History and Political Culture in Early Modern Europe* (London, 1975). Jim Bulpitt's 'The
    problem of the "North Parts": territorial integration in Tudor and Stuart England'. University
    of Warwick, Politics Working Paper No. 6, illustrates the differing interpretations by histo-
    rians of this important aspect of English development. Samuel E. Finer's 'State-building,
    state boundaries, and border control', *Social Science Information*, 13 (415) is an important
    paper by a political scientist on this general topic yet practically every point made by Finer
    would be disputed by some British historians.

13 Otto Hintze, 'The formation of states and constitutional development' (1902), reprinted in
    Felix Gilbert (ed.), *The Historical Essays of Otto Hintze* (New York, 1975), p. 171.

14 See J. R. Stayer, *On the Medieval Origins of the Modern State* (Princeton, 1970), pp. 36–49;
    P. Anderson, *Lineages of the Absolute State* (London, 1975), Chapter 5; P. S. Lewis, *Later
    Medieval France* (London, 1968), Chapters 1 and 5.

15 F. R. H. Du Boulay, *An Age of Ambition: English Society in the later Middle Ages* (London,
    1970), Chapter 2: J. R. *Lander, Conflict and Stability in fifteenth-century England* (London,
    1969), Chapter 7.

16 For Tudor policies see: G. R. Elton, *England Under the Tudors* (London, 1955) and *Policy
    and Police* (Cambridge, 1972); L. Stone, *The Crisis of the Aristocracy 1558–1641* (Oxford,
    1965); Penry Williams, 'Rebellion and revolution in early modern England' in M. R. D. Foot
    (ed.), *War and Society* (London, 1973).

17 See Bulpitt, *op. cit.*

18 Elton, *England Under the Tudors*, p. 176.

19 P. Anderson, *op. cit.*

20 For the 'court/country' distinction see: H. R. Trevor-Roper, 'The general crisis of the seven-
    teenth century' in T. Aston (ed.) *Crisis in Europe 1560–1660* (London, 1965); P. Zagorin,
    The Court and the Country (London, 1969); Lawrence Stone, *The Causes of the English*

Revolution 1529–1642 (London, 1972) pp. 85–8 and 105–9; J. S. Morrill, *The Revolt of the Provinces* (London, 1976), pp. 13–31.

21 J. P. Kenyon, *Revolution Principles: The Politics of Party, 1689–1720* (Cambridge, 1977); J. H. Plumb, *The Growth of Political Stability in England 1675–1725* (London, 1967); H. T. Dickinson 'The eighteenth-century debate on the sovereignty of parliament', *Transactions of the Royal Historical Society* (1976).

22 J. S. Morrill, *op. cit.*; Derek Hurst, *The Representative of the People? Voters and Voting in England Under the Early Stuarts* (Cambridge, 1975); C. Russell, *The Origins of the English Civil War* (London, 1973), pp. 12–13; J. R. Western, *Monarch and Revolution: the English State in the 1680s* (London, 1972).

23 A. B. White, *Self-Government at the King's Command* (London, 1933).

24 For the eighteenth-century 'system' in England see: Lewis Namier, *England in the Age of the American Revolution* (London, 1966); J. H. Plumb, 'Political man', in James C. Clifford (ed.), *Man versus Society in eighteenth century Britain* (Cambridge, 1968); L. P. Curtis, *Chichester Towers* (New Haven, Conn., 1966); J. R. Western, *The English Militia in the Eighteenth Century* (London, 1965); E. P. Thompson, *Whigs and Hunters: the Origins of the Black Act* (London, 1975).

25 Poynings' Law required all bills introduced into the Irish parliament to be submitted for approval, modification or rejection to the king and privy council in England. Those approved or modified were then represented to the Irish parliament which could accept or reject them, but not amend them. By the Declaratory Act, 1720, the British parliament reaffirmed its right to legislate for Ireland. See J. C. Beckett, *The Making of Modern Ireland* (London, 1966), pp. 51 and 164.

26 See T. C. Smout, *Scottish Trade on the Eve of the Union* (London, 1963).

27 Quoted in E. N. Williams, *A Documentary History of England*, II (London, 1965), p. 131.

28 C. R. Russell, *op. cit.*

29 W. Ferguson, *Scotland's Relations with England* (Edinburgh, 1977), pp. 126–7. An exception to this generalisation on religion would be Westminster's attempt in the 1650s to propagate Puritanism in the 'dark corners of the land', which included Wales. See C. Hill, *Change and Continuity in seventeenth-century England* (London, 1974), pp. 32–44. A more important exception to this rule was James II, both as King and as Duke of York. As one commentator has recently put it 'James was a mature imperialist who wished to rationalise his inherited complex of kingdoms and colonies and to strengthen the grip of the central royal administration over them'. See Bruce Lenman, *The Jacobite Risings in Britain* (London, 1980), p. 52.

30 For Scotland see Ferguson *ibid*; for Ireland, E. M. Johnston, *Great Britain and Ireland 1760–1800* (London, 1963); for Wales, G. Roberts, 'Wales and England: antipathy and sympathy, 1282–1485', *Welsh Historical Review* (1960–3); R. A. Griffith, 'Wales and the Marches' in S. B. Chrimes (ed.), *Fifteenth-Century England* (London, 1976).

31 To the basic Union statutes must be added the consolidatory Act for Wales of 1542 and the 1706 Scottish Act for Securing the Protestant Religion and Presbyterian Church Government. Catholic emancipation was also promised by Pitt during the Anglo-Irish Union negotiations but was not achieved until 1829.

32 In the language of Chapter 2 above, this can be alternatively expressed as a perceived or

threatened decline in the effectiveness of the external support system.

33 See G. A. Hays McCoy, 'Royal supremacy and the ecclesiastical revolution' in T. W. Moody *et al.*, *A New History of Ireland* (Oxford, 1976), iii, p. 40.

34 W. Rees, *The Union of England and Wales* (Cardiff, 1967). The Scottish connection posed problems in the 1540s and 1550s with the 'rough wooing' followed by the Guise interlude when Scotland was temporarily ruled by the French interest.

35 P. W. J. Riley, *The Union of England and Scotland* (Manchester, 1978), pp. 52–9.

36 V. T. Harlow, *The Founding of the Second British Empire* (London, 1964), Chapter 10; N. T. Phillipson, 'Scottish public opinion and the Union in the age of association' in N. Phillipson and R. Mitchison (eds.), *Scotland in the Age of Improvement* (Edinburgh, 1970); V. Bogdanor, *Devolution* (Oxford, 1979), pp. 3 and 4; J. C. Beckett, *op. cit.*, Chapters 10 and 11.

37 D. Fieldhouse, 'British imperialism in the late eighteenth century' in K. Robinson and F. Madden (eds.), *Essays in Imperial Government* (Oxford, 1963).

38 Cited in Phillipson, *op. cit.*, p. 126.

39 In the House of Commons Wales was represented by twenty-six MPs, Scotland forty-five and Ireland 100. In the House of Lords, sixteen Scottish peers were to be elected by their colleagues. Ireland was represented by four lords spiritual and twenty-eight temporal peers.

40 Cited in Oliver Macdonagh, *Ireland: the Union and its Aftermath* (London, 1977), p. 17.

41 See Phillipson, *op. cit.*; R. Pares, 'A quarter of a millennium of Anglo-Scottish Union', *History* (1954); P. Williams 'The Welsh borderland under Elizabeth', *Welsh History Review* (1960–3); D. Williams, *A History of Modern Wales* (London, 1950), Chapter 6; M. Hechter, *op. cit.*, Chapter 4.

42 In addition to the Robinson and Gallagher literature cited above, this point can be plausibly inferred from the following: D. A. Low, *Lion Rampant: Essays on the Study of British Imperialism* (London, 1973); Ronald Hyam and Ged Martin, *Reappraisals in British Imperial History* (London, 1975); G. W. Martin, 'Was there a British Empire?', *Historical Journal* (1972); F. Madden, 'Some origins and purposes in the formation of British colonial government' in K. Robinson and F. Madden, *op. cit.*

43 N. Gash, *Mr Secretary Peel* (London, 1960), especially pp. 149–51; R. Cooke and J. Vincent, *The Governing Passion* (London, 1974), pp. 17–19.

44 Richard Shannon, *The Crisis of Imperialism, 1865–1915* (London, 1974), p. 11.

45 David W. Miller, *Queen's Rebels: Ulster Loyalism in Historical Perspective* (Dublin, 1978).

chapter four | the old order challenged: the modernisation of territorial politics, 1870–1926

The Celts are having their revenge upon the brutal Saxon.[1]

There is absolutely no grip anywhere.[2]

INTRODUCTION

The United Kingdom was manufactured in a pre-industrial and pre-democratic era. The operation was mounted by traditional landed elites to meet particular problems at particular times and was designed to reconstruct as much of the pre-Union structure of territorial politics as was possible in changed and dangerous circumstances. The imperial character of the exercise was twofold: it was pushed through by the court or Centre without much positive support from the English periphery; and the system of government applied to the celtic periphery was essentially the English system of territorial management as it had developed in the sixteenth and seventeenth centuries. Hence, the Union was a ramshackle affair in which a weak Centre managed its estate via local elite collaborators in times of normalcy and what amounted to a gunboat diplomacy in times of emergency.

It seems reasonable to suppose that this structure of territorial politics would be radically altered (or 'modernised') by the new social, economic and political forces which emerged in the nineteenth century. The advent of an industrial society and a more democratic polity would bring about a 'great transformation' in the pattern of centre-periphery relations. This chapter attempts to discover whether such a transformation occurred in practice. Within this general framework the analysis has three aims: to identify the major challenges to the old order which emerged after about 1870 and their possible political outcomes; to chart the development of these challenges up to the mid-1920s; and to assess their overall impact on the structure of territorial politics by that date. Of necessity this sort of exercise must be highly inferential in character. Three principal problems are encountered: it is (once again) difficult to confine the discussion within the accepted parameters of territorial politics; there is little agreement among historians and social scientists concerning the nature and outcome of the modernisation challenge;[3]

and, more specifically, it is hard to find generally agreed criteria by which the strengths and weaknesses of the Centre can be assessed. Nevertheless, the period has to be examined, since it represents an important transition stage, a critical juncture, in the development of territorial politics in the United Kingdom. The argument, in brief, is that in this period modernisation took a very peculiar form with an even stranger outcome. By the middle of the 1920s the challenges to the traditional territorial order had been either defeated, emasculated, or swept under the carpet. Territorial modernisation was a very conservative process, leading to what can be called a 'suspended revolution'.[4] The consequences of this are still with us today.

CHALLENGES AND OUTCOMES

The period to be examined, 1870 to 1926, requires some preliminary justification. It could be argued that while the latter date signifies nothing in particular, the former appears to follow Dicey's now discredited views concerning the decline of individualism and the onset of collectivism.[5] In addition, why date the onset of the modernisation challenge so late in the nineteenth century? This sort of periodisation seems to take no account of the social consequences of industrialisation and urbanisation earlier in the century, the extension of the parliamentary franchise in 1832, developments in municipal government, the Poor Law and public health after 1834, the emancipation and repeal campaigns of O'Connell in Ireland, the rise of Nonconformity in Wales, the first demands from 'respectable' opinion in Scotland in the 1850s to alter or improve the operation of the Union settlement, and what many now perceive to have been a revolution in government ideology and action in the mid-nineteenth century.[6] The argument here is that while individually these developments may have had contemporary significance, their general impact by 1870 was only a partial one. In 1870 the main lines of the traditional territorial order remained intact. Nothing had been permanently settled and everything was still to play for. After 1870 the challenges to the old order became individually more intense, and, in combination, more dangerous. By 1926, however, a settlement in response to these challenges had been reached, a new territorial regime had begun to operate.

Five principal challenges emerged (or increased in salience) after 1870. First, the successful strategic and economic *external support system* constructed by successive United Kingdom governments after 1815 and regarded as an essential prop to domestic political tranquillity, was threatened by economic competition from, and the international power ambitions of, the United States, Germany and Russia. Secondly, *social change* posed a double threat. Industrialisation and urbanisation, plus the continued decline of the agricultural community, suggested the political emergence of new social groups which could not be easily accommodated into the existing patterns of territorial management. In addition, improved transportation and education facilities plus the advent of new forms of popular media communication seemingly pointed to a more homogeneous territorial society, in which local and regional loyalties would decline in strength. Thirdly, *mass party mobilisation*, resulting from the franchise extensions of 1867 and 1884, appeared to signify that the traditional and informal elite-operated system of Centre-periphery relations would be relegated to the attic. Fourthly, after 1870, a number of demands for institutional reform and legislation were placed on the political agenda which, if accepted, seemed to herald the development of a *new territorial constitution*, one allowing more effective and democratic government within the periphery and a more formally autonomous relationship with the Centre. Finally, these challenges hinted at an enforced *change in the nature of the Centre*, in terms of its ideology, resources and power relations with peripheral forces.

These challenges to the traditional territorial order have been presented in a deliberately open-ended fashion in terms of their possible political outcomes. This contrasts with the line taken by the early comparative literature on political modernisation and the accepted academic orthodoxy regarding territorial development in Britain, if not Ireland. Both these argue that social change stimulates social mobilisation which in turn produces mass party mobilisation, resulting in a more homogeneous society with a nationalised political system dominated by class cleavages, in which an enlarged and more assertive Centre succeeds in supervising and controlling peripheral communities more effectively than before. It is now accepted that this was only one possible outcome of the challenge listed above. Other models of this process and impact 'logically of equal status' to the traditional model, now exist.[7] Indeed, the only academic consensus at present is that modernisation will promote radical change in the structure of territorial politics. This said, the range of possible outcomes from the challenge of territorial modernisation in this period can be listed as follows:

1. The emergence of a dominant central authority basing its power over the periphery on one or more of the following resources:
(a) an hegemonic Unionist culture, the United Kingdom 'one and indivisible';
(b) a comprehensive constitution covering all territorial sections, increasing the Centre's authority and obstructing the efficient articulation of peripheral demands;
(c) an extensive and expert central bureaucratic machine with a significant presence in the field, permitting effective supervision and control of peripheral governments and communities;
(d) a system of mass political parties spread throughout the periphery, controlled by politicians at the Centre and establishing a more subservient set of local collaborators;
(e) an external support system allowing the political elite at the Centre sufficient time and resources to efficiently manage peripheral affairs.

2. The development of an internal colonial situation in which the most modernised region (England) exploits, politically, economically and culturally, the less advanced regions of the periphery.

3. The establishment of a federal system symbolically altering the constitutional

terms of the Union in favour of the periphery.

4. The development of a structure of territorial politics in which Centre-periphery relations are mediated by a set of powerful brokerage institutions, such as:

(a) directly elected Home Rule Assemblies;

(b) administrative devolution arrangements which permit efficient decentralised administration and a powerful peripheral voice at the Centre;

(c) a form of territorial consociational democracy, involving a cartel of peripheral elites at the Centre, whose power rests on their political dominance in their own sections, and able to bargain effectively within the central institutional complex.

5. The emergence of a periphery-dominated Centre, which ceases to have any political existence independent of peripheral forces.

6. The secession from the Union of one or more territorial sections.

TERRITORIAL POLITICS 1870–1926

It is clear that the outcome of the process called territorial modernisation was potentially a very open one. Which of these possible end results occurred in the United Kingdom? There are two possible methods of approaching this question. One is to chart the development of the various challenges to the old order over the whole period. The other is to examine the nature and outcome of two territorial crises which occurred during these years, the crisis of the 1880s and that of the period 1910 to 1926. Both these approaches will be pursued below.

The challenges: five types of ambiguity

The external support system

After 1870 the territorial impact of the external changes was potentially twofold. Either a besieged and weakened Centre would stimulate the growth and influence of peripheral dissident groups, or the Centre would be provoked into a counter-offensive to assume greater control over peripheral affairs in order to construct a more secure home basis to bolster its external operations. In practice the external challenge in this period was beaten off with the assistance of imperialism and the Great War. Since this particular story is well known and largely accepted the general argument needs only brief discussion. However, some qualifications need to be raised concerning the precise link with domestic territorial development.

Imperialism, or the move to formal Empire, was undertaken largely as a defensive reaction to the United Kingdom's declining international power position. The Empire became a military resource to be called on in times of emergency, a supplier of raw materials and a market for industrial goods. It also acted as an outlet for emigration and, more generally, exerted a profoundly conservative influence on British society and politics.[8] The Great War cashed the strategic advantages of Empire in explicit terms, defeated a major rival, Germany, and seriously weakened and preoccupied that potentially awkward challenger to the United

Kingdom's Middle East and Indian interests, namely Russia. The results of all this, so the argument runs, favoured a more territorially integrated home base. While the Empire provided an important symbol to capture territorial loyalties, the outbreak of the Great War halted the slide to civil war in Ireland and suspended disputes over Welsh disestablishment and Home Rule All Round. Moreover, the course of the war unleashed a surge of patriotic fervour in Britain and its victorious settlement extended the boundaries of the Empire, boosted the domestic prestige of the central elites, and tied the periphery even closer to the established Union.

The admitted exception to this happy tale was of course, Ireland. From the 1880s, Irish nationalism was sustained by American-Irish money and anti-British feeling, a development which British politicians found difficult to counteract. Before 1914 Irish demands for Home Rule were a constant challenge to the internal cohesion of the Empire. Moreover, Redmond's magnanimous gesture in 1914 to call off the Home Rule agitation in order to assist the war effort was obliterated by the Easter rebellion of 1916 and the subsequent necessity to grant the bulk of Ireland dominion status in the early post-war period.

Although the broad outlines of this thesis can be accepted, several points require further discussion. First, we must be careful not to over-emphasise the degree to which the Centre faced these external challenges with any preconceived general plan of operation. Clearly, the Great War was not part of any such plan. Where imperialism is concerned the matter is more complex than the above thesis suggests. Imperialism certainly assumed great symbolic importance, but the Empire itself had little coherence. It was never a major outlet for British goods and investment and it never developed a uniform centralised structure. Moreover, given the parsimonious attitude of the Treasury towards colonial government and the predilection for indirect rule there was often doubt as to whether the British were the *ruling* imperial power.[9] Significantly, those who pushed the idea of greater imperial integration, such as an imperial federation, never received much support at home or abroad. In this respect it was not the Empire which influenced the domestic Union, but the reverse. The official mind of imperialism in this period looks remarkably like the traditional domestic territorial code. In short, the Empire was a welcome addition to the United Kingdom's international power resources, but it did not alter them fundamentally and relatively few attempts were made to develop imperial integration.

This reluctance on the part of the Centre to innovate governmentally in face of the external challenges can be illustrated by two further points. One is the continued commitment, despite internal pressures, to free trade. The United Kingdom was the only major country after 1870 not to adopt high tariffs on either agricultural or industrial goods. Free trade, of course, was the external dimension of the domestic *laissez-faire* ideology and consequently indicates the degree to which the Centre did not use the external challenge to expand the general role of government. Even tariff reformers were often embarrassed by the imperial content of their theories.[10] The second point concerns the nature of Unionism as an ideology.

Apart from 'moral force' Unionism in Ireland, this seems to have been designed for external consumption, as a prop to external management, rather than something with real substance in terms of domestic territorial politics. Home Rule for Ireland was objected to on the grounds of security from external threats, the danger of Irish tariffs and the awkward example it could set for the Empire. Similarly, it was often not clear whether politicians at the Centre (even more the mass public in Britain) regarded Ireland as an integral part of the domestic Union, or as a troublesome colony which happened to be in the backyard of the mother country.

The second qualification to the conventional thesis concerns the difficulty of finding hard evidence to support the arguments regarding attitudes towards, and the benefits obtained from, imperialism within the United Kingdom. Finance capital and the professional bourgeoisie may have benefited from the imperial connection, but the balance sheet for agricultural and industrial capital and the working class is less easy to draw up. Again, attitudes towards the Empire and its political impact may have differed between the various parts of the United Kingdom. And on *a priori* grounds there seems no reason why a diffuse sense of patriotism and togetherness in relation to the outside world should not co-exist with continuing regional and sub-national loyalties. In short, as a force for territorial integration imperialism was generally significant, but its precise dimensions are difficult to specify. Finally, there are a number of loose ends regarding the impact on territorial politics of the Great War. Once again, arguments concerning its integrative impact seem plausible. But it should not be forgotten that the war also created that political culture of 'tiredness' and preoccupation with new problems which allowed the Centre to pursue policies permitting secession in Southern Ireland and Home Rule in the north. Moreover, the integrative force of the war in Britain may not have survived very long without the important changes in the party system which occurred after 1918. More generally, as will be argued in the next chapter, the war and the peace settlement, by overloading the United Kingdom with external responsibilities in a difficult world, created an environment in which no drive for further integration would come from the Centre.

Social change
As noted above, most existing theories emphasise the radical potential of social change for territorial politics in this period. Either social change presaged the establishment of a more homogeneous society with a nationalised political structure, or it would provide the stimulus for a peripheral counter-mobilisation against the modernising pressures from the Centre. On the basis of the available evidence a plausible case can be mounted to suggest that in Britain, at least, neither of these two developments took place. Instead, a new territorial equilibrium between Centre and periphery emerged. Put another way: neither the quality nor the quantity of social change after 1870 was sufficient to support any radical territorial outcome.[11] The arguments to support this view run as follows.

First, developments in transportation, education and the mass media provided the form but not the substance of a homogeneous, nationalised society. Too much stress, perhaps, has been placed on railways and motor cars in this period as the creators of a national society with national loyalties. For most people both were expensive forms of transport and, in the case of the motor car, poor roads, inefficient engines and unreliable tyres militated against extensive use for long journeys. Bicycles and motor cycles were probably more important and both these facilitated local travel and contacts rather than regional or national ones. In early twentieth-century Lancashire, for example, 'easy movement between neighbouring centres was not a pronounced feature of its way of life'.[12] More generally, there seems no reason to think that because travel facilities are available people will make use of them or, if they do, that this will have any significant impact on their political attitudes and behaviour. Similar comments can be made about mass media developments in this period, such as national newspapers, radio and the cinema. In many parts of the country these were often not easily available even to those who desired them, and when they were their message was probably merely added on to existing local sentiments, rather than destroying those sentiments. In short, in this period, local parochialisms could continue to exist alongside nationalising and even internationalising forces. The Great War is a good example. Clearly it was a force favouring national integration in many countries.[13] Yet the United Kingdom fought the war with county regiments made up, in many cases, of 'pals battalions' from local communities. Indeed, it was probably the very density of local mourning which provided the national integrative force of the experience.

Secondly, if any aspect of peripheral culture was weakened by social change during this period it was probably the old regional cultures. The uneven spread of industrialisation created greater intra-regional differences; south Wales, west central Scotland and the conurbations in England are examples of this phenomenon. In Wales, for example, the divisions between north and south became so significant that the Welsh Football Association had to select the national team on the basis of a strict 6:5 player formula.[14] Hechter's emphasis on the importance of industrial enclaves within the periphery is probably correct, not however in the sense of providing positive instruments of central penetration but of simply weakening the homogeneity of regional interests. Some regional cultures were not only diversified, they also declined in popular esteem. The best example is the English north. Industrialisation in the nineteenth century provided the resources and *élan* to sustain a proud regional culture. Economic depression after 1918 reversed that development. Wigan was not only unfortunate but comical. The 'north' became a place which produced talented sportsmen and music-hall comedians. The rural areas of the north also lost many of their traditional landed elite after the Great War when the more wealthy began to sell their estates and move to the Home Counties or Kenya.[15] All these developments weakened regional cultures and sentiments. On the other hand, there is little evidence to suggest that the Centre engaged in any positive *Kulturkampf* against peripheral loyalties. Sport is again a good illustration. In this period Scotland, Wales and Ireland all developed separate associations and national teams for major sports. These quickly became important symbols of sub-British loyalty, even Anglophobia. Any Centre wishing to pursue territorial integration in a meaningful fashion would have attempted to obstruct such developments in favour of national, United Kingdom teams.

It seems reasonable to conclude that social change after 1870 did not produce a national homogeneous society. Local, if not regional, loyalties continued to be important. But such sentiments were essentially corporate or defensive, in character, because they were politically weak. They were politically weak because increasingly the party system did not choose to articulate or foster such sentiments. Britain continued to be a highly localised society which 'lived with' a national class-based party system.

In Ireland the process and impact of social change were different. The bulk of Ireland, outside Belfast and its hinterland, did not experience industrialisation. Nevertheless, Ireland after 1870 underwent a real social revolution and one with very awkward political repercussions.[16] Social change, assisted by government help in the form of the Land Acts, struck at the foundations of the Protestant ascendancy, the Centre's collaborative class. A peasant society was manufactured in Ireland by political action, both from within Ireland and from the Centre. At the same time Ireland developed three successful counter-mobilisation movements against the Centre and, for two of them at least, the idea of Britishness; the Land League and Home Rule movement, Sinn Fein and Ulster Unionism. Ireland, then, underwent more profound social change than Britain, but much of this was sponsored by the Centre's policies regarding landlordism. These policies may well have thrown up the new collaborative class so desired by successive administrations in London. That they failed in the bulk of the island is obvious, but the reason for their failure lies in history, politics and external forces. In its paradoxical way Ireland, in this period, only emphasises the unimportance of social change as an influence on territorial politics.

Popular government and party mobilisation, 1870–1914
The extensions to the parliamentary franchise in 1867 and 1884, plus the intervening Ballot Act of 1872, are generally taken to mark the birth of democratic politics in the United Kingdom. In territorial terms one of the consequences of these franchise extensions, the development of nationally organised mass political parties, provoked at the time a number of fears concerning possible changes to the traditional pattern of Centre-periphery relations. On the one hand, extra-parliamentary mass parties threatened to provide politicians at the Centre with an instrument by which they could continuously penetrate and control peripheral affairs and thus attack the relative autonomy of local elites. On the other hand, the advent of the local party caucus threatened to eliminate the traditional local collaborators, politicise many aspects of local government, mobilise peripheral communities against the Centre and allow peripheral interests to achieve significant influence over Westminster politics and politicians.

In Britain some developments gave support to these fears. Local branches of the national parties were established in almost all constituencies and they often attempted to increase the range of local party activity beyond the traditional functions relating to parliamentary elections.[17] Again the newly-enlarged electorate voted increasingly for candidates of the national parties and, as a result, the period saw a decline in the number of independent MPs. It is also clear that these new mass parties did attempt to structure local government elections, particularly in urban areas, around national party concerns and that in some areas, notably Wales and London, their entry into local politics represented an important attack on the power of traditional elites. Nevertheless, in general terms it is difficult to support the contention that the new mass parties brought about a fundamental change in the structure of territorial politics in Britain. This was primarily because, as Lowell put it, there was a considerable element of 'sham' surrounding their operations.[18] After 1870 the parties did not significantly assist central penetration, the politicisation of local government, or the decline of Westminster politics. Indeed, the reverse is more plausible: the depoliticisation of the periphery and the increased autonomy of Centre politics from peripheral influences was associated, in Britain, with the rise of mass parties. Some of the reasons for this paradoxical development were as follows.

First, in suffrage terms what developed after 1867 was not democracy but popular government, something more open and electorally uncertain than the post-1832 system, but still falling short of a modern democratic electorate in terms of the numbers of people allowed to vote.[19] After 1884, for example, some adult groups, women and those in receipt of poor relief, were still explicitly excluded from the franchise. Equally important, about forty per cent of adult males did not receive the vote as a result of the complicated provisions regarding registration requirements and the registration procedures themselves, which were dominated by the local party agents. In practice the vote was still 'the reward of known loyalty to a political party rather than the disinterested exercise of a citizen's rights'.[20] In 1914, then, Britain was the only major western democracy not to have achieved a practical universal male suffrage, and it was not until 1918 that this system of 'democracy tempered by registration' was abolished.

Secondly, several aspects of the electoral 'constitution' in this period had a more specific relevance for territorial politics. The complex registration procedures just mentioned made effective local party organisation essential: canvassing not only persuaded voters, but determined who could vote as well. In these circumstances divisions within local parties could have serious electoral results. Local government elections were similarly affected by these procedures. Lists of committed registered voters ensured relatively high polls: before 1914 turnouts of less than fifty per cent were rare in local elections.[21] The 1883 Corrupt and Illegal Practices Act also affected local party activity. It prescribed limits to election expenses, made the party agents responsible for policing such limits, and shifted the burden of electioneering from professional to voluntary workers. For a time it turned grass-roots politics into an uncertain, yet attractive, game, something which stimulated the participation of both sexes.[22] The 1885 Redistribution Act had a different impact. By splitting the provincial cities into single-member constituencies it ensured that they lost much of their old political coherence.

Moreover, the Act was based on the principle of equal constituency size. As a result, parliamentary constituencies sometimes became artificial creations, designed to bolster parliamentary legitimacy rather than represent real local communities. All this represented a psychological loss to local, particularly big city, interests. The electoral system employed was also relevant. Although it changed the franchise, the United Kingdom stuck by the single member, simple majority system. It did not adopt proportional representation. This may have been important, since it has been argued that PR assists central penetration of local politics and, at the same time, stimulates local politicisation by giving parties a chance of gaining seats in any constituency.[23]

Thirdly, a major reason why local parties did not succeed in penetrating Westminster politics or politicising local government was the attitude of the party elites at the national and local levels. Disraeli, Salisbury and Gladstone all wished to avoid any loss of Westminster power to local forces. Most of their colleagues agreed. Only Joe Chamberlain took a different view and for reasons explained below his actions and attitudes after 1886 were less important than they might have been. Local party elites, though prepared to devote time and energy to the organisation of parliamentary elections, rarely attempted to control MPs or bring continuous pressure to bear on their national leaders. Neither did they support a more positive role for local parties in local government. A relevant factor here is the decline during this period of the *ad hoc* authority, the most politicised section of local government.[24]

The exception to all this was, once again, Ireland. Irish conditions were important because after 1870 the major British parties never managed to establish themselves there, because Ireland was over-represented in parliament, and because the Irish question and Home Rule dominated Westminster politics after 1880. The Irish Nationalist party was particularly effective in terms of mobilising and controlling mass support, penetrating Westminster politics, disciplining the parliamentary group and politicising local government. Drawing on the successes of O'Connell earlier in the century, the 1879 plan of campaign represented an effective organisational combination of American funds, Land League extra-parliamentary agitation, and parliamentary demands for Home Rule. Indeed, the Land League represented 'one of the most effective and sophisticated movements of rural agitation in the nineteenth century'.[25] All these aspects of mass political mobilisation were subject to strict central control by the Irish parliamentary leadership. These developments were later paralleled by the Ulster Unionist Party in the early twentieth century with its Orange Order link and the Solemn League and Covenant mobilising the Protestant community against Home Rule. Ireland then was the only territorial section in the United Kingdom to develop effective mass parties and both of these were designed to challenge the Centre's authority. The British played at mass party politics, the Irish took these matters seriously, more seriously perhaps than anywhere else in the Western world.

Demands for a new territorial constitution

The principal demands for changes in the territorial constitution which surfaced or increased in salience after 1870 were as follows:

(i) the specific demand for the disestablishment of the Church of Wales and, more generally, 'Disestablishment All Round';[26]

(ii) the reform of local government throughout the United Kingdom on the basis of directly elected most-purpose authorities, the municipalisation of local government;

(iii) Scottish and Welsh demands for more effective and democratic 'national' administration, improved representation in the government, and more efficient arrangements for the discussion of Welsh and Scottish business in parliament;

(iv) legislation to reform land tenure in rural Wales, the Scottish Highlands and the bulk of Ireland;

(v) demands for educational reforms in Wales and Ireland to take account of and protect distinctive national cultures;

(vi) the Home Rule policy advocated by the Irish Nationalist party;

(vii) the more general demand for 'Home Rule All Round' covering Scotland and Wales and perhaps England, or the English regions; and

(viii) the Sinn Fein policy of secession from the Union and the establishment of an independent united Ireland.

It can be seen that these demands were based on a variety of political principles, ranging from the removal of specific economic and cultural abuses (land tenure and education) to the break up of the existing Union. The majority, however, were concerned to produce more efficient and democratic territorial government and grant peripheral interests more formal weight at the Centre. They also varied in terms of the degree of trouble they posed for the Centre. Clearly, 'Disestablishment All Round', Home Rule and secession were, from the Centre's point of view, the most dangerous and least bargainable issues. What happened to these demands? How many were successful? In the present context, detailed treatment of these questions must be avoided. Nevertheless, the general point can be made that by the mid-1920s many of these matters appeared to have been resolved as a result of positive action by the Centre. Welsh disestablishment was on the statute book, elected, most-purpose local authorities had been established everywhere (apart from the City of London) and a Scottish Secretary (soon to become a Secretary of State) had been appointed with a permanent place in the Cabinet. Further, some initial moves to decentralise administration to Wales had been made, the land tenure systems in Ireland and the Scottish Highlands had been radically altered, a University of Wales created, and finally, Southern Ireland had seceded from the Union and Northern Ireland granted a Home Rule regime within it.

These primarily institutional developments in the years after 1870 are difficult to assess in isolation from the wider workings of the structure of territorial politics. The most obvious 'non-decision' was the absence of any positive move towards Home Rule for Scotland and Wales, or Home Rule All Round. However, as we shall see below, this was 'a damned close run thing'. Equally significant, perhaps, were those demands which peripheral dissidents tended to neglect. It is possible, for example, that their interests might have been better served if they had given more support to those schemes for electoral and House of Lords reform which were popular in the early decades of the twentieth century, on the grounds that proportional representation and a powerful regionally-based second chamber would have done more to protect and promote peripheral interests than many of the reform schemes which were supported. This merely points to the important distinction between constitutional form and political substance. The developments in party organisation discussed above, for example, were a major factor ensuring that local government reforms never provided an effective base to protect and promote peripheral interests.[27]

Again, although national sentiment undoubtedly increased during this period in Scotland and Wales, it was weak from an organisational point of view. A major reason for this was the internal divisions in Scotland and Wales. Another was the electoral importance of the Scottish and Welsh Liberal Parties. In these circumstances the political motor behind Welsh and Scottish nationalism in this period was Ireland and the Irish Nationalist Party. Irish demands for Home Rule dominated British politics in the thirty years before 1914. But this issue had some unfortunate consequences for those hoping for some beneficial spill-over effects. Irish nationalism produced the counter-ideology of Unionism. Admittedly, this was designed primarily for external consumption, but it hardened attitudes at the Centre and set constitutional thinking in the doctrinal straight-jacket of parliamentary sovereignty from which it has still to recover.[28] Again, for much of the period Irish nationalism was dominated by Parnell. To Unionists, Parnell was a rogue politician determined to use extra-parliamentary means to attack the Centre. In fact, he was less an Irish 'Bismarck' and more a parliamentary wheeler-dealer.[29] More to the point, he was not interested in assisting Welsh and Scottish political demands. Hence the 'motor' was never a particularly high-powered one and produced as many problems as benefits. In waiting for the Irish question to be resolved, Scottish and Welsh Home Rule supporters waited too long. The world had changed by the time they got to the front of the Home Rule queue.

A changing Centre?
Thus far we have emphasised the degree to which the various challenges to the traditional territorial order failed to produce any radical change in the structure of territorial politics in Britain during this period. Even developments in Ireland had a conservative impact in Britain. Most of the analysis has pointed to the increasing political weakness of peripheral forces. It seems plausible to assume therefore that the Centre would take advantage of this. In other words, those radical changes which did occur in the territorial politics arena in this period would occur at the Centre, which would adopt a more positive role and increase its political and bureaucratic resources so as to control the periphery more effectively.

If this is the hypothesis to be tested then it is worth reiterating the traditional nature of the beast which would experience such change. In the previous chapter the Centre was defined as the court, that body of politicians and officials surrounding the monarch, which determined policies in the 'High Politics' arena, assumed overall responsibility for domestic administration, and in general carried on the king's government. It was argued that as a result of events in the seventeenth century this Centre had few resources for continuous direct intervention in the periphery and thus, for its territorial management, relied on a complicated system of indirect rule via local elites. However, since these elites were well represented in parliament, this body was of crucial importance for the Centre's management designs. Parliament became the essential intermediary between court and country. The result, in practice, was that Westminster, although not a part of the Centre, often determined much of the Centre's policies and actions towards the periphery. It is not surprising then that according to the Whig interpretation of territorial politics Westminster was the Centre. As the Duke of Devonshire put it as late as 1893, 'Parliament... does actually and practically in every way, directly govern England, Scotland and Ireland'.[30] This, of course, was incorrect in so far as Devonshire wanted to argue that parliament dominated the Cabinet. Nevertheless, it reflected what many believed the position ought to be and as such was a significant influence on the Centre's operations.

Although there is some dispute between historians on the matter (fuelled by a lack of generally accepted criteria by which to assess the point), it is not hard to find evidence which supports the view that after 1870 the Centre did experience a radical change in character, such that it was able to assume a more dominant role in relation to the periphery. The argument can be summarised as follows.

First, well before 1870 the location of the Centre had shifted from the court to the Cabinet and Whitehall. The development of a constitutional monarchy meant that the Centre gained independence from the Crown whilst at the same time inheriting its old prerogative powers. This, plus the increased legitimacy resulting from the creation of a more democratic franchise, meant that the United Kingdom Centre was able to claim authority from both democratic and more traditional constitutional sources. Secondly, after 1870, and especially during the Great War, the range of social and economic matters for which the Centre accepted at least ultimate responsibility considerably increased. As a result employment in the public sector expanded, as did public expenditure as a percentage of the gross national product. The extent to which the Centre was prepared to intervene in society was illustrated by the package of policies associated with 'moral force' Unionism in Ireland after 1886.[31] Thirdly, to cope with these increased responsibilities it became both more expert and more cohesive. The decline of political patronage and the creation of a career civil service, appointed and promoted on merit, the increasing efficiency and pervasiveness of Treasury control, the refining and strengthening of the principles of Cabinet and ministerial responsibility, the creation of the Cabinet secretariat in 1916, even the Official Secrets Acts of 1911, can all be taken as developments which increased either the Centre's expertise or internal cohesion, or both.

Fourthly, in the course of the nineteenth century the Centre had developed some efficient instruments to control local governments in Britain, namely the judicial doctrine of *ultra vires*, Exchequer grants, and central inspection of key local services. In addition, the establishment of the Local Government Board in 1871 (and the Scottish Office in 1885) provided the basis for a more systematic relationship with local authorities. In Ireland, of course, the administrative devolution structure at Dublin Castle was well established and gave the Centre (so it could be argued) a degree of control over local communities not attempted in Britain. The Centre's control over British local government was assisted by two other factors. Increasingly, intellectual and political opinion at the Centre adopted a patronising attitude towards the institution. John Stuart Mill regarded local authorities as rather dreary institutions in which the lower orders could learn that politics was only the art of the possible. Salisbury, and probably many others, did not believe that men would be prepared to die for 'municipal liberties' Bluntest of all was Bagehot:

> ...In a country like England where business is in the air, where we can organise a vigilance committee on every abuse and an executive committee for every remedy ...we need not care how much power is delegated to outlying bodies, and how much is kept for the central body. We have had the instruction municipalities could give us: we have been through all that. Now we are quite grown up, and can put away childish things.[32]

Again, although the old landed classes, the traditional collaborators of the Centre, were in 1870 at the beginning of a long process of decline and abstention from local government, they were quickly replaced in this period by another, and more deferential, local elite of 'social leaders', drawn from the ranks of industrialists and tradesmen.[33] Hence, in Britain, unlike Ireland, a collaborative 'vacuum' never developed at the local level. Finally, before 1832 the Centre had usually controlled parliament, though it had to work hard to achieve that control. Between 1832 and 1867, however, the Centre's influence over the Commons declined considerably as a result of the confused party situation. After 1867 the Centre regained its traditional party influence over Westminster. Indeed, it increased it, since in this period it came to dominate the parliamentary timetable, developed controls over debates and exerted a more systematic call on back-bench loyalties via the Whips. In so far as Westminster was the crucial intermediary between Centre and periphery, then the latter lost a powerful resource in its battles with the Centre.

This argument concerning the rise of a stronger more interventionist Centre in the period after 1870 sounds plausible. It is also convenient. Liberals, Marxists and peripheral nationalists have all had good reason to accept it. However, there are several reasons why the argument should be treated with some caution. To begin with, even if the Centre did gain in terms of expertise, cohesion and functions, there is no reason why similar developments should not have taken place in local government. In fact, there is good reason to think that this is exactly what happened: after 1900 the advent of the most-purpose local authority, with increasing functions, an expanding professional-based bureaucracy and serious-minded councillors, all contributed to an increasingly expert and cohesive system of elected local government. In short, as with social change, a new equilibrium was established, both central and peripheral government altered to meet changing circumstances. An alternative and equally plausible thesis is that the Centre was more adversely affected by changing circumstances than the periphery. Its range of responsibilities and the problems facing it on both the domestic and external front were greater than the coherence and expertise it gained. More specifically, neither the Local Government Board nor the Scottish Office became dynamic innovative departments, and in the case of the Irish administration it was sometimes uncertain which set of lunatics were in charge of the asylum.

Further, in so far as administrative developments favourable to the Centre did take place they were incredibly slow. Efficient Cabinet records did not appear until the birth of the secretariat in 1916 and civil service reform and Treasury dominance were both more difficult to achieve than sometimes suggested. Again, the first government with a general interventionist approach was not elected until 1906. Hence, those who argue that not much had changed at the Centre by 1914 are probably right.[34] The Great War certainly changed matters but its impact was only temporary. After 1918 there was a general move to return to normalcy (pre-1914) and economy campaigns such as the Geddes axe ensured that there was never enough money to pursue radical policies. Perhaps the major change in the Centre's position was the new servility of parliament. This certainly made life easier, but it had some awkward implications. Taken with the decline of political patronage, the disappearance of local elites with contacts at Westminster and the peculiar depoliticised mass parties which had developed, it meant that the Centre was in danger of losing contact with the periphery. Yet contact was essential if political control was to be established. Above all, however, the Centre lacked the support of any positive coherent doctrine of an independent, community-orientated state.[35] There were simply too many political groups who objected to such a development, including many working-class organisations with memories of the Poor Law. Moreover, the place of parliament in the political culture acted as an obstacle to theorising about the state. As a result *laissez-faire* may have lost its former intellectual hegemony, but nothing more positive or coherent arose in its place.

TWO TERRITORIAL CRISES

The specific challenges to the old order are only one part of the story. For the most part, to chart their progress and impact (or lack of it) tells us what didn't happen. But there is more to the story than that. It also involves politicians at the Centre reacting to some of these challenges, ignoring others and trying to construct or reconstruct a viable system of territorial management in an awkward world. In short, the politics of territorial challenge must be examined as well. On this perspective, two periods, the 1880s and the years from 1910 to about 1926, are of particular significance, since in both, politicians at the Centre were faced with situations in which the pressures for change were particularly acute, amounting to conditions of territorial crisis. The ways in which these crises were resolved are important because they give us the more positive elements in the story, they tell us what did happen. Of the two crises, that of 1910 to 1926 was the more serious because in that period the conditions of territorial political instability, which had given rise to the three Union settlements, reappeared on the scene. However, the events of the 1880s, more particularly of 1886, cannot be ignored, for although this crisis was less dangerous, its outcome was significant for the general development of territorial politics, and for the Conservative Party in particular.[36]

The territorial crisis of the 1880s

This was caused by the problems of Irish agriculture, the Irish Nationalist demand for Home Rule, and the embarrassment of extra-parliamentary party growth in Britain. The challenges from external forces, social change and a more positive Centre, provided no more than a backcloth to these problems. These Irish and party questions involved a threat to the sovereignty of Westminster politics and they produced different responses from key politicians; Parnell, Chamberlain, Gladstone and Salisbury. It was these responses which largely determined the outcome of the crisis.

The Irish challenge was important because by the early 1880s Parnell (with a little help from his friends) had constructed an efficient political machine which sheltered under the same roof tenant agitation and nationalist sentiment in Ireland, plus a legislative caucus at Westminster which obstructed parliamentary business and demanded Home Rule, a demand which had obvious attractions for dissident groups in Scotland and Wales. Most important of all, by 1885 Parnell had managed to persuade a leading United Kingdom politician, Gladstone, that Home Rule was the only solution to the Irish problem. The party question concerned the internal power structure of the Liberal and Conservative parties, an issue with awkward implications for the continuing authority of their parliamentary leaders. On this matter the major threat came from the West Midlands in the shape of Joe Chamberlain and the Birmingham Liberal caucus. Chamberlain and his friends had already annoyed local conservative opinion in his own area. According to one opponent they 'came out of Birmingham at election time, black-coated, gamp umbrellaed, cotton gloved à la Stiggens and interfered with the farm hands'.[37] By the mid-1880s Chamberlain wanted to interfere with more than rural labourers; his aim was to control the Liberal leadership at Westminster.

The crisis was precipitated by the general election of 1885. Called by a caretaker Conservative ministry the results gave the eighty-six Irish Nationalist MPs the balance of power in the of House of Commons. Gladstone's post-election public conversion to the cause of Irish Home Rule led Parnell to overturn the Conservative government and support a Liberal ministry pledged to introduce a Home Rule bill. The results in the first half of 1886 have been described in the following terms:

> The struggle over the first Home Rule Bill lasted for nearly six months. That brief period saw ancient alliances crumble and disintegrate almost overnight; new confederations suddenly arise; political colleagues of many years in violent opposition to one another; and lifelong opponents uniting under a single banner.[38]

As a result of defections from his own party, Gladstone's Home Rule gambit was defeated in the Commons, and the general election which followed brought Lord Salisbury and the Conservatives to power with a majority resting on support from the new Liberal Unionist Party. With one short interruption Conservatives were to maintain this new-found parliamentary hegemony until 1906. Thus the results of the crisis were far-reaching: it defeated Home Rule, it brought the Conservatives to power, and in doing so it was to provide the Centre with an operational code for territorial politics which was to remain influential well into the twentieth century.

The specific results of the crisis can be summarised as follows. First, peripheral dissidents and those national politicians who supported them were seriously weakened. The Liberals were split between Gladstonian Home Rulers and the Liberal Unionists under Hartington and Chamberlain, respectively the leaders of the old Whig and radical factions in the Liberal Party. Chamberlain's defection was crucial. He brought much needed popular support to the Unionist cause and yet his alliance with Salisbury reduced his radical impact. Since the Conservatives ensured that his extra-parliamentary party influence was confined to his West Midlands 'duchy', his threat to internal party management was reduced. Secondly, Parnell's position regarding his ultimate aim of Home Rule now rested on the Liberal Party alliance. Given the new popularity of the Conservative Party, plus the backstop of the House of Lords and the lukewarm attitude of many Gladstonian Liberals towards the issue, this represented a weakening of his tactical position. On the other hand, the formal Liberal commitment to Home Rule allowed the party to assume the leadership of Scottish and Welsh nationalism for over thirty years, without committing itself irrevocably to that cause in either section – 'a feat of political legerdemain that effectively stultified the national movements for a generation'.[39] Thirdly, 1886 and the Unionist cause provided the Conservative Party with an occasion and an issue which allowed them to break Whig/Liberal hegemony for the first time in the nineteenth century. In the process the Conservative Party became the court party, the party of central defence, an important reversal of its traditional role in British politics.

Finally, this crisis enabled Salisbury, the Conservative leader, to impose his own territorial management code on both his party and the United Kingdom. Salisbury's general strategy was to delay and weaken the forces of 'aggressive democracy' in order to protect property rights and the established institutions of Crown, Church and the House of Lords. To do this he favoured a two-party system and moderate Conservative policies. The proper management of territorial politics was also a means to those ends, and unionism was helpful if it assisted that proper management. In return for the Centre's autonomy in matters of 'High

Politics', Salisbury was prepared to allow considerable operational autonomy to peripheral forces *within* the periphery. Hence, local governments, local parties and Dublin Castle were permitted to pursue their own interests as long as these did not threaten parliamentary supremacy and through that the Centre's own autonomy. Thus territorial politics involved a division of labour principle: peripheral or 'Low Politics' matters for peripheral people and central or 'High Politics' matters for centre people. For Salisbury all peripheral cats (even English ones) looked grey in the dark; he was Unionist to the extent that he sought to keep all of them away from the Centre. Of course this code was not original: it had been an element in the English official mind for centuries. Salisbury's importance is that he decided to pursue the code with renewed vigour in the latter part of the nineteenth century. Since it seemed to work and received support from many sources it had a considerable impact on the Conservative Party. After Salisbury, few Conservatives bothered to formulate an alternative code: until the 1960s Conservative ideas on territorial politics both began and ended with Lord Salisbury's code.

Territorial crisis 1910 to 1926
Salisbury's system obstructed radical change for twenty vital years. In the early part of the present century it began to decline. The Boer war eventually posed questions about the nature of United Kingdom government which many Conservatives found difficult to answer. The old master retired from politics and was replaced as Prime Minister by his accident-prone nephew Balfour. Chamberlain then split the Conservative Party and united the opposition over the question of tariff reform. The result was the general election of 1906 at which the Liberals were returned to power with a massive majority.

Thus, one aspect of the impending crisis was the collapse of the twenty-year Conservative parliamentary hegemony. Although the Conservatives improved their position in the two elections of 1910, their chances of regaining office remained slim given that a minority Liberal government could rely on the parliamentary votes of the Irish Nationalists and Labour Party. More positive forces were emerging, however, to challenge the traditional order of territorial management which Salisbury had done so much to preserve. Omitting for the moment problems on the external front, we can identify after 1910 five forces which challenged the old order: the positive state ideology of the new liberalism; the advent of a formally democratic constitution as a result of the Parliament Act, 1911 and the Representation of the People Act, 1918; the third Irish Home Rule Bill of 1912 and the concurrent idea of 'Home Rule All Round'; the new industrial and political power of the Labour movement; and the Sinn Fein revolution in Ireland after 1916 and the consequent demand for an independent republican Ireland.

Most of these challenges have been discussed above. Two points still require some brief discussion, however. The first relates to the challenge emanating from the Labour movement, particularly the Labour Party. This challenge was fourfold: it seemed to represent an important and dangerous force favouring extra-parliamentary politics; its ideology appeared to suggest an attack on private property and the traditional institutions of social and political control; its early commitment to Home Rule for Scotland and Wales provided support and encouragement to those groups advocating such changes; and its belief that local authorities should pursue policies favourable to the working class (Poplarism) and act as a political base from which to capture power at Westminster threatened to politicise local government in ways not attempted before.[40] Secondly, if these challenges are combined and related to the more general workings of the political system then it can be argued that these years saw the reappearance on the scene of the conditions of territorial political instability which gave rise to the three Unions discussed in the previous chapter. In other words, in the period after 1910 there existed a perceived decline in the autonomy of the state from external forces, political instability, including reform notions and a lack of elite consensus at the Centre, and the decline of peripheral collaborative arrangements resulting from the activities of the Ulster Unionists, Sinn Fein and the Labour Party. But there was now an additional condition: peripheral dissidents possessed what appeared to be plausible alternative ideas regarding the nature of the Union, ranging from secession to Home Rule and Poplarism.

Thus a very real territorial crisis developed. The forces favouring a fundamental change in the structure of territorial politics appeared both numerous and influential. To take Home Rule All Round as an example, the Liberal Party, the Labour Party, the Scottish TUC, many intellectuals and even some Conservatives came to support the idea. Asquith formally promised such a measure in his speech on the Ireland Bill in 1912 and the principle was supported in the report of the Speakers' Conference on Devolution of 1920. In addition, the many private bills presented on the subject in the Commons usually received majority support from Welsh and Scottish MPs. Despite this, and owing for the secession of Southern Ireland and the granting of Home Rule to Northern Ireland, the eventual outcome of this crisis cannot be described as radical. Indeed, the reverse would be nearer the truth.

What were the principal causes of this peculiar development? Some of the answers to this question can be inferred from the discussion in the earlier part of this chapter. At this point three other factors which influenced the resolution of the crisis need to be mentioned.

First, the Irish settlement of 1920/1 had a profoundly conservative impact on territorial politics. It removed the principal motor behind Welsh and Scottish nationalism, dramatically reduced peripheral interference in Westminster politics, served to highlight for both elite and mass opinion the dangers and complexities inherent in territorial disputes, and finally, removed a major obstacle to Conservative supremacy in parliament, the Irish Nationalist/Liberal Party alliance. Secondly, the contribution of the Labour Party after 1918 to the resurgence of territorial conservatism was important in three respects. It progressively dropped its commitment to Home Rule and Poplarism – its peripheral strategy to power – in favour of capturing the Centre and implementing policies from the Centre to favour the working class. In pursuing this strategy it assisted in the elimination of the Liberal Party as a major political force and took over its role as the protector of Scottish and Welsh interests. Hence, like the Liberals after 1886 it was able to pose as a party of peripheral defence whilst at the same time pursuing a fundamentally centrist strategy. In this sense, it served to negatively integrate Britain.[41] Its final contribution stemmed from its electoral defeat of 1924 and the fiasco of the 1926 general strike. These events ensured that although Labour had developed into a major political force, its normal parliamentary role was to be in opposition.

Thirdly, the party to benefit from these developments was the Conservative Party which lost an embarrassing issue (the Irish question) and gained an opponent in the territorial arena far more in tune with its basic aims than the Liberal Party. In addition, the 'blind and unrewarding negativism' of its pre-war strategy and the coalitionism of post-1915 was dropped, in 1922, for a return to the old Salisbury strategy of aiming for national power within a two-party system and pursuing moderate policies. This acceptance by Baldwin, and those who followed him, of Salisbury's electoral and policy strategies also involved accepting his territorial code. This will be discussed in the next chapter.

By 1926, therefore, the various challenges to the old territorial order had worked themselves out. It had been a close run thing, but the eventual outcome was a United Kingdom dominated by territorial conservatives: a strange alliance of Ulster Unionism, the Labour Party and the Conservative Party now operated. The period of potential upheaval was over.

CONCLUSIONS

This chapter has been concerned with a number of dogs which didn't bark, an exercise in what might have been. Territorial modernisation in this period was a partial and ambiguous affair. In terms of the possible outcomes detailed earlier the position in the United Kingdom by the mid-1920s was peculiar. Apart from the Irish settlement involving secession and Home Rule no other option had developed. Obviously many things were responsible for this, but it is hard not to conclude that primary responsibility must rest with that political coalition composed of Lord Salisbury, Sinn Fein and British social democracy. It would be difficult to imagine a stranger 'alliance' to defeat the forces of territorial radicalism and ensure the depoliticisation of the periphery than this one. A more detailed analysis of the outcome of this strange alliance forms the subject matter of the next chapter.

NOTES

1 Lloyd George in 1890. Cited in Kenneth O. Morgan (ed.), *Lloyd George Family Letters 1885–1936* (London, 1973).

2 Sir Henry Wilson in 1919. Cited in Keith Jeffrey, 'Sir Henry Wilson and the defence of the

British Empire, 1918–1922', *Journal of Imperial and Commonwealth History*, V (1976/7).

3 Dean C. Tipps, 'Modernisation theory and the comparative study of societies: a critical perspective', *Comparative Studies in Society and History* (1973).

4 This term is used by Peter Amann in 'Revolution: a redefinition', *Political Science Quarterly*, LXXVII (1962).

5 A. V. Dicey, *Lectures on the Relation between Law and Public Opinion in England during the Nineteenth Century* (London, second edition, 1914).

6 For good summaries of this debate see Henry Parris, *Constitutional Bureaucracy* (London, 1969), Chapter 9; Arthur J. Taylor, *Laissez-Faire and State Intervention in Nineteenth-Century Britain* (London, 1972); G. Fry, *The Growth of Government* (London, 1979).

7 Richard Rose and Derek W. Urwin, *Regional Differentiation and Political Unity in Western Nations* (London, 1975), p. 40. See also S. M. Lipset and S. Rokkan, *Party Systems and Voter Alignments* (New York, 1967); Michael Hechter, *Internal Colonialism* (London, 1975); Joseph Lee, *The Modernisation of Irish Society 1848–1918* (Dublin, 1973); A. Lijphart, 'Consociational democracy', *World Politics* (1968/9); Tom Garvin, 'Political cleavages, party politics, and urbanisation in Ireland: the case of the periphery-dominated Centre', *European Journal of Political Research* (1974).

8 Perry Anderson, 'Origins of the present crisis', in Perry Anderson and Robin Blackburn (eds.), *Towards Socialism* (London, 1965).

9 William Roger Louis (ed.), *Imperialism: The Robinson and Gallagher Controversy* (New York, 1976), p. 59; Ged Martin, 'Was there a British Empire?', *The Historical Journal* (1972).

10 Peter Alexis Gourevitch, 'International trade, domestic coalitions; and liberty: comparative responses to the crisis of 1873–1896', *Journal of Interdisciplinary History* (1977); Geoffrey K. Fry, *op. cit.*, p.153.

11 Walker Connor, 'Nation-building or nation-destroying?', *World Politics* (1972); 'Ethnonationalism in the first world: the present: historical perspective', in Milton J. Esman (ed.), *Ethnic Conflict in the Western World* (New York, 1977).

12 Grace Jones, *National and Local Issues in Politics: A Study of East Sussex and Lancashire Spinning Towns, 1906–1910* (unpublished University of Sussex D. Phil. Thesis, 1965), p. 28.

13 Eugen Weber, *Peasants Into Frenchmen: The Modernisation of Rural France, 1870–1914* (London, 1977), p. 477.

14 Maurice Golesworthy, *The Encyclopaedia of Association Football* (London, 1973), p. 207.

15 J. M. Lee, *Social Leaders and Public Persons* (Oxford, 1963), p. 92.

16 Joseph Lee, *op. cit.*

17 H. J. Hanham, 'The reformed electoral system in Britain', *Historical Association* (1968); J. Garrard, 'Parties, members and voters: A case study', *The Historical Journal* (1977).

18 A. Lawrence Lowell, *The Government of England*, I (London, 1910), p. 491.

19 Peter Marsh, *The Discipline of Popular Government: Lord Salisbury's Domestic Statecraft, 1881–1902* (Sussex, 1978); Neal Blewett, 'The franchise in the United Kingdom, 1895–1918', *Past and Present* (1965).

20 Richard Shannon, *The Crisis of Imperialism, 1865–1915* (London, 1974), p. 395. These registration requirements did not operate in Scotland. See Lowell *op. cit.*, I, p. 483.

21 J. M. Lee, *op. cit.*, p. 54.

22 A. B. Cooke and John Vincent, *The Governing Passion* (Brighton, 1974).

23 S. Rokkan, *Citizens, Elections, Parties* (New York, 1970), p. 191.

24 J. M. Lee, *op. cit.*, p. 50, and generally Derek Fraser, *Urban Politics in Victorian England* (Leicester, 1976).

25 Joseph Lee, *op. cit.*, p. 89.

26 The Church of Ireland was de-established in 1869.

27 Another factor was probably the decline of patronage/corruption in local politics. Patronage constructed local political systems out of organisational chaos earlier in the nineteenth century. See D. Fraser, *op. cit.*

28 A. V. Dicey's *England's Case Against Home Rule* (London, 1886), is a good example of this kind of constitutional thinking.

29 The Bismarck point is made by Oliver Macdonagh, *Ireland: The Union and Its Aftermath* (London, 1977), p. 61.

30 H. J. Hanham, *The Nineteenth Century Constitution* (Cambridge, 1969), p. 22.

31 L. P. Curtis Jnr., *Coercion and Conciliation in Ireland 1880–1892* (London, 1963), Chapter 15.

32 J. S. Mill, 'Centralisation', Edinburgh Review (1862); Lord Salisbury, 'The Commune and the Internationale', *The Quarterly Review* (1871); Walter Bagehot, *The English Constitution* (Fontana, 1963), pp. 264–5.

33 J. M. Lee, *op. cit.*

34 G. K. Fry, *op. cit.*; John P. Mackintosh, *The British Cabinet* (1977), p. 4; A. J. P. Taylor, *English History 1914–1945* (Oxford, 1965), p. l.

35 H. J. Hanham, op. cit., p. 294; Tom Nairn, *The Break-Up of Britain* (London, 1977), Chapter 1; Kenneth Dyson, *The State Tradition in Western Europe* (Oxford, 1980).

36 For a more detailed treatment of these crises see Jim Bulpitt, 'Conservatism, Unionism and the problem of territorial management', in R. Rose and P. Madgwick (eds.), *The Territorial Dimension in United Kingdom Politics* (London, 1982).

37 Cited in M. C. Hurst, *Joseph Chamberlain and West Midland Politics 1888–1895* (Oxford, Dugdale Society), p. 4.

38 Robert Rhodes James, *Lord Randolph Churchill* (London, 1959), p. 221.

39 J. C. Banks, *Federal Britain* (London, 1971), p. 79.

40 Ross McKibbon, *The Evolution of the Labour Party 1910–1924* (London, 1974); M. Keating and D. Bleiman, *Labour and Scottish Nationalism* (London, 1980); B. Keith-Lucas, 'Poplarism', *Public Law* (1962); E. Briggs and A. Deacon, 'Local democracy and central policy: the issue of pauper votes in the 1920s', *Policy and Politics* (1974).

41 M. Hechter, *op. cit.*, p. 392.

chapter five | *l' ancien régime*: the anatomy of a dual polity

It is like a great factory wherein two sets of machinery are at work, their revolving wheels apparently intermixed, their bands crossing one another, yet each set doing its own work without touching or hampering the other.[1]

Local politics have remained more separate from national politics than in almost any other country.[2]

INTRODUCTION

By the mid 1920s a kind of normalcy had returned to United Kingdom politics. The general election of 1924, the Locarno Pact (1925), the return to the gold standard (1925), and the defeat of the general strike in 1926 marked this return in terms respectively of party politics, foreign affairs, economic management and industrial relations. In the territorial arena the acute challenges of the previous decade and a half had worked themselves out. The tripartite agreement of December 1925, in which the government of the new Irish Free State recognised the existing boundaries of Northern Ireland, was perhaps the best indication that the period of challenge and crisis had come to an end.[3] Thus 1926 can be taken as the beginning of a new territorial era, one which was to last for nearly forty years. Given the outcome of the modernisation process described in the previous chapter what were the major characteristics of territorial politics in these years? The argument presented here is that a very peculiar and subtle system of Centre-periphery relations functioned. With hindsight this period can be labelled the United Kingdom's *Ancien Régime* and the distinguishing feature of this regime was that it operated as a *Dual Polity*. This meant that the degree of political inter-penetration between Centre and periphery was low. In other words, they had relatively little to do with each other, relative, that is, to the situation in the past, the future and to other countries at the same time.[4]

As an aspect of territorial politics, duality was briefly mentioned in Chapter 2 above, in connection with the central autonomy model of centralisation. Such autonomy was an important aspect of the Dual Polity but it was only one aspect.

In general terms, during the *Ancien Régime* duality was the product of the co-existence of a politically weak periphery and a weak preoccupied Centre, resulting in a relationship of mutual deference and frigidity. This distinguishes the regime from dual federalism situations where the lack of interpenetration between the two levels is the result of a relatively strong periphery facing a weak Centre. The suggestion is not that there were no contacts between Centre and periphery in this period, merely that those that existed (and there were many) were primarily bureaucratic and depoliticised in character. There were also variations in the degree of duality between different territorial sections and different policy arenas. Nevertheless, the argument is that these were differences of degree only. Again, at certain times, notably during the Second World War, interpenetration between Centre and periphery increased significantly, though this was largely administrative and bureaucratic in character. The central proposition, however, is that taking the period as a whole, political duality was its major characteristic, the dominant code of politicians at the Centre and accepted by politicians in the periphery. National and local politics were largely two separate worlds. After 1961, or thereabouts, the Dual Polity went into decline because interpenetration began to increase. That story is pursued in the next chapter.

TERRITORIAL POLITICS 1926–61

The major features of territorial politics in this period can be examined under three broad headings; the external support system, peripheral politics and the nature of central management.

The external support system
In this period the United Kingdom's external economic relations were always fragile, and its security position was often awkward and sometimes precarious. In a dangerous world, its limited resources did not match its extensive responsibilities. Equally important and awkward, from the very beginning there existed 'a quite terrifying contrast' between elite perceptions of these problems at the Centre and the mass electorate's perceptions of the United Kingdom's position in the world.[5] The public perceived great power status, enjoyed that status, and yet at the same time was rarely willing to sanction the expenditure and military actions required to maintain it. For a country whose national elite had always recognised the vital link between external success and domestic tranquillity these problems ensured that foreign affairs and the construction of a viable external support system would remain a priority matter. In fact, external affairs and their management had a generally integrative impact on domestic territorial politics, at least until the early 1960s, and in one important respect they made a significant contribution to the construction and maintenance of the Dual Polity.

One obvious reason for their integrative impact was that war and the threat of war provided British nationalism with something to react against. In the domestic context the positive meaning of Britishness may have been ambiguous but it was clear what it didn't represent, what it objected to. The actions of Germany, Japan and later Russia, also served to emphasise the importance of those institutions, such as the armed forces and the Commonwealth, which had traditionally bound the United Kingdom together. Even Northern Ireland benefited. As one commentator on the effects of the Second World War put it, 'for a contentious people we were remarkably unified in face of the dangers of war'.[6] Moreover, external dangers produced a political climate unfavourable to peripheral dissidence. The traditional nostrums of secession and Home Rule appeared to most people to be both dangerous and irrelevant, attractive only to cranks on the political fringe. Serious politics was about other matters. Thus, nationalism lacked intellectual support. It was regarded as a suspect cause, responsible for European political instability in the pre-war years, and for much suffering thereafter. Significantly, both the Scottish National Party and Plaid Cymru became divided on issues related to these problems in the 1930s and early 1940s.

The newly-independent state in southern Ireland also made an important contribution to territorial integration within the United Kingdom. If secession meant Irish economic dependence 'Britain's ranch' – then it did not appear a worthwhile cause to pursue. More positively, after 1932 successive governments in Dublin pursued a number of policies – gaelicisation, a 'special position' for the Catholic Church, trade war with Britain, neutrality in the Second World War and finally the declaration of a republic outside the Commonwealth in 1948 – which appeared designed to weaken even further its appeal to the majority community in Northern Ireland whilst at the same time embarrassing its friends in Britain and the United States.[7] Neutrality was generally regarded throughout Britain as an act of gross disloyalty, while the decision to quit the Commonwealth produced from Westminster the 1949 Ireland Act which not only regularised this new stage in Anglo-Irish relations, but included a proviso that Northern Ireland would be detached from the United Kingdom only with the consent of its parliament. In short, both Northern Ireland Protestants and the United Kingdom Centre had reason to be grateful for the territorial impact of policies followed in Dublin.

Above all, external forces were integrative because the Centre seemed so successful in managing them. It survived the 1930s with less political and economic trouble than other countries, it 'won' the war, established the welfare state, 'the envy of the world', and subtly transformed the Empire into a self-governing Commonwealth association, with the United Kingdom at its head. In addition, the 'special relationship' with the United States provided both a wealthy benign protector and continued front-rank status in international politics. All this was achieved without the awkwardness resulting from membership of any alliance or supranational organisation able to penetrate directly and continuously domestic politics and act as an alternative source of loyalty and economic benefits. In short, the United Kingdom Centre, against all the odds, constructed and maintained a highly favourable external support system. In doing so it considerably enhanced its domestic prestige. It also ensured that membership of the Union brought tangible economic and political benefits.

A price was paid for this success however, and one which had all important influence on the structure of territorial politics. External management required the commitment of scarce time and resources. During the *Ancien Régime* the Centre was preoccupied with this management. Indeed, in many ways it became obsessed with it. Maintaining the external support system became the highest of 'High Politics'. Successive Prime Ministers, even Baldwin and Attlee, found that defence, foreign policy and the protection of sterling dominated their lives. Churchill and Eden discussed little else but defence and foreign policy, while those who previously had emphasised the need for domestic reforms, such as Chamberlain and Macmillan, were either forced, or grew into positions where these ideas had to be pushed to one side. By the time Macmillan became Prime Minister, 'Foreign affairs was his vocation, economics his hobby'.[8] Although these external preoccupations began as an essential instrument to achieve domestic tranquillity, ultimately they became an end in themselves. For most politicians at the Centre this arena *was* politics. There were two unfortunate results. On the one hand, the elite at the Centre divorced itself from the dreary details of territorial politics; it had neither the resources nor the interest to devote time to this aspect of its own backyard. On the other hand, peripheral interests were increasingly adversely affected by external policies. Domestic economic policy was one obvious example.[9] External policies favoured finance capital in the City, physically close to the Centre, rather than industrial capital in the periphery. Another example was immigration from the black Commonwealth. Although this produced peripheral protests very early on in the 1950s, the Centre refused to obstruct the process on the grounds that the Commonwealth as a principle implied free entry and/or that any move to restrict it would embarrass the Centre's position within an organisation so necessary to its international power strategy. Local authorities and peripheral working-class communities were left to cope with the problems as best they could. The Centre was not interested: considerations of 'High Politics' overruled peripheral protests, even those that reached parliament.[10]

Peripheral politics
For nearly forty years, the periphery mounted no serious challenge to the Centre's authority. Its principal operational characteristic was its docility. What explains this peripheral political quiescence? At the time, and later in the 1960s, three popular explanations were advanced: quiescence was the result of societal homegeneity, citizen demands for uniform service standards, and the Centre's control over peripheral governments and politicians.[11] Homogeneity produced a class–based politics in which territorial forces and issues were unimportant, demands for uniform services suggested that local and regional governments merely reflected the interests of their citizens which were everywhere the same, and central control indicated local governments and politicians with little freedom of action and, so it was inferred, further pressures from above towards uniform service standards. It is not hard to produce data which cast doubts on these arguments. Indeed, few periods have experienced such a gap between academic explanations and reality.

The negative response to the academic orthodoxy for the period runs as follows.

First, the analysis of United Kingdom territorial development thus far does not suggest that there existed any tradition of a powerful state machine at the Centre able to impose its will on the periphery and enforce quiescence. This situation had not evolved by the mid-1920s and did not change over the next four decades. In power terms we are studying a period of Central retrenchment, not expansion. Secondly, as commonly presented, the homogeneity thesis was theoretically ambiguous, conceptually confused and empirically weak. It was plausible only because it omitted Northern Ireland and placed heavy emphasis on comparisons with a single country, the United States. Moreover, it inferred societal homogeneity from what were perceived to be major *natural* characteristics of the party system, namely two parties relying on class-based electoral support. In following this line it made no allowance for the fact that electoral choice may not have been natural but enforced; that the two-party predominance was the result of the electoral system plus the organisational resources and policy manoeuvres of Conservative and Labour Party elites at the Centre and in the periphery. Above all, as a description of society and its values in this period the homogeneity thesis simply did not fit the facts. The United Kingdom, even England, was riddled with local and regional cultural particularisms and marked economic disparities.[12] Whether these were greater or less in comparative perspective than the United States, France, Denmark and New Zealand is not important. What is significant is that in this period they failed to enter any serious political arena. The formal title under which the state operated on the international front, the United Kingdom, was meaningless to most people. More important the sense of British national identity was only partial and superimposed on other identities, English, Welsh, Scots, Irish and Ulstermen. At a time of extreme national danger, in September 1939, Leo Amery's famous parliamentary cry of 'Speak for England, Arthur!', only served to highlight the problem of national identity.[13] Similarly, the available evidence appears to show that alongside confusions regarding national identities there existed, in both Northern Ireland and Scotland, considerable sentiments favouring radical change to the nature of the Union. In short, not only did societal homogeneity not exist, but the cultural and political bonds of Union were less than imagined.

Two further points regarding central control and uniform policy demands need to be noted. It is true that throughout this period the unitary nature of the constitution was generally accepted by those interested in such matters. This unitary theme was expressed in two constitutional principles, the sovereignty of parliament and the supremacy of the Crown's executive power. These principles were buttressed by the constitutional conventions of collective Cabinet and ministerial responsibility. On this basis Dicey would have been happy in his grave: the ultimate authority of parliament and the Crown was still safe. However, in terms of the operation of government this unitary constitution contained two major anomalies. The 1920 Government of Ireland Act had bestowed on Northern Ireland a Home Rule or legislative devolution constitution. This meant that the Province possessed a parliament and a Cabinet responsible to that parliament. It also involved a separately appointed civil service and judiciary. At the same time, Scotland continued to operate a distinct legal system, distinct in the sense that the personnel of the Scottish legal world, the organisation of the courts and the general principles underlying Scots law, were all different from those south of the border. Moreover, the apparatus of administrative devolution involving the Scottish Office and the numerous *ad hoc* agencies with special Scottish responsibilities continued to expand and gain in prestige (at least in its bureaucratic dimensions) during this period. Clearly, where Scotland and Northern Ireland were concerned the Centre accepted that some degree of special governmental autonomy was required. Consequently, its control over these two territorial sections was bound to be less intensive than in England and Wales where such arrangements were absent. Few departments in London, for example, were able to exercise their responsibilities both directly and autonomously in Northern Ireland and Scotland. Either they had no 'presence' in those sections or they were forced to act concurrently with Scottish and Ulster based civil servants and politicians.[14]

These separate institutional arrangements also suggest an acceptance by the Centre that distinct policy patterns were either required, or to be allowed, in Northern Ireland and Scotland. The Government of Ireland Act had devolved a considerable range of functions to the Stormont parliament and it is clear that Ulster politicians took advantage of this. For historical reasons service standards were lower in the Province than in Britain. But both the Northern Ireland policy agenda and the content of policies run concurrently with Britain exhibited considerable variations from the rest of the kingdom. Policy differences also occurred in Scotland though to a lesser extent. More important, the available evidence points to many policy content variations and considerable disparities in service standards throughout Britain, not just in Scotland.[15] Since most services of direct relevance to the citizens' everyday lives were provided either by elected local authorities or nominated *ad hoc* agencies with some form of territorial organisation, this is of considerable relevance. Thus, territorial governments did not produce uniform policies or policy standards anywhere in the United Kingdom.

Hence, peripheral political quiescence in this period cannot be explained in terms of social homogeneity or successful demands for uniform services. In addition, doubts are raised about the notion of central control by the existence of legislative and administrative devolution in Northern Ireland and Scotland respectively, and variations in policy content and standards suggest a Centre either unable or unwilling to impose policy.

The argument pursued below suggests that the causes were to be found primarily in the world of peripheral politics, particularly party politics. The matter can be discussed under three broad headings: the weakness of peripheral dissidents, the nature of collaborative politics, and the failure of most peripheral forces to penetrate and influence the Centre. These suggest a combination of circumstances highly favourable to the Centre. In fact, a degree of peripheral docility obtained greater than ever before, and one highly unlikely to occur again.

Peripheral dissidents

Old dissidents had declined, lost their way, or renounced their traditional commitments. New dissidents lacked popular appeal, organisational resources, and suffered from internal divisions. That is a reasonable summary of this aspect of the regime's story. The result was a pattern of territorial politics throughout the United Kingdom in which Unionist, or better, territorial conservative forces dominated the periphery.

The old dissidents were the Liberal Party, the Irish Nationalists, the Labour movement generally, and the Independent Labour Party and Scottish Trade Union Congress in particular. Although the Liberals continued to win votes (five million in 1929) the electoral system ensured that they would never again hold power on their own at the Centre. Moreover, with some exceptions, their organisational resources in the periphery were almost non-existent. Throughout this period they were a parliamentary caucus in search of a grass-roots base. Their decline had a twofold doctrinal impact. It meant, for example, that the ideas traditionally associated with them, Home Rule and, more generally, local democracy as a serious base for political action, suffered an eclipse. Perhaps more important, with all their faults, the Liberals were the only party whose doctrines suggested that they could have united a belief in a welfare-promoting Centre with a viable system of local democracy and effective local government. The only other candidate for this task was the Independent Labour Party, the most peripheral-orientated of all the groups affiliated to the Labour Party. However, the ILP was never a major national force and its enforced departure from the Labour alliance in 1932 meant not only that it was relegated to the political fringe, but a potential source of territorial radicalism within the Labour movement was lost.

The Irish Nationalists lost their way in the political thicket of partition and a Unionist dominated Northern Ireland. The only source of respectable opposition within the Province during this period, they lacked both organisation and a viable political strategy. The remnants of a once great party could never make up their minds whether to accept partition and play the game of normal politics or sulk in their tents awaiting a united Ireland. Such attitudes only increased Unionist dominance and effectively depoliticised the minority community. The Labour Party's conversion from a party of territorial radicalism to one pursuing a Centre strategy was noted in the previous chapter. It is difficult to find evidence to support any contention that the parliamentary leadership or the TUC considered territorial politics a serious matter during this period. Some residue of its original radicalism in this arena remained in its Scottish and Welsh organisations, but this was never important on the national stage. Home Rule Assemblies in Scotland and Wales had potentially awkward implications for the Party's Westminster ambitions. Moreover, economic problems suggested the need for nationally conceived solutions. By 1930 the STUC 'was seriously considering the possibility of amalgamating with their English counterpart, a suggestion which would have been inconceivable a decade earlier'.[16]

The new dissidents were Plaid Cymru, the Scottish Nationalist Party and the

Communist Party. The latter needs to be mentioned if only to illustrate how favourable the conditions for territorial conservatism were in Britain, compared with, say, France and Italy. In those countries, particularly Italy, the Communist parties after 1948 played a significant role in territorial politics. It is true that the strength of the Italian Communists was one reason why many of the provisions for regional government in the 1948 constitution were not activated until the late 1960s. Nevertheless, at the communal and provincial level the PCI played an important role. Its strategic emphasis on the importance of grass-roots politics as the basis for achieving national success in Rome injected an element of organisational power, politicisation and policy innovation into Italian local government completely lacking in Britain. Thus the absence of a powerful and intelligent Communist party had a considerable conservative impact on peripheral politics throughout Britain. Plaid Cymru was founded in 1925 and the National Party of Scotland in 1928. The latter merged with the Scottish Party in 1934 to establish the Scottish National Party. Both nationalist parties were founded because of the failure of the old Home Rule programmes. The unfavourable intellectual climate in which they were forced to operate was described above. It would be wrong to say that national sentiment and ideas for reforming the structure of the Union were completely dead in Scotland and Wales during this period. Nevertheless, neither party made any really lasting impact on parliamentary or local politics. Both lacked active supporters and both were unclear or divided about political tactics and ultimate aims. The important thing is that they survived (like the Conservative Party in the nineteenth century) and were able to take advantage of the more favourable political conditions in the 1960s.

Collaborative politics
Thus, peripheral political activity was dominated by territorial conservatives, by groups favourable to the existing state of the Union. Peripheral politics was also collaborative politics: governments and local parties in the periphery were run by people who were either concerned to avoid conflicts with the Centre or administer its policies as best they could. These points tell us something about the general nature of the *Ancien Régime*. They indicate the sources of peripheral quiescence. But we need to know more than that. We need to know something about the style of local politics. This will throw some light on another key feature of the regime, the peculiar weaknesses of the collaborators themselves. Two models of collaborative politics operated, one in Northern Ireland and the other in Britain. In terms of their impact on peripheral communities they were completely different. In terms of their relations with the Centre they were broadly similar; those differences which existed were differences of degree not of kind.

The main outlines of Northern Ireland politics in this period are well known. Its boundaries had been drawn to provide a secure Protestant majority, the electoral system employed ensured that this majority voted for a single Unionist party at local, regional and parliamentary elections, and a variety of devices were used, especially at the local government level, to sustain Protestant supremacy. The major actors, the policy agenda, and style of Ulster politics, were all different from British politics. Indeed, in matters such as the relationship between elected representatives and their constituents, Northern Ireland practice resembled the state of affairs in the south of the island more than that in Britain. The Unionist Party and its ally the Orange Order governed the Province in what they perceived to be the Protestant interest. This was a one-party statelet with powers of control and coercion unknown in the British periphery. From the viewpoint of the minority community (and most of the comment in the British media in the late 1960s was from their point of view), Northern Ireland was an example of strong, even immoral, peripheral government. Again, Unionist Party hegemony combined with a Home Rule constitution and the absence of a British party (and to some extent administrative) presence in Northern Ireland suggested a troublesome relationship with London government. In theory this was the territorial section in the United Kingdom where the Centre could not be assured of a docile periphery and the absence of conflict. In practice, of course, the reverse was true. For almost fifty years there was no major public conflict between London and Belfast. One reason for this was undoubtedly the policies followed by successive governments at the Centre towards the Province; another was that Unionist supremacy was less clearcut than it appeared.

The Unionist Party elite ruled over a disparate coalition brought together solely by the partition issue. As a result they were less autonomous from 'pressures from below' than peripheral politicians in Britain. On the other hand, they faced a minority community more antagonistic to their rule than any in Britain. One method of dealing with this antagonism was coercion. But the more usual practice was to follow the code of every good veterinary surgeon, 'leave well alone'. Thus, at one and the same time, the Unionist elite were subject to more internal pressures and forced to grant more autonomy and special favours to rival groups than peripheral politicians in Britain.[17] To these internal complications must be added weaknesses on the external front of Unionism. By definition the Unionists lacked the ultimate weapon of any party of territorial defence, the threat of 'exit'. Of course, in times of crisis the contractual nature of the Union could be emphasised. As a symbol, like 'no surrender', it had its uses. But there was really nowhere else to go, other than to a united Ireland. To this general weakness of the Protestant elite on the external front must be added a specific and related one. The knife-edge nature of Northern Ireland politics meant that to preserve its prestige the Unionist elite could not afford to lose disputes with the United Kingdom Centre. As a result, it was very reluctant to initiate conflict situations, and above all to publicise them. The joke is that on this point it had a lot in common with the Centre itself. Thus the Ulster Unionists were ideal collaborators: stable, quiescent, efficient, and yet fundamentally weak in their relationship with the Centre. The Northern Ireland model was sustained by the Centre's indifference, not by peripheral strength.

In Britain the state seemed similarly set for a pattern of peripheral politics dominated by party considerations, in this case a dual Conservative and Labour Party hegemony. They had branches scattered throughout the country, their

candidates represented most parliamentary constituencies, and no alternative parties, nation-wide or regionally based, existed to challenge their supremacy. On this
basis it would be plausible to argue that collaborative politics during the *Ancien
Régime* was the politics of nationally-organised mass parties, able to mobilise the
electorate and colonise all aspects of peripheral government and political activity.
Of course, the analysis in the previous chapter casts doubts on this sort of argument in terms of Conservative Party developments after 1870. Nevertheless, it is
reasonable to suppose that even if the Labour Party had renounced its commitment
to territorial radicalism, it would at least develop during this period an organisation with sufficient resources to politicise local affairs and colonise local government in the Labour interest. On this basis the Conservatives would have been
forced to respond, to behave in a similar fashion. Thus, whatever the
Conservatives had not done before the mid-1920s, they would be forced to do
afterwards in order to combat the tactics of their major rival. However, matters did
not develop this way. In Britain, throughout the *Ancien Régime*, the conditions of
effective party peripheral government did not exist.[18] There were three principal
reasons for this.

To begin with, the agencies of peripheral government were highly fragmented.
Three types existed: elected local authorities, *ad hoc* agencies with a territorial
structure, and field offices of the central departments. There was no *system* of
peripheral government because these agencies followed no common boundaries,
operated largely in separate compartments, and possessed their own special
'publics'. Moreover, with the exception of the Scottish Office, no institutions existed to take a general view of their operations and enforce some co-operation. There
were no elected regional governments as in Northern Ireland and no prefects as in
France and Italy. *Within* each category of peripheral government there was a similar lack of coherence. The most obvious, and perhaps the most important example,
was the world of elected local government. It is true that in 1929 the last of the old
nineteenth-century elected *ad hoc* authorities, the Poor Law boards, were abolished. But by the mid-1950s there were still over 1,800 elected local authorities in
Britain, excluding parish councils, with over 40,000 elected posts to fill. And only
in the large towns was there just one elected authority providing all local government services: in the county areas a two-tier system of local government operated.
In addition, there were deep social and political divisions between urban authorities on the one hand and suburban and rural authorities on the other, making co-
operation between them difficult. To this lack of integration between local authorities must be added the fragmented character of their internal organisation. A formal political executive was absent: the basic operational unit for council work was
the department and 'its' committee. In a sense, the nineteenth-century ad hoc principle persisted within the so-called all-purpose local authorities.

Because peripheral government was so fragmented the public did not understand it: it knew little about local authorities and even less about the *ad hoc* agencies and field offices. Their various services were consumed in a passive way,
rates, rents and service charges were paid, but the differences between the Gas

Board, Middlesex County Council, the non-county Borough Council of Wembley, and the local office of the Inland Revenue, were barely understood and their precise location often unknown. It is not surprising that in these circumstances public participation in peripheral government affairs was low. And the structure was not designed to produce it. Apart from local authority elections there were few other formal procedures through which a half-interested citizen could easily participate. Peripheral governments, then, were largely divorced from the general body of citizens. This fragmented structure also affected the local parties. They were not presented with an integrated system to rule; they had to create one, and, as we shall see, the task was beyond them.

Another factor which influenced party activity was the local political culture, particularly as it applied to local authorities. The argument here is that throughout Britain this culture possessed a number of features which obstructed strong party government.[19] First, although elected local governments were regarded as reasonably efficient providers of services (though housing would not be included in that generalisation), neither they nor their elected personnel were particularly popular. Certainly it would be difficult to find evidence to support the orthodox contention that local governments and local councillors, because 'closer' to the people, received greater citizen support than national institutions and representatives. A shopping-list of items to support this argument runs as follows: many uncontested local elections and low voting turnouts (far lower than many countries in western Europe in this period); in urban areas voting behaviour increasingly determined by national party loyalties and national political issues; relatively few citizen contacts with councillors, especially senior ones, and a preference to seek advice and help from council officials; a general belief that councillors pursued their own economic interests or, more strongly, were corrupt ('they're like bananas, they start off green, end up yellow, and are always bent');[20] a lack of citizen concern about fears of increasing centralisation (shared, however, by many councillors and officials); the popular idea that councils spent too much and the belief that rates were an unfair tax; the feeling in some working-class communities that local councils represented 'them' not 'us'; and intense fears from middle-class interests about certain local decisions, particularly the siting of council house estates. This list is by no means conclusive and some points can be employed to support the opposite argument. But, given the available evidence, it is good enough. Councils and councillors were not very popular; they did not have much positive public support.

Secondly, considerable confusion existed concerning how the local political process ought to operate. On this point two conflicting cultures occupied the stage. One argued that local politics should be consensus politics. Serious political conflicts within local communities should be avoided either because the subject matter of local government (drains, dustbins etc.) was simply about administrative efficiency, not differences of principle, or because disputes between neighbours were liable to be too intense. This latter theme dated back to eighteenth-century ideas concerning 'the peace of the county'. The other culture was deliberately more divisive. It perceived two major actors in the local political process; the 'ratepayers' and the 'rest', or the 'haves' and the 'have-nots'. In some senses this was merely the national class conflict model of politics transferred to the local level. But the ratepayers theme, the more important of the two, was more than that. It represented the survival of pre-democratic ideas in the twentieth century: local politics and local councils were regarded as the preserve of private property owners who paid a local tax, the rate, directly. The rest, principally council house tenants, were not perceived as legitimate local citizens; in some way they had acquired the suffrage by trickery and misunderstanding. Since local councils spent the ratepayers money, only those who paid the rates directly should be allowed to participate in the local political process. There is no doubt that until the 1960s this divisive ratepayers' culture continued to be of considerable importance.[21] Its practical impact was not only to divide the community but to place restraints on local council policy-making. Since these were the trustees of the local ratepayers, they were not expected to do much beyond providing the bare essentials of local service provision.

Both the points discussed so far, the lack of positive support for elected local government and the conflicting cultures concerning the local political process, sustained an awkward environment for active party government in the periphery. But there was a more direct cultural restraint in this period. In many areas, and amongst many groups, the intrusion of political parties into local politics was regarded as both unnecessary and illegitimate. The extent of this anti-party feeling is difficult to gauge. Sometimes it was against any type of political organisation in local politics, at other times it merely objected to national parties. Certainly in many areas of Britain organised parties were absent from local government affairs. But whether this was because electors favoured that situation or did not have the chance to vote for parties is unclear. In the 1970s the Houghton Committee found that fifty per cent of their sample agreed that parties (national ones) 'were not necessary in local politics'.[22] What is clear is that in this period many sections of the local press, textbooks on local government and many councillors and local officials were doubtful about the entry of party into local government. In other words, the elite world of local government either objected to political parties or was embarrassed about their entry into the field. These attitudes were more prevalent in Conservative circles than Labour ones, but Labour itself did not entirely escape this culture, especially one of its sub-themes – the local party organisation should not control council group policy-making.

The final obstacle to strong party government in the periphery was the nature of the parties themselves. Several characteristics of local Conservative and Labour party life during this period require some comment.[23] To begin with, they rarely scored highly in terms of organisational resources. They lacked active members, finance, the expertise of professional agents and, in many cases, pleasant and clean party premises. All this would be generally accepted for the Labour Party. However, matters were not all that different with the Conservatives. That party only scored on organisational criteria because the comparison was with Labour.

Equally important, during this period, the local parties were not primarily interested in party political activity, at least not in the sense that such activity is commonly portrayed in the textbooks. A culture of *apolitisme* dominated local party operations. This was the result of three factors: the overwhelming concern with raising money, either to sustain their own activities or, as in the case of the Conservative Party after 1945, to support the national party organisation; the concern to put on a good 'show' administratively at parliamentary and the numerous local elections; and the realisation that local activists were often deeply divided on doctrinal matters. The result was that fund-raising operations dominated all local parties and the administration of these operations took so much time that more openly political matters were relegated to minor positions on the meeting agendas of wards and branches, general management committees and executive councils. This served to unite members in a negative fashion: it avoided serious discussion about matters on which there were deep divisions. The parties were also privatised organisations, divorced from the outside world and defensive in their attitudes towards it. In this respect they resembled one description of the French family:

> For the French each family circle is peculiarly self-enclosed, with the family members closely bound to one another and a feeling of extreme wariness about intrusion from outside.[24]

Similarly, one of the best descriptions of local party life during the *Ancien Régime* summarised the position in the following terms:

> local party organisations…are self-perpetuating and self-contained, busy with their own affairs, not greatly troubled from day to day by party leaders, party bureaucracy, or even by party policy… It would be unwise to be dogmatic about what their business is: sometimes it is local government, sometimes social life, sometimes personal rivalries and ambitions, often a mixture of all three.[25]

Local parties in Britain were such a closed world that any search for new members or organisational resources was usually a national party concern, one which intruded awkwardly on the placid privatised life of their local branches. New members posed a threat both to *apolitisme* and the established power of local office holders. As Ron Hayward put it much later, 'Some parties don't want new members. They have got a nice comfortable clique and don't want new faces to upset them'.[26]

Apolitisme and privatisation were both furthered by the fragmented nature of local party organisations. 'A place for everyone and everyone in their place' was the operational code. Thus, surrounding the main-line organisational chart of branches/wards, executive councils/general management committees and financial and general purposes committees/executive committees were a variety of auxiliary organisations, youth groups, womens' organisations, political discussion groups, social activity groups. On top of these were city parties, county federations, and, even more remotely, area and regional organisations. Moreover, the parties increasingly lost contact with their own natural support groups, trades councils and local business and ratepayer organisations. Only at times of parliamentary elections did the local constituency parties operate as integrated units. A Conservative woman might never meet a Conservative man, and a Labour alderman could successfully avoid his ward secretary.

The fragmented structure of peripheral government, the non-supportive political culture, and the peculiar life of local parties ensured that the conditions for effective party government did not exist in the British periphery during this period. Local parties operated like brothels mistakenly sited next door to nunneries; there was an air of embarrassment and apology surrounding all their activities. The results in terms of peripheral government were three. First, party colonisation of peripheral government was incomplete: they exerted little influence over the operations of the *ad hoc* agencies or field offices of the central departments. Consequently, these functioned in a kind of political vacuum divorced from both national and local political pressures. Secondly, party colonisation of elected local government was only partial; many local councils, particularly the smaller ones and those in rural areas, either had no national party representatives at all or only in derisory numbers. Independent and 'local party' politics (the politics of purely local parties) were sufficiently prevalent to ensure that the national party style was never dominant. Thirdly, even where the national parties dominated local elections and the majority of council incumbents were their representatives, party government was often not meaningful. Council caucus groups were either not very disciplined, or if they were, the group as such was free of local party control. In many places the situation was worse than this. Policy making was the preserve of a small group of committee chairmen working closely with their chief officials. This 'court' faction relegated all other councillors to a 'country' party role, *party* government was forgotten. In short, during the *Ancien Régime* the local branches of the national parties failed to colonise the periphery in Britain.

Peripheral failure to penetrate the Centre

This was the third foundation of peripheral quiescence and a major force in sustaining territorial duality generally. In the past, although the Centre may have desired autonomy from peripheral forces to pursue 'High Politics', it had always been forced to reckon with powerful peripheral representation in parliament and influence in Whitehall on matters of 'Low Politics'. In this period peripheral influence at the Centre and Westminster was generally weak. The principal reasons for this were as follows.

By the beginning of our period the logic of some nineteenth-century and early twentieth-century constitutional developments had begun to affect territorial politics in ways detrimental to a powerful peripheral presence at the Centre. The elimination of electoral corruption in Britain, the decline of the House of Lords, the rise of a career civil service, the establishment of the Scottish Office, and the advent of Home Rule in Northern Ireland had all contributed to a situation in which the Centre did not require the political assistance of peripheral elites, where there were fewer institutional cracks for peripheral forces to exploit, and where peripheral pressures could be hived off to regional administrative and political outposts. It is true that Scotland possessed a Secretary of State with a place in every Cabinet, but the calibre of those holding this office was variable and their influence depended on special circumstances (Tom Johnston in wartime), or their political friendships (James Stuart and Churchill).

The Northern Ireland Unionists faced a dilemma. There was no Secretary of State for Northern Ireland and the Province had only a small number of MPs (thirteen then twelve). One possible strategy in terms of external relations would have been to play politics at Westminster; to switch their parliamentary support to favour those governments which promised benefits for Northern Ireland. Unfortunately, there were few occasions during this period when their votes were important to a government. In addition, Unionist distrust of the Labour Party meant that this ploy was difficult to follow. In practice, the Ulster Unionist strategy involved a low-intensity parliamentary alliance with the Conservative Party and a concentration on bureaucratic contacts with the Treasury. Most Ulster politicians stayed at home; few, if any, played politics at Westminster or Whitehall. With hindsight it can be argued that this strategy was a mistake. It meant that the Unionist cause was not articulated at Westminster. Even worse, Ulster had few friends at the Centre. The Unionist elite were to suffer from this after 1968.

In England and Wales there was a marked absence of territorial pressure groups with any great influence at the Centre. Local industrial and commercial interests, for example, did not possess peak organisations sufficiently strong to make any significant impact. It is true that a variety of important local government pressure groups existed. But these tended to operate as if representing some *general* local government interest or particular local authority *services*: they ignored the specific interests of separate local communities. Hence the pressure group world was divided between local groups and national groups and the two rarely combined. Amongst trade unions there developed an increasing division of labour between the national interests of the TUC and individual union leaders on the one hand, and the purely local interests of district officials and shop stewards on the other.[27]

The analysis of local party activity in the previous section did not indicate any sound base for peripheral influence at the Centre. Local parties were neither sufficiently strongly organised on a mass basis nor in possession of any powerful machine bosses to facilitate their penetration of the Centre. Moreover, in different ways the national representative organs of both the Conservative and Labour parties prevented the successful articulation of peripheral interests. The party conferences were increasingly concerned with national issues and largely controlled by their respective parliamentary leaders. The executive council of the Conservative National Union was separate from the party in parliament, did not control Central Office (it was not certain that the leaders did either), and had only an advisory capacity in terms of policy making. The Labour Party's National Executive Committee gave no formal representation to local government interests and, in practice, the constituency section was filled by MPs, not representatives of the local parties.

Above all, by this period, the House of Commons had declined as the prime arena for major peripheral interest articulation. This was not because party discipline forced MPs to vote against the interests of their constituencies. On constituency matters MPs had considerable freedom in the Commons. Nor was it the case that they lost complete contact with their constituencies. Indeed, even among Conservatives, they tended to devote more and more time to constituency affairs. It was the nature of these contacts that mattered: they were essentially depoliticised connections. And they were depoliticised because in this period MPs developed a double identity: they were party politicians at Westminster and welfare officers in their constituencies. The two roles were kept separate. Politics was a Westminster activity, the rest was 'pub admin'. The result was that most MPs avoided constituency politics (and many their constituency parties) and few, if any, became local *notabili*, persons of political consequence in the periphery, with a political power base in and beyond their own constituencies. In this respect British politicians differed significantly from their colleagues in other western states in this period. Herbert Morrison may be cited as an obvious counter to this argument in terms of his continued interest in London politics, but he was an exception and regarded as such by his colleagues. A more typical example was Roy Jenkins. In the 1960s, because of his importance in the Labour government, Jenkins could have become an extremely powerful figure in West Midlands politics. However, he chose not to build a regional power base; he remained a Westminster politician with Fleet Street connections.

This development, the Westminsterisation of British MPs (Northern Ireland MPs kept closer to local politics), is difficult to account for. On *a priori* grounds a variety of possible causes can be offered: the lack of a constituency residence rule, the relative unimportance of local issues with electors at parliamentary elections, the intellectual dominance of the Burkean view of an MP's role, the deferential attitudes of local constituency parties, and MPs' fear of local caucus domination. Whatever the reason, it was one of the most important forces in the making of the Dual Polity. During the *Ancien Régime* the House of Commons became a 'house without windows', a national legislature largely divorced from peripheral politics.[28]

Central management

Thus far, our examination of territorial politics in this period has discovered a precarious, preoccupying, yet successfully handled external support system, and a structure of peripheral politics marked by quiescent, weakly organised collaborative groups, with a low displacement both in parliament and at the Centre. What then were the principal characteristics of the Centre during this period? More specifically, did it take advantage of this politically weak periphery to construct a regime more centralised than in the past, one in which it assumed more direct control over peripheral communities and governments? The argument runs as follows.

Throughout this period the Centre was both stable and cohesive. It was stable because in general political terms a *series* of consensus situations operated within the Centre and through it in the electorate as well. A consensus situation is defined here as one in which there exists a broad political programme acceptable to the leaders of the major political parties and the public at large. It does not mean the absence of party conflict, merely that these conflicts will be restricted in scope and intensity. The sequence of consensus situations covered the Baldwin consensus of the late 1920s and 1930s, the Attlee consensus in the 1940s, and the consensus of the 1950s summed up by the term Butskellism.[29] It should be noted that for the most part these situations were Conservative-directed, if not Conservative-inspired. The fact that the Conservatives were in office at the Centre for most of this period, assisted by the anti-Labour coup of 1931, was a relevant factor in terms of the stability of the Centre and its style of territorial management. The *Ancien Régime* was not only territorially conservative, it was a period of Conservative Party 'system' hegemony as well.

Elite consensus made its contribution to the Centre's cohesion. But there were other factors at work. One was that parliament had achieved the status of 'the ever-present outsider', a talk-shop, easily managed and a useful source of legitimacy for Centre policies.[30] Another was the increasing importance of the higher civil service, the 'men between' as they have been called.[31] These years were probably the golden age of civil service influence over governments: the Treasury was officially recognised as the top department, publicly articulated opposition to the bureaucracy was not extensive, and the parties were unable to provide or find alternative sources of expert advice in an age which increasingly required expert knowledge. Most of all, the Centre was cohesive because it was so small, because so few belonged to it, and those that did shared common assumptions and calculations not only about policies but administrative practice as well. It was best defined as a political-administrative community of Cabinet ministers and their senior civil servants, with opposition parliamentary leaders waiting in the wings.[32] And within this community it was necessary to distinguish between an inner and outer circle. The former was composed of civil servants and politicians from the Treasury, Foreign Office, service departments, Cabinet Secretariat plus the Prime Minster. Their responsibilities were either more general or regarded as more important than those of the domestic spending departments, whose personnel formed the outer circle. The result was that if the British Empire 'was governed by Christian names' then so too was the United Kingdom, at least at the Centre. It was managed by 'chaps', 'sound chaps' in London, who did their best to get on with equally sound, but sometimes socially suspect 'chaps', in the periphery.[33]

But if the Centre was stable and internally cohesive it was not strong, at least in terms of its external relations with the periphery. We have already noted that it was preoccupied, even obsessed, with managing the external support system. Thus it had little time, and even less inclination, to devote to the details of territorial politics. That was 'Low Politics'; 'High Politics', defence, foreign affairs, the management of sterling, were its prime responsibilities. Equally significant, it lacked many of the resources necessary for positive direct control of peripheral governments and politics. Beyond Whitehall and Westminster the Centre was weak. The resources the Centre lacked are listed below:

(a) It had never developed any positive Unionist culture. The idea that the United Kingdom was 'one and indivisible' was absent. Moreover, it could not call on any popularly accepted doctrine that the state existed as an independent promoter of community welfare.

(b) There existed no dominant territorial department at the Centre, no Napoleonic-style Ministry of the Interior. Relations with Northern Ireland were divided between the Home Office and the Treasury, and, in Scotland the Scottish Office had to compete with British-orientated departments with Scottish interests. In England and Wales a variety of departments had a variety of functional interests in peripheral affairs. Given departmental rivalries this situation was unlikely to lead to any co-ordinated policy of peripheral management. Even within the same department, peripheral management policies could differ between sections.[34]

(c) There was no extensive *system* of field administration. Such a system was built up during the war but was disbanded afterwards. Hence not only did relatively few civil servants work in the periphery (especially senior ones), but those who did work there found it difficult to co-operate since their administrative boundaries differed and no institution existed to integrate their activities. This meant that the Centre's capacity to supervise the operations of local authorities and *ad hoc* agencies, even its ability to acquire basic data, was not very high, except perhaps in Scotland where the Scottish Office was closer to all peripheral governments than any department in England and Wales.

(d) Two of the major instruments by which the Centre was supposed to control local authorities, financial controls and *ultra vires*, were less effective than commonly realised. *Ultra vires* was no danger to any intelligent local government lawyer with a good knowledge of statute law. Financial controls were macro-controls only: they operated on the total expenditure of all local governments. Put another way, the Centre did not possess any easy methods for controlling the overall budgets of individual local authorities.

(e) The headquarters of the national parties had only minimal powers over their local branches in Britain. The Conservative and Labour party organisations in Scotland operated in practice as quasi-independent units. In England and Wales local parties had considerable political autonomy, not surprisingly, since the national headquarters provided them with few important services. This local party autonomy was particularly marked in terms of the selection of parliamentary candidates and local government operations.

Thus the Centre was stable, cohesive, preoccupied with external problems, and yet lacking many of the resources necessary to control peripheral affairs closely. One other restraint on its actions needs to be mentioned. Most of its members throughout this period subscribed to an ideology best labelled territorial liberalism.

As practical men they did not allow such sentiments to dominate their work and the positive content of this ideology was never very great. Nevertheless, it gave them some idea of what *not* to do: continuous and high-handed interference in the affairs of the periphery was not a part of this ideology, nor was any deliberate attempt to treat one territorial section less fairly than another. To this extent the Centre was more liberal, more Unionist, and more concerned about the ideals of local democracy than many sections of the periphery, and it was certainly no less committed to those ideals than parliament. Moreover, since it rightly perceived itself to be weak in relation to the periphery, it tried to avoid territorial conflicts on the grounds that it might well lose them and, in doing so, lose face.

However, the Centre did receive one notable boost to its resources during this period. A doctrinal package, plus appropriate instruments of rule, was developed which was ideally suited to the Centre's official mind. This boost was provided by the Keynesian revolution in economics.[35] Keynesian economic management was concerned to achieve control over key economic aggregates such as output, employment and prices, by regulating total demand in the economy through the instruments of fiscal, credit and public expenditure policies. For the United Kingdom Centre these ideas had two advantages. Their formal acceptance in the early 1940s became associated with post-war economic prosperity. To the extent that this promoted general domestic political tranquillity, then the Centre clearly gained. More specifically, macro-demand management appeared to give the Centre the opportunity to control the economy by an automatic pilot located in the Treasury. Once the appropriate fiscal, credit and public expenditure levers were pulled the economy could be expected to react accordingly. Thus, difficult economic problems could be tackled within the Centre and without the necessity to bargain with interested groups or pay much attention to the supply side of the economy, something which would have forced the Centre into more detailed economic intervention. Of course, Keynesian management never worked precisely in these ways: bargaining with employers and trade unions did occur, economic interventionism was never entirely absent. But the Keynesian system worked well enough. It provided the Centre with a degree of relative autonomy in the economic arena (and doctrinal backing for it) which had important spillover effects for territorial politics. Firms, employers, trade unionists and all the problems associated with production and the supply side of the economy, existed in the periphery. Demand management gave the Centre an instrument of rule which enabled it to avoid much contact with the periphery. Keynesian economics possessed no regional or territorial dimension; its concentration on economic aggregates suggested that only national trends were important. Hence, it was a perfect support for a Centre with a tradition of seeking autonomy from peripheral forces.

In this period the Centre accepted a system of territorial management handed to it on a plate by history, external affairs, peripheral weakness, its own lack of resources and the Keynesian revolution in economics. This was a Centre which did not attempt to innovate, but passively accepted the considerable advantages which went with the *status quo*. It sought nothing more than quiet deference from the periphery via the established methods of indirect rule from collaborative local elites. For its part, open displays of what power it had were avoided in order to bolster the prestige of its peripheral collaborators. Moreover, whenever possible it attempted to appease the periphery. Northern Ireland was appeased by constantly increasing financial subsidies. Scotland was appeased by accepting the principle that 'in the absence of convincing evidence to the contrary, the machinery of Government should be designed to dispose of Scottish business in Scotland'.[36] Local government was appeased by removing the wartime regional commissioners, increasing grants-in-aid to assist expanded services, and above all, by a failure to move positively on the awkward subject of reform. Only the Welsh were forgotten, although the Ministry of Education did its best to promote the Welsh language against the opposition of many local education authorities in the Principality. By these various methods the Centre attained its desired autonomy from peripheral forces and was thus in a position to concentrate on more important matters, on 'High Politics', above all the management of the external support system.

CONCLUSIONS

The United Kingdom entered the second half of the century operating, in the territorial arena, a Dual Polity; structure of territorial politics in which Centre and periphery had relatively little to do with each other. The most extreme of this duality was Northern Ireland. Nevertheless, the situation in Britain differed only in degree, not in kind. Unionism existed in terms of this common duality. Some policy fields, such as town and country planning in Britain, do not easily fit the duality thesis, although it could be argued that the Centre's peculiar willingness to interfere in those matters stemmed from a desire to maintain political tranquillity within the periphery. Overall, however, the period is remarkable for the degree to which *political* activity at the Centre and in the periphery were separate worlds. Central autonomy, a major support of duality, resembled the code of a traditional absentee landlord. As a political doctrine its origins lay with the Conservative Party.[37] In this period, however, the Labour Party played a key role in sustaining that autonomy. In terms of the centralisation definition offered in Chapter 2 above, the *Ancien Régime* can be described as centralised. However, given the very peculiar characteristics of this regime, peripheral weakness allied to Centre autonomy, it is probably better to regard the Dual Polity as a distinct form of territorial politics, a model to be added to the existing ones in this field.

NOTES

1   James Bryce, *The American Commonwealth*, I (London, 1889), p. 318.
2   Ian Gilmour, *The Body Politic* (London, 1969), p. 336.

3 F. S. L. Lyons, *Ireland Since The Famine* (London, 1963), pp. 492–3. In 1924 the last of a long series of back-bench sponsored Scottish Home Rule Bills was defeated. In 1926 Neville Chamberlain finally began to get on top of Poplarism. See Keith Feiling, *Life of Neville Chamberlain* (London, 1946), pp. 138–42.

4 The idea of territorial duality has connections with some other analytical approaches in the social sciences. One is Eldersveld's idea of 'stratarchy', the autonomy of local party activists from higher levels of party organisation. See S. Eldersveld, *Political Parties* (New York, 1964). Another is the Marxist idea of the 'relative autonomy of the state'. See Ralph Miliband, *Marxism and Politics* (Oxford, 1977), pp. 74–110; John Dearlove, *The Reorganisation of British Local Government* (Cambridge, 1979), Chapter 9. Gregory Henderson's *Korea: The Politics of Vortex* (Cambridge, Mass., 1968), is interesting because it describes the reverse situation, a society with no peripheral politics.

5 Michael Howard, *The Continental Commitment* (London, 1974), p. 80.

6 John A. Oliver, *Working at Stormont* (Dublin, 1978), p. 68.

7 See Lyons op. cit., Part IV, Section A.

8 Samuel Brittan, *The Treasury Under The Tories* (London, 1964), p. 195. For Churchill and Eden see James Barber, *Who Makes British Foreign Policy?* (Milton Keynes, 1976), p. 7.

9 Andrew Shonfield, *British Economic Policy Since the War* (London, 1958); Stephen Blank, 'Britain, the politics of foreign economic policy', *International Organisation* (1977).

10 Paul Foot, *Immigration and Race in British Politics* (London, 1965); E. J. B. Rose *et al.*, *Colour and Citizenship* (Oxford, 1969), pp. 209–20; J. Edwards and R. Batley, *The Politics of Post Discrimination* (London, 1978), pp. 29–30.

11 J. Blondel, *Voters, Parties and Leaders* (London, 1965); R. J. Lawrence, *The Government of Northern Ireland* (Oxford. 1965); W. A. Robson, *Local Government in Crisis* (London, 1966).

12 Richard Rose, *The United Kingdom as a Multi-National State* (Glasgow, 1970) and Michael Hechter, *Internal Colonialism* (London, 1975) are the most important general presentations of this argument.

13 He was addressing Arthur Greenwood, deputy leader of the Labour Party, as he rose to speak in the debate on the German invasion of Poland.

14 Richard Rose, *The United Kingdom as an Intellectual Puzzle* (Glasgow, 1977).

15 C. Brett, 'The lessons of devolution in Northern Ireland', *Political Quarterly* (1970); W. D. Birrell, 'The Stormont-Westminster relationship', *Parliamentary Affairs* (1972–3); James G. Kellas, *The Scottish Political System* (Cambridge, 1975); John Dearlove, *The Politics of Policy in Local Government* (Cambridge, 1973), Chapter 1.

16 Keith Webb, *The Growth of Nationalism in Scotland* (Glasgow 1977), p. 45.

17 On the pressures from the Protestant community see Michael Farrell, *Northern Ireland: The Orange State* (London, 1976). On educational favours to the Catholic community see Lawrence, op. cit., Chapter 6.

18 For one list of such conditions see Richard Rose, *The Problem of Party Government* (London, 1976), pp. 372–5. As Rose says, the conditions are 'onerous'. In fact, we may be expecting too much from political parties – like Playboy's view of women. Nevertheless, even if the conditions were relaxed it would still be difficult to argue the case positively for peripheral party government in this period.

19 Very little work has been done on this subject and what has been done is not very good. For

one survey of the literature see John Gyford, *Local Politics in Britain* (London, 1976), Chapter 5.

20 *The Times* (26 October, 1976), carried an item on a letter which had appeared in *The Western Mail* the previous day from Leo Abse, MP, opposing devolution on the grounds that the Welsh were so 'friendly' that they were unable to distinguish between 'the disinterested favour' and the 'corrupt act'.

21 See J. G. Bulpitt, *Party Politics in English Local Government* (London, 1967).

22 Committee on Financial Aid to Political Parties, *Report* (Cmnd. 6601, 1976), p. 43.

23 For a more extensive treatment of this subject see Jim Bulpitt, *English Local Politics: The Collapse of the Ancien Régime?* (Political Studies Association Annual Conference Paper, 1976). The analysis here is based on the twin views that, though differences between the parties did exist the similarities were more important and that local party politics in Scotland and Wales resembled English conditions in most important respects.

24 Mark Kesselman, *The Ambiguous Consensus* (New York, 1967), p. 10.

25 A. H. Birch, *Small Town Politics* (Oxford, 1959), p. 44.

26 *Labour Weekly* (14 April, 1972).

27 See Eric Wigham, *What's Wrong with the Unions?* (London, 1961); Royal Commission on Trade Unions and Employers Associations, *Report* (Cmnd. 3623, 1968).

28 Nathan Leites, *The Game of Politics in France* (Stanford, 1959).

29 Northern Ireland was not a part of these consensus situations, though the Unionists elite attempted to follow 'step by step' the major developments in the Centre's welfare policies.

30 Hugh Heclo and Aaron Wildavsky, *The Private Government of Public Money* (London, 1974), p. 244.

31 Keith Middlemas in his introduction to *Thomas Jones, Whitehall Diaries, III* (London, 1972).

32 Here I follow a major theme of Heclo and Wildavsky, *op. cit.*

33 The British Empire quotation is cited in W. L. Guttsman, *The British Political Elite* (London, 1965), p. 319.

34 J. A. G. Griffith, *Central Departments and Local Authorities* (London, 1966).

35 For a discussion of the political implications see R. Skidelsky 'The political meaning of the Keynesian revolution' in R. Skidelsky (ed.), *The End of the Keynesian Era* (London, 1977).

36 Royal Commission on Scottish Affairs, *Report* (Cmnd. 9212, 1954), para. 13.

37 Jim Bulpitt, 'Conservatism, Unionism and the problem of territorial management' in R. Rose and P. Madgwick (eds.), *The Territorial Dimension of United Kingdom Politics* (London, 1982).

chapter six | duality challenged: remodernisation and territorial politics, 1961–79

It is frequently a prior condition of reform that it should, not necessarily with a pious regard for the truth, discredit the system which it seeks to replace...[1]

If we want things to stay as they are, things will have to change.[2]

INTRODUCTION

From the early 1960s a number of forces emerged to the Dual Polity structure. This chapter attempts to identify and account for the major developments (and non-developments) in United Kingdom territorial politics between 1961 and 1979.[3] It argues that from a Centre perspective these years represent a particular phase in the story of territorial management. The policies pursued by the Conservative government elected in 1979 and, more importantly, the problems it encountered, mark another stage in that story and require separate treatment.

In terms of what happened after 1961, three preliminary comments are necessary. First, a Centre perspective, a view of our subject matter which concentrates on the problems facing the authorities in the capital city and their attempts to resolve those problems, skews the analysis in favour of certain conclusions. It suggests that between 1961 and 1979 peripheral dissidents were less important as a force challenging the traditional territorial order than the changing codes and actions of politicians and civil servants in London (initially in Belfast as well) and the impact of those changes on collaborative elites in the periphery. Secondly, this analysis of territorial development cannot be divorced from the nature of the regime which preceded it. In other words, whatever happened in this period happened to the Dual Polity. It follows, once again, that those accounts which have sought to explain the events of the 1960s (and 1970s) in terms of a series of autonomous peripheral revolts against an *existing* all-controlling and exploiting Centre, or have linked United Kingdom developments with a general western-wide phenomenon of peripheral nationalism, must be treated with considerable scepticism. The Dual Polity was *sui generis* in the western world and its nature precluded positive Centre dominance over peripheral affairs.

Thirdly, if the key to understanding the events of this period lies with accepting political duality as its base-point characteristic, then it is necessary to itemise some of the hidden penalties embedded in that structure in terms of its ability to cope with changing circumstances. These can be summarised as follows:

(a) The Dual Polity was constructed to avoid problems, not solve them. A 'suspended revolution', it contained a Pandora's box of trouble waiting to get out. Awkward questions concerning the boundaries of state action, the meaning of local self-government, the role of extra-parliamentary party organisations and the political tactics open to aggrieved minorities, had been pushed to one side by the banal slogans of mid-twentieth-century English liberalism – 'the mixed economy', 'the central-local partnership', 'parliamentary government' and 'freedom under the law'.[4]

(b) The operational code of the Polity – Centre autonomy and territorial duality – had never been formally articulated to the wider public. It remained an 'efficient secret' understood only by a few. Hence, if the regime came under concerted attack, appropriate intellectual support would be lacking. On the other hand, the very smallness and cohesiveness of the court elite in London enormously facilitated the rapid adoption and spread of new ideas once they were accepted as necessary by that elite. In this sense a new code or governmental paradigm could be imposed from above without consulting peripheral collaborators, or, indeed, any serious consideration of the possible territorial consequences.

(c) The Dual Polity was Conservative-inspired but sustained by the Labour Party's willingness to work it at both the Centre and in the periphery. Hence, if at any time the Labour leadership adopted a different territorial code and/or the party's collaborative capacities declined in the periphery (especially in Scotland and Wales), then trouble was likely to follow.

(d) Territorial duality was hardly an appropriate political base for any policy programme demanding more positive, more efficient and more democratic government. A court/country, territorial distinction allied to a practical separation of powers in London did not provide the necessary political integration for such a programme. The Centre lacked resources to control, and information about, the periphery, while the passive collaborative talents of the established local elites were not suitable for more positive government. Moreover, in many ways the collaborative system had worked too well. By the late 1950s many local elites were divorced from their local communities: collaborators with few grass-roots contacts cannot be relied on to drum up much active support for the Centre.

(e) Territorial conflict was not a major characteristic of the *Ancien Régime*. Consequently a generation of politicians had grown up lacking the skills necessary to deal competently with such issues. In particular, peripheral dissidents had been largely absent from Westminster and this absence came to be regarded as a normal feature of United Kingdom politics. Hence their reappearance on the Westminster scene was liable to provoke an overreaction from the Centre, parliament itself and, above all, the mass media.

(f) Apart from its passive and increasingly weak collaborative peripheral elites the Centre, or court, possessed no effective territorial political base. The regime survived because of the weakness of its enemies rather than the strength of its supporters. Thus, despite its appearance of solidity, in reality little stood in the way of determined and intelligent territorial dissidents if and when they emerged in one or more parts of the periphery. Nevertheless, the Dual Polity possessed a certain negative strength. Throughout the United Kingdom the general public appeared not to want a more dynamic system of territorial politics. They disliked positive and politicised local government as much as an active interfering Centre. To this extent peripheral dissidents would both gain and lose from any successful attempt to politicise peripheral affairs.

This said, the discussion which follows will concentrate on two sets of questions. First, what sort of forces emerged in this period to challenge the old Dual Polity? Put another way, what was the anatomy of territorial political change after 1961? Secondly, how did these challenges develop? More specifically, how did successive groups of civil servants and politicians at the Centre, plus their intellectual hangers-on, react to these challenges?

THE ANATOMY OF TERRITORIAL CHANGE

One method of identifying the major challenges to the old regime is to sketch the position as it would have appeared to a frightened supporter of the Dual Polity in the spring of 1977, that is just after the defeat of the Labour government's first devolution bill in the House of Commons.

First, the laboriously constructed and maintained external support system seemed to have collapsed. The most obvious manifestations of this were the lost potential for major independent military action (Suez and the 1960 failure of the Blue Streak rocket) and Dean Acheson's remark in 1962 that 'Great Britain had lost an empire and has not yet found a role...'[5] In terms of domestic politics, however, a number of other developments were equally and more specifically important. By the mid-1970s the United Kingdom economy was one of the weakest in the western world, requiring massive loans from international organisations (culminating in the 1976 International Monetary Fund rescue operation) to stay afloat.[6] Moreover, many of the old regime's most important external supports, the Commonwealth, the Sterling Area (plus the 1944 Bretton Woods international monetary agreement) and the special relationship with the United States had apparently lost their effectiveness. As a result, the relative autonomy of the United Kingdom polity from direct and overt penetration by external forces in its domestic affairs, appeared lost. As well as its membership of the European Community, United Kingdom sovereignty was now seemingly heavily qualified by the actions of multinational companies, the United States Treasury and State Departments, NATO, the International Monetary Fund and the Organisation of Petroleum Exporting Countries. Of these the European Community represented for many the greatest threat. Not only did membership mark a formal attack on parliamentary sovereignty, but the whole debate on Europe had caused a decline in elite consensus regarding foreign policy, a decline which in turn adversely affected the Centre's traditional 'High Politics' autonomy in this field. In the past the external support system had made important contributions to both domestic tranquillity and the political prestige and cohesiveness of the Centre elite. By 1977 these traditional benefits had either vanished completely or declined considerably.

Secondly, from the Centre's viewpoint, the periphery was no longer politically supportive: the easy supremacy of the traditional collaborative elites had gone. Unionist opinion in Northern Ireland was no longer organised by a single party and the Labour and Conservative parties in Scotland and Wales were weakened by internal disputes over the devolution issue. Indeed, throughout Britain the old dual Conservative-Labour hegemony appeared in decline: their once secure bases of voting support had been replaced by a highly volatile, more discriminating, electorate; both parties faced severe problems in terms of declining membership, finance and organisational resources; and policy divisions within their respective leadership groups unsettled, or were directly reflected among, the grass-roots activists.[7] In Northern Ireland the knife-edged quiescence of the *Ancien Régime* had been replaced by inter-communal armed conflict and an IRA-directed 'war of liberation' against the Union. Parts of the Province could no longer be continuously and effectively penetrated by the security forces of the United Kingdom state.

'Normal' politics in the periphery was now contested by a variety of forces outside the traditional ruling parties. In Northern Ireland the Democratic Unionist Party, the Social Democratic and Labour Party and the Alliance Party, had become important components of the party political scene. In Scotland and Wales the Scottish National Party and Plaid Cymru had made significant advances. Indeed, the popularity of the SNP threatened to overturn the whole traditional basis of Scottish politics.[8] In England the Liberals, the National Front and an increasing number of local citizen welfare and environmental groups had become actors on the peripheral politics stage. The result was that in terms of their relations with local citizens and political organisations many peripheral governments had lost a part of their old autonomy. This trend was assisted by two further developments. On the one hand, elected local governments, especially in urban areas, now pursued policies in the housing, highways and planning fields more likely to bring them into contact and conflict with local citizens.[9] On the other hand, more local authorities than ever before in Britain were subject to elections and councillors influenced by national party considerations; except in a few remote rural areas, the independent and 'local party' styles of local government politics had been eliminated. Thus, despite their many problems, the Conservative and Labour parties had finally succeeded in colonising, at least in formal terms, most of the new local authorities established by the structural reforms of 1974 and 1975. Moreover, some local authorities were prepared to venture into open dispute with the Centre: successive governments' plans for comprehensive education were disputed by local education authorities and the Housing Finance Act in the early 1970s had provoked the Clay Cross affair.[10] Above all, peripheral dissidents were now a significant force at Westminster. The October 1974 election had produced a total of twenty-six MPs representing purely territorial parties, not allied with either Conservative or Labour, while, in addition, there were thirteen Liberal MPs. The influence of all these was increased by the Labour government's minority position in the House of Commons after the spring of 1976. Thus not only had peripheral dissidents arrived at Westminster, the Centre had lost control of that institution as well.

Thirdly, by the mid-1970s the United Kingdom had experienced nearly two decades of positive action from the Centre. After the early 1960s successive governments pursued policies which increasingly departed from the old autonomy principle. One obvious example was the restructuring of peripheral government. Beginning with the reform of London government in 1963, the Centre, in the early 1970s, proceeded to suspend the Northern Ireland parliament, radically alter the pattern of local government throughout provincial Britain, and make important changes to the management structure of the National Health Service and the administration of water resources and supplies. In addition, the field administrative network was extended and partially systematised via the creation of the Welsh Office in 1964, constantly expanding the functions of the Scottish Office, and the establishment of regional economic planning boards in the mid-1960s. Regional planning experiments represented a major policy break with the Dual Polity in terms of both central penetration and the necessity to mobilise support for such schemes through the network of regional economic planning councils, on which regional notables were represented.[11] Another break with traditional practice was the decision to advise and then enforce the comprehensive principle in secondary education in England and Wales, a significant attack on local autonomy in this field. Moreover, the various prices and incomes policies pursued by successive administrations at the Centre in the 1960s and 1970s must be regarded as a significant new form of intervention in the affairs of both governments and economic organisations in the periphery.

However, the break with the old central autonomy code was not a one-way process. We have already seen that by the mid-1970s the Centre faced a less quiescent, more politicised periphery throughout the United Kingdom, and a less supportive House of Commons. Two other developments with awkward implications for the Centre's territorial management need to be noted. One was its increasing difficulty in effectively controlling public expenditure, particularly local government expenditure in Britain.[12] The many local protests in 1974 and 1975 against increased rate demands by local authorities were one aspect of this problem. More important were the difficulties posed for efficient central economic management by the increasing displacement of local authority expenditure, investment, taxation and employment, in the economy as a whole, another example of traditional 'Low Politics' issues affecting customary 'High Politics' concerns. The other development involved what was seen at the time as *the* major break with the traditional conventions of territorial politics in Britain. The strength of Scottish, and to a lesser extent Welsh, nationalism had seemingly forced the Centre after 1974 to work on, and then introduce in parliament, proposals granting directly elected regional Assemblies to Scotland and Wales, involving, where the former was concerned, the devolution of legislative powers. Yet such was the parliamentary weakness of the Centre at the time that the Labour government's first devolution bill was defeated in the House of Commons in February 1977, a defeat which seemingly did little to arrest the spread of nationalist and regionalist opinion in Scotland and Wales.

This sketch of the major developments in territorial politics between the early 1960s and the spring of 1977 serves to emphasise one important point. Territorial change was not simply a matter of Welsh and Scottish nationalism or the troubles in Northern Ireland. The whole structure of the Dual Polity had seemingly suffered radical alteration. In less than twenty years the Centre had increased the range of its responsibilities, had begun to intervene more directly in peripheral affairs, and yet at the same time had become more subject to pressures from the periphery than before.

THE PROCESS OF TERRITORIAL CHANGE

Three questions arise from the discussion above: How did this situation develop? Was the story as radical as the analysis above suggests? What happened to territorial politics between 1977 and 1979?

The events of the period can be properly understood only if the various phases of territorial development after the early 1960s are examined in terms of the principal challenges facing the Centre, the main lines of the Centre's response to those challenges, and the impact of those responses on peripheral politics and politicians. The period can be divided into three, each phase marked by a particular characteristic in terms of its relation with the old Dual Polity. The three phases were: *(i)* the decline of duality, 1961 to 1968; *(ii)* the threatened collapse of duality, 1968 to 1977; and *(iii)* the partial reconstruction of Centre autonomy, 1977 to 1979.

(i) The decline of the Dual Polity (1961–8)
In the early 1960s leading politicians and civil servants in both London and Belfast decided to subscribe to political modernisation, or better, remodernisation programmes. This modernisation theme, a broad attempt to update the economic and political systems of Britain and Northern Ireland in order to confront a variety of new problems and challenges, was a key feature of United Kingdom politics in the 1960s, at least until about 1968 by which time it had become a spent force. The London programme, accepted in its essentials by both the major parties, was not designed with Northern Ireland in mind; an indication of the extreme political duality which existed at the time between London and Belfast. The Northern Ireland programme, a Unionist elite strategy, was influenced by its counterpart in Britain. But that was only one influence, and the intended results were

viewed entirely in terms of Ulster politics. The important point is that both modernisation programmes affected territorial politics, mostly in ways not intended by
those who initiated them.

In Britain, modernisation was born in 1961. This was the year in which both
the Plowden Report on 'The Control of Public Expenditure' and Michael Shanks'
Penguin Special, *The Stagnant Society*, were published. It was also the year of the
Selwyn Lloyd credit squeeze and pay pause, new discussions on long term economic planning which led to the creation of the National Economic Development
Council, and the first application to join the EEC. Although there were good
domestic reasons for this 'great reappraisal',[13] increasing unemployment and a
reasonable performance by the SNP at a Glasgow by-election (Orpington in 1962
had a greater impact), the principal impetus appears to have come from changing
perceptions concerning Britain's position in relation to the outside world. In particular, Britain's relative economic decline was perceived to be adversely affecting her international power position, which in turn threatened domestic tranquillity. Thus, modernisation was initially adopted to preserve the external and internal
status quo. In the domestic context broad agreement existed between the major
parties as to what modernisation involved. The consensus emphasised the need for
planned economic growth, more efficient public administration and a more democratic political process. As a result planning, efficiency and participation became
the key symbols of the decade. On the external front the meaning was less clear.
For the Conservative elite it meant entry to the EEC. Labour however, did not formally adopt this strategy until 1967.

This first phase of modernisation was dead by 1968, killed by the unsuccessful attempt to protect sterling and de Gaulle's second EEC veto. The general story
does not concern us here. What is important is that by 1968 modernisation had had
a profoundly unsettling effect on territorial politics. The argument can be summarised as follows.

First, the programme was associated with a sustained attack on the existing
institutions, procedures and personnel of territorial politics, on the grounds that
they were administratively inefficient, insufficiently democratic and over-cen-
tralised. A popular solution to these problems was to emphasise the need for a
greater element of 'regionalism' in British politics. Although differences of opinion existed regarding the relative weighting to be given to the administrative efficiency and greater democracy requirements, and the meaning of 'regionalism' was
often ambiguous, the important point was the attack itself. For reasons detailed
above, the *Ancien Régime* could draw on little support or understanding to combat these criticisms. Thus, a political culture was created in which it was commonly accepted amongst informed opinion that territorial politics was one of those
'dignified' parts of the constitution in need of drastic reform. This new culture was
initially formulated and publicised by academics and journalists hoping to influence public policy. It was accepted by the political administrative community at
the Centre as a convenient item to incorporate into its wider programme. In this
sense, 1960s-style territorial modernisation was designed *at* the Centre *for* the

periphery. Technocratic and managerial in character, with little organised political support outside Whitehall, it lacked any awareness of the political problems likely to be encountered when implementing such aims. It sought 'improvement' without politics, a philosophy better suited to the operations of Marks and Spencers than to the complex and fragile affairs of territorial politics.[14]

Secondly, modernisation meant that the Centre was forced to drop its old autonomy code: it became interested in many aspects of peripheral activity. For example, a concern for economic efficiency resulted in an interest in the supply side of the economy, which in turn necessitated more detailed information about, and encounters with local governments, employers and trade-unionists in the periphery. It was not that the Centre had eliminated the distinction between 'High' and 'Low politics', rather that to sustain its 'High Politics' interests required more attention to its own backyard than before. Symbolic of this new interest was Lord Hailsham's appearance, complete with cloth cap, in the north-east of England early in 1963, charged with special ministerial responsibility for the region. This abandonment of the autonomy code took a very awkward form. Under the pressure of electoral competition the sum total of the Centre's policy announcements in this period suggested its acceptance of a form of territorial contract with the periphery: it had a duty to pursue and achieve territorial justice between the various parts of the periphery. The latter's responsibilities in this contract were unclear. Even less clear, and potentially very awkward, was how the periphery should react if the Centre failed to fulfil the new contract.

Thirdly, in the process of attempted modernisation both the Centre and its peripheral, collaborative elites lost face; the latter because the structure which they managed was pronounced in both theory and practice as incapable of meeting the demands of more active government and the former because under the direction of both major parties it had failed to achieve modernisation, failed to fulfil its contract with the periphery. Consequently, by the second half of the 1960s a credibility gap had appeared in the politics of both Centre and periphery. In these circumstances it is not surprising that there was some sort of political revolt in the periphery, notably in Wales and Scotland where the collaborative system was weakest. This revolt was marked not only by the rise of nationalist parties, but by the growth of a situation in which most of the established 'corporations' of Scottish and Welsh politics, (churches, business, trade unions and professions) began to take a more critical attitude towards the existing nature of the Union.

The argument then is that in this period the Centre made a major contribution to the decline of the Dual Polity. This is not to deny the importance of other factors such as the impact of television, the growth of house and automobile ownership, and the increasing organisational skills of peripheral dissidents. But at this stage these were less important than the programmatic failure of the Centre and its effects on established peripheral elites. Perhaps equally important (at least for the future) was the hasty response of the major parties to incipient political unrest in Wales and, above all, Scotland.[15] Mr Heath's 'Declaration of Perth' in May 1968 gave a vague commitment to an elected Scottish Assembly without consulting the party in England. Labour, on the other hand, with more parliamentary seats to lose, resorted to the classic device of a Royal Commission to inquire into all aspects of territorial politics in the United Kingdom.

A similar, though more intense and sorry story took place in Northern Ireland.[16] From the late 1950s Unionist governments in the Province were confronted with three major problems: increasing unemployment resulting from the decline of the traditional industries of textiles and shipbuilding; industrial unrest and the beginnings of a move by the Protestant working class to vote for the Northern Ireland Labour Party; and the British modernisation programme described above. This diminished the regional aid advantages offered by Northern Ireland governments, whilst at the same time highlighting the failure of the Unionist elite to produce a similar policy package to deal with broadly similar economic problems. In 1963 Lord Brookeborough, Prime Minister since 1943, resigned and his place was taken by Terence O'Neill. Whether O'Neill was the liberal moderniser his autobiography suggests is open to question. What is important is that his programme of economic progress through planning, more efficient government and the suggestion that sectarian divisions should decline, represented modernisation in the context of Ulster politics.

Predictably, O'Neill was faced with opposition from the Unionist grass-roots. Equally important, some Labour MPs under the guidance of Paul Rose and later Gerry Fitt (elected to Westminster as Republican Labour MP for a Belfast constituency in 1966) began to press parliament to take a closer interest in Northern Ireland affairs. O'Neill faced two further problems: he promised the minority community more than he was prepared or able to give; and the Nationalist Party, the official opposition after 1965, was an ineffective, even deferential, articulator of Catholic interests. The result was that elite politics at Stormont became increasingly isolated from grass-roots opinion in both communities. On the Catholic side, political activity was increasingly channelled into the new civil rights movement. The subsequent marches and riots which took place between August and October 1968 spelt the end of the *Ancien Régime* in Northern Ireland: liberal opinion in Britain was not prepared, in the late 1960s, to accept the televised scenes of violence at the Londonderry demonstration of 5 October. As a result, Northern Ireland re-entered British politics. The joint meeting of Northern Ireland and British government ministers at Downing Street in November 1968, called to discuss the problems of the Province, symbolically confirmed this. O'Neill was forced to accept the broad outlines of a reform programme, the details of which he later announced at Stormont.[17] Thus, once again duality had been broken by an attempt to impose modernisation from above, without an appropriate political support structure.

(ii) The collapse of duality? (1968–77)

By 1968 the Dual Polity had declined throughout the United Kingdom. It is possible to argue that between 1968 and 1977 it collapsed. Indeed, for some commentators at this time the whole system was on the verge of breaking up into its separate territorial parts. As Tom Nairn put it, 'There is no doubt that the old British state is going down'.[18] The discussion above concerning the anatomy of territorial change could also be taken as suggesting that by 1977 the United Kingdom was experiencing the reappearance of the traditional conditions favouring territorial political instability, namely: a perceived decline in the autonomy of the state from external forces; reforming consensus-lacking governments at the Centre; a marked decrease in the effectiveness of collaborative operations in the periphery; and the emergence of plausible alternatives to the existing nature of the Union among peripheral dissidents.

It would be difficult to deny that in this period the Centre faced a number of serious problems regarding its 'estate' management: the old duality with its supports, peripheral collaboration, central autonomy and a favourable external support system, was severely compromised. But the position was extremely complex. Duality survived in peculiar places and any thesis concerning a general self-propelling peripheral revolt against the Centre must be heavily qualified. A number of points need to be raised here.

On the surface there seems no better illustration of the collapse of duality in these years than Northern Ireland. The presence after 1969 of the army and British officials, the London-sponsored reforms between 1968 and 1972, the suspension of Stormont and institution of direct rule and sporadic IRA campaigns in Britain, these developments all suggest a more complete integration between Ulster and British politics. There, is, however, another side to the argument. The initial decision to commit the army was taken with extreme reluctance and yet considerable casualness, even naivety, in terms of considering the eventual outcome. At one and the same time it was the minimal possible response to disorder in the Province with the maximum potential for further trouble. It bore some resemblance to Gladstone's equally reluctant and casual commitment of troops to Egypt in 1882 and the consequent long term responsibilities which followed in that imperial province.[19] The Ulster peacekeeping force was similarly thought to be an unfortunate but temporary expedient. Again, apart from the first five months of 1974, the Centre, after the 1972 suspension of Stormont, managed the Province directly via the Northern Ireland Office. But direct rule was a low intensity operation. Ulstermen continued to play an important part in security affairs and the British politicians heading the Northern Ireland Office sat on top of an organisation staffed overwhelmingly by Northern Ireland, not British civil servants. In many ways this was the nineteenth-century Dublin Castle model transferred to twentieth-century conditions. And whatever administrative integration followed direct rule was not paralleled in the world of party and group politics. British parties and pressure groups still did not penetrate Northern Ireland and showed few signs of wanting to do so. The only major departure from direct rule, the Whitelaw power-sharing constitution, can be viewed as an attempt to offload the problems of the Province onto a new home-based executive. Despite the powers which remained with the Secretary of State, it was essentially a scheme to reconstruct indirect rule, but with a new set of peripheral collaborators. Its failure merely emphasised the

Centre's principal continuing problem in the Province: its inability to build up a new collaborative elite.

Perhaps more important than these points was the peculiar British political culture concerning the Northern Ireland problem which developed in this period. From 1969 opinion polls indicated relative majorities favouring action by the Centre to encourage Northern Ireland to secede from the Union and join with the Republic and, after the summer of 1974, polls always found majorities in favour of withdrawing 'British' troops from the Province. Of course, in the 1970s no major politician from the Conservative and Labour parties publicly supported these views. Nevertheless, there is some evidence to suggest that the views of the electorate were reflected in the private conversations of politicians.[20] Equally significant, a number of policies pursued by the Centre indicated either a less than complete commitment to Northern Ireland's continued presence in the Union, or a very real recognition that it needed to be treated as a separate unit. The publicly announced principle that Northern Ireland could leave the Union if a majority of her citizens supported such an action (a principle institutionalised every ten years by the Border Poll) was one example of a less than complete commitment, so too were sporadic backstairs negotiations with the IRA and the acceptance, after 1973, of an 'Irish dimension' to Northern Ireland politics. Separate treatment was illustrated by the Centre's reluctance to support the power sharing executive during the Ulster Workers' Council strike in 1974[21] and the passing of the Prevention of Terrorism Act in the same year which allowed undesirable 'immigrants' from Northern Ireland to be excluded from Britain.

In short, political duality between the Centre and Northern Ireland continued despite the troubles and the institution of direct rule. This duality was supported by the bipartisan commitment at Westminster to two principles: opposition to schemes for more formal and extensive administrative integration with Britain and a determination not to allow the Northern Ireland problem to affect British party politics. In terms of the Centre's principal medium-term aims, its Northern Ireland policy in this period was a success. The problems of the Province were not solved, but political duality was maintained.

What sort of forces emerged to challenge the old territorial regime in Britain during this period? Developments were even more confused and ambiguous than in Northern Ireland. Initially, these years were marked by a resurgence of the Centre's authority and autonomy, and when the crisis did come it was less extensive than it once threatened to be and owed more to political circumstance and the actions of successive governments at the Centre than the strength of peripheral revolt.

In 1968, the major peripheral threat to the Centre appeared to come from Scottish and Welsh nationalism. This was not sustained in the next parliament. Although both the SNP and Plaid Cymru gained votes at the 1970 general election, the latter lost its sole Westminster representative, while the former was forced to exchange Hamilton for the Western Isles. In fact, neither peripheral nationalists nor peripheral governments (with the small exception of Clay Cross) posed any real threat to the Heath government for most of its term of office. It was able to ignore its 1970 manifesto commitment concerning devolution to Scotland and at the same time radically alter the structure of local government, the National Health Service and water management throughout Britain, with no great threat from the peripheral forces involved. Moreover, these new structures, following the modernisation prescriptions of the 1960s, were based on highly technocratic, efficiency-orientated principles.[22]

All this represented a great triumph for the Centre after the failures and back-slidings of the previous decade. If we include the Northern Ireland changes, then the whole institutional design of the *Ancien Régime* was abolished 'at a stroke'. Whatever its practical implications (discussed below) no other central government in the western world has been able to restructure territorial government so comprehensively and so quickly. Peripheral weakness in face of this new policy of *'Thorough'* was fully exploited. So too was the enforced acquiescence of territorial governments to the Centre's prices and incomes policies.

Despite this it is doubtful whether the Heath government ever had a considered general territorial strategy. Its principal preoccupations were always related to the European Community gambit, industrial relations reform and macro-economic management, hence its most important non-decision: its willingness, despite many doubts, to allow the Royal Commission on the Constitution 'to meander on'.[23] During the government's early Selsdon strategy it had tried to reconstruct (in the name of efficiency) a general autonomy for the Centre. In its later corporatist phase it attempted, in clumsy though probably sincere fashion, to re-establish contact with those powerful economic estates of the realm, the TUC and CBI. The problem here was that these estates had little control over their members.[24] At all events, the refusal of the trade unions to play this particular game resulted in a Centre more isolated from the outside world than any time in the twentieth century. Downing Street became 'a most closed society' where the 'shutters were fastened and the door open only to a select few...'.[25] By the autumn of 1973 the Centre had retreated once more into its traditional redoubt. The opposition of the miners to the prices and incomes policy, the electoral defeat of the Heath government in February 1974, the Wilsonian social contract and SNP successes in both the elections of 1974, put an end to this brief period of renewed Centre autonomy. The challenges of the 1960s had now seemingly reappeared in strengthened form. On this view we reach, at last, the great events surrounding the territorial crisis of the 1970s: duality finally succumbs to peripheral revolt. As indicated, this perspective on the events of the period requires considerable qualification.

To begin with, the striking thing about British politics in the 1970s, and above all between 1973 and 1977, was not the extent of territorial conflict and threatened collapse of Centre-periphery relations, but the threat of collapse to the whole system. The Centre became 'overloaded' with problems of all kinds resulting in a degree of 'ungovernability' in the system not experienced since the period prior to the First World War.[26] Huge increases in world commodity prices (not just oil), the collapse of the post-war international monetary system, the decline of United

States power and a depression in world trade represented a significant deterioration of the external support system. In the domestic arena union militancy, rising unemployment and inflation marked the collapse of domestic economic tranquillity. And these problems were compounded by a decline in elite consensus both within and between the parties. One reason for this was the collapse of the Keynesian economic paradigm and the seeming absence of any viable alternative. Another was the abrasive style of the Heath government plus the specific impact of its European and industrial relations policies. A general syndrome of conflict and despair hit the political elites at the Centre; an atmosphere which the SNP caught in the introduction to its October 1974 election manifesto – 'London has lost confidence in its ability to master events. There is a hint of Weimar in the English autumn'.[27] Two points arise from this discussion. First, in so far as the general system came under considerable strain in this period, then it becomes difficult to abstract the purely territorial aspects of this strain. Secondly, these were circumstances highly favourable to peripheral dissidents. If they didn't mount a major challenge to the Centre's authority in this period, they never would.

In practice it was surprising how many peripheral dogs did not bark. Even if we adopt a wide definition of our subject matter and include, as potential peripheral challenges to the Centre, 'unofficial' grass-roots trade-unionism, the various warring groups involved with the race issue and extra-parliamentary dissidents within the major parties, it is still difficult to see this period as one in which these forces posed *serious* problems for the established territorial order and the Centre's authority. On this perspective the only significant developments occurred *within* the House of Commons, the traditional intermediary between Centre and periphery. Not only did the Centre eventually lose control of that institution in terms of holding a single party majority, but, equally important, an increasing number of Conservative and Labour MPs became more resistant to the threats and blandishments of the Whips.[28] This was certainly an important change, with considerable significance in terms of the outcome of the crisis. But we should recognise it for what it was: a Westminster revolt with territorial implications, and largely independent of organised mass support outside, rather than a direct challenge from the periphery to the Centre's authority.

On a narrower definition of our subject matter, there existed, after 1974, three other potential sources of challenge to the traditional territorial order – local government, Plaid Cymru, and the Scottish National Party. As indicated above, local government presented a threefold threat: local authority expenditure was becoming increasingly difficult for the Centre to control and, at the same time, was politicising the ratepayers; the new local authorities which came into operation after 1974 (1975 in Scotland) were more subject to party colonisation than their predecessors; and the Centre's organisational resources to deal with these problems were still deficient. However, these problems failed to develop any significant challenge. The issue of local authority finance was emasculated via a series of *ad hoc* expedients; the new Consultative Council on Local Government Finance, the appointment of the Layfield Committee of enquiry (and then ignoring its subsequent report) and the appeasement of domestic ratepayers by increasingly pushing the burden of local taxation onto commercial and industrial ratepayers. Again, formal party colonisation of the new local authorities did not radically alter their relations with the Centre in this period. Overburdened with organisational problems, financial shortages and theories of corporate management, the parties in local government found it difficult to increase their role in its operations. Indeed, in many ways, the impact of party government at the local level may have declined in the period immediately following the structural reforms of the early 1970s.[29] Finally, with the possible exception of its Scottish dimension, the Centre carried out no serious reorganisation of its own resources to deal with local government more effectively.[30] In short, although the Centre continued to expand its responsibilities in this field, the degree of *political* duality remained pretty much the same.

Similar conclusions can be drawn about the threat from Plaid Cymru. In winning two and then three seats at the general elections of 1974 the Blaid's parliamentary representation became greater than ever before, but these victories were backed by only ten per cent of the Welsh vote. In fact, fewer people supported the party in 1974 than in the 1970 election. Moreover, Plaid Cymru's emphasis on cultural goals and protection of the language only served to divide opinion in Wales. Again, lacking the support of any major natural resource the Blaid's ultimate 'exit' option never appeared attractive. There may well have been many grievances in Wales but in so far as these were represented by Plaid Cymru then the Centre could afford to treat them as an irritant, not a major threat. The political fortunes of Welsh nationalism were linked to events elsewhere.

This leaves us with the SNP, from the Centre's viewpoint the major symbol of Scottish dissidence. The electoral advances of the SNP in 1974 are well known. By October of that year the party had eleven Westminster MPs and over 800,000 voters in Scotland, representing thirty per cent of the regional vote. In addition, it was placed second in forty-two of the seventy-one Scottish constituencies. At the time this was regarded as 'easily the biggest nationalist advance in recent British electoral history'.[31] The SNP had become the second largest party in Scotland. These electoral successes stemmed to some extent from the party's organisational abilities and publicity flair. They were also associated with a number of other developments in Scottish politics: a diffuse sense of grievance concerning the way Scotland was governed, a decline in the collaborative capacities of the major parties in Scotland, and a general growth in Scottish national sentiment. On the other hand, it is important to note that throughout this period the overwhelming majority of Scottish voters continued to support 'Unionist' or British orientated parties. Moreover, in terms of the various policy options regarding governmental reforms Scottish opinion was, and remained, deeply divided. Neither the independence nor devolution options had any positive majorities behind them. Equally important, few politicians and civil servants in London had supported greater devolution of power to Scotland before 1973, and even after that date most remained hostile to the principle. Further, English public opinion was either indifferent or hostile to the idea.[32]

Thus the key question is not what caused the rise of the SNP, but why the Centre in this period took its challenge so seriously? Why was it moved to initiate devolution legislation for both Scotland and Wales? The answer is that between October 1973 and February 1977 the political situation in London was highly favourable to the SNP. Like the Conservatives in the early 1930s the SNP could sit back and reap the benefits bestowed on it by a variety of events and enemies. These favourable circumstances can be itemised as follows:

(a) Oil price rises during and after the Yom Kippur war in the autumn of 1973 suddenly made North Sea oil (discovered in the early 1970s) an economic proposition and a very necessary resource for the United Kingdom Centre. The salience of Scottish politics within the system was automatically increased by these events. They also provided the SNP with both a continuing grievance about where and how the oil revenues were to be spent within the Union and an attractive independence scenario outside it. The consequent change in the relative economic power of England and Scotland was as significant in its short term political implications as the discovery of gold in the Transvaal in 1886.[33]

(b) At the very moment when the oil factor became politicised (the autumn of 1973) the long delayed report of the Royal Commission on the Constitution was published. Its recommendations were divided and its analysis often little better than a first-year undergraduate essay. Nevertheless, although initially greeted with ridicule in the House of Commons, the changing nature of territorial politics produced a great reversal. The report suddenly became an important state paper outlining policies which needed to be taken seriously by everyone. For the first time, Home Rule, especially its Scottish dimension, gained intellectual respectability.[34]

(c) Shortly afterwards, at a time of industrial conflict and maximum political confusion, the Heath government decided to appeal to the country on the 'who governs?' issue. Not surprisingly in these circumstances the SNP won seven seats and twenty-two per cent of the Scottish vote at the general election of February 1974.[35]

(d) The election produced a minority Labour government and the prospect of yet another appeal to the people later in the year. In the course of this 'short parliament' both the major parties, for reasons of electoral expediency, made frantic efforts to attract Scottish votes. The Conservatives resurrected their 1970 policy of an indirectly elected Scottish Assembly. The minority Labour government, with more seats to lose in Scotland, directed a large amount of 'pork barrel' benefits north of the border. In addition, the National Executive of the party forced its Scottish counterpart to accept the idea of a directly elected Scottish Assembly. This policy was then published in a White Paper just prior to the October 1974 election.[36] In these circumstances, whatever the merits of secession, a vote for the SNP could be seen to bring benefits to Scotland within the Union. Thus, the SNP successes at the October election were not surprising; they were a direct result of panic at the Centre and the pressure of party competition in a 'first past the post' electoral system.

(e) The European Community issue also favoured the SNP in this period. It is true that the party was against Scotland's membership as long as it was part of the Union. Nevertheless, the issue itself produced several benefits. It provoked divisions in the Labour and Conservative parties, particularly the former. Equally significant, it also offered the prospect of a new and larger market for Scottish goods, automatic entry into the English market and an alternative source of government benefits, if Scotland became independent and then joined the Community. In short, it removed the economic necessity for Union with England. Moreover, some EEC officials were not slow to point up additional advantages for Scotland within the Community. As one member of the Commission declared during the 1975 referendum campaign: 'It will be much easier to alter the United Kingdom constitution in favour of decentralisation in the context of the EEC than in the framework of Britain alone'.[37]

(f) The Labour Cabinet's devolution legislation was finally produced in November 1976. But by that time the government was too weak to push it through the Commons successfully. The bill's defeat in February 1977 was not only embarrassing to the government's parliamentary business managers; it meant, in effect, that the Labour leadership had broken its October 1974 contract with the Scottish voters. The subsequent withdrawal of SNP support from the minority government seemingly put the survival of the Labour administration at stake. A general election appeared imminent, with the twin prospects of the Conservatives under Mrs Thatcher returned to power and a further expansion in the number of SNP parliamentary seats.[38]

To conclude, there was only one major peripheral challenge to the Centre's authority in this period, that emanating from the SNP from the autumn of 1973 to the spring of 1977. In Wales and, above all in England, the traditional territorial order remained largely undisturbed. Even in Northern Ireland the Centre, though it failed to solve the problems of the Province, managed to preserve to a considerable extent that desired political duality so characteristic of the old London-Belfast connection. The Scottish phenomenon was clearly different. Nevertheless, it is difficult not to conclude that what can be called the SNP's opportunity, embodied in the highly favourable political circumstances described above, was primarily the result of awkward and rapid changes in the external support system, the decline of traditional collaborative elites in Scotland, and a sense of panic and political expediency on the part of politicians, particularly leading members of the Labour Party, in London. If there was a territorial crisis in the mid-1970s it was a crisis of territorial appeasement from the Centre, involving a loss of political nerve in relation to future electoral prospects in Scotland. Its significance lies in exposing the sheer lack of territorial principle (and knowledge) within the leadership of the major parliamentary parties. The intellectual basis of the old Dual Polity was territorial indifference in Whitehall: in a paradoxical way the 'crisis' of the mid-1970s only confirmed the continued existence of that indifference. The political elite was prepared to engage in all sorts of tinkering with the territorial constitution to maintain or gain power at the Centre.

(iii) The Centre's reprieve (1977–9)

Between February 1977 and May 1979 the Centre recovered from its previous position of territorial weakness. This was not entirely due to its own policies and actions. Equally important were a number of developments, some fortuitous, which, combined, led to the 'withering away' of the political advantages previously enjoyed by the SNP. This brief period is also significant because it throws interesting light on the Centre's devolution ideology: what in the end it was prepared to give up to regional assemblies in Scotland and Wales and how it perceived or hoped they would work.

One reason for the Centre's recovery was that after the spring of 1977 the external environment became, temporarily, more favourable. The disruptive influence of the European Community issue appeared to have been solved by the referendum held in the dark days of 1975 (showing incidentally that even at this time the SNP had limited influence on Scottish voters). More important, the intensity of the 1973/4 oil crisis diminished and world economic activity began to adjust, astonishingly easily so it seemed, to an OPEC-dominated international economic order. World commodity prices stabilised and sterling began to recover much of its exchange value lost in the debacle of 1975/6. In fact, the external problems of the early and mid-1970s, particularly the sterling crisis of 1976, bequeathed a number of benefits to the Centre's politico-administrative community. They had indicated in very clear terms to the public at large the extent to which the country's international power position had declined and the close proximity of national bankruptcy. As a result, a new realism began to permeate both elite and mass attitudes to foreign affairs. From the Centre's point of view they had also emphasised the degree to which Western economic interdependence forced the other powers to bail out the United Kingdom economy and the extent to which external pressures could be employed to impose unpopular domestic policies, for example public expenditure cuts, on political groupings normally opposed to them.[39] In other words, after the mid-1970s external weakness became a convenient support to the Centre's authority and changing domestic strategies; a significant reversal of the position during the *Ancien Régime*. An important example of this new trend was Mr Callaghan's public recognition in the autumn of 1976 that old-style Keynesian demand management was no longer a viable method of controlling inflation and defeating unemployment.

The Lib-Lab parliamentary pact, born in March 1977 and operating formally until June 1978 (and informally until April 1979) also provided the Callaghan government with some much needed security in terms of its Westminster manoeuvres.[40] It is true that one consequence of this was the government's renewed commitment to devolution legislation, but overall Labour gained more from the pact than the Liberals. It also revealed the autonomy of the Labour leadership (and to a lesser extent their Liberal counterparts) from the extra-parliamentary party. Neither the NEC nor the annual conference played any part in this court strategy.

Again, no other peripheral force emerged in this period to challenge (or assist) the SNP's position as the principal threat to the Centre's authority. Welsh nationalism continued to rely on its Scottish motor, and the worlds of local government, grass-roots trade-unionism (until the winter of 1978) and extra-parliamentary party activists remained largely quiescent. The race issue, in the form of National Front and Anti-Nazi League conflict, was a partial exception to this pattern of peripheral quiescence. But both parliament and the Centre could afford, on the whole, to ignore the struggles between two sets of *white* extremists. In one important respect peripheral problems appeared to improve. After the failure of the Northern Ireland Constitutional Convention in 1976, the Centre attempted no further major policy innovations in the Province. This 'benign neglect', plus divisions in the IRA, the abortive Loyalist strike in 1977 and the firm security policies pursued by Roy Mason as Secretary of State, ensured a period of relative tranquillity in Northern Ireland. Indeed, the Centre's sole policy initiative, Mr Callaghan's casual commitment in the spring of 1977 to increasing the Westminster representation of the Province, seemed only to re-emphasise the continuing importance of the Unionist tradition.

Thus, by the summer of 1978 the Centre appeared to have recovered from its previous fragile position. The Labour government had not only survived, but its macro-economic strategy, its struggles against inflation, unemployment, industrial relations unrest and the weaknesses of sterling seemed remarkably successful. Public opinion polls now indicated that over forty per cent of the electorate approved of the government's record. On the territorial front no new challenges to the Centre's authority had emerged and the second and successful devolution gambit appeared to have satisfied Scottish and Welsh opinion. It is important to note that all this had occurred at a time of significant shifts in the Centre's operational code. From the mid 1970s the beginnings of a new economic orthodoxy slowly emerged. The Centre began to concern itself with such matters as controlling the money supply, limiting government borrowing, and cash limits and restraints on public expenditure. In other words, 'hard times' were precipitating an intellectual revolution regarding both the Centre's objectives and its control mechanisms over spending by public agencies. In its public expenditure dealings at least, the Centre now had the *potential* to be a much harder, more interfering, creature than ever before.[41]

These developments posed a number of problems for the SNP. 1978 was a disappointing year for the party. What has been called the changing psychology of North Sea oil meant that fewer Scots now regarded that natural resource as the sole solution to Scotland's problems. Even the failure of Scotland's football team in the World Cup suggested the continued existence of the old Scot's disease, premature ejaculation. Moreover, opinion polls and local election results in Scotland, plus Labour's victories at the Garscadden, Hamilton and Berwick by-elections, all indicated the 'withering away' of the political advantages previously enjoyed by the party. Nevertheless, it could still look forward to the prospect of a directly elected Scottish Assembly and reasonable successes at the forthcoming general election. In the event, even these hopes were unfulfilled. Devolution proved to be a highly ambiguous gift in terms of both what it offered the SNP (and Plaid

Cymru) and its impact on their subsequent electoral performance.

After the failure of the first devolution bill the SNP, accepting the conventions of parliamentary and Cabinet government, waited for the Callaghan administration to produce a new set of proposals. In the autumn of 1977, with Liberal Party support, two separate devolution bills for Scotland and Wales were introduced in parliament and were finally approved in the summer of the following year. However, opposition from Labour MPs had ensured that their coming into force was conditional on support from at least forty per cent of the Scottish and Welsh electorates in advisory referendums on the legislation. Despite these concessions the devolution package appeared to represent a radical change in the Centre's territorial code. In fact, the Centre's position on the matter was highly ambiguous. Admittedly, the devolution legislation had to take account of considerable parliamentary opposition and many technical and constitutional problems which emerged in the course of devising the schemes. Moreover, in political terms, devolution was bound to be 'a leap in the dark'; its operation would depend on the development of intergovernmental conventions and, above all, on the nature of party control over the new Assemblies. Nevertheless, an examination of the contents of the two bills provides some interesting clues regarding the Centre's devolution ideology.[42] The following brief comments are relevant.

First, the devolution package obviously did not represent a general change in the United Kingdom's territorial constitution: England and Northern Ireland were omitted from this particular game. Moreover, even though an elected Assembly was to be established in Wales, its powers were limited to those subsumed under the concept of executive devolution: it would merely execute the laws laid down at Westminster. In constitutional terms at least, the Welsh Assembly was meant to be little more than an enlarged county council. Secondly, although legislative powers were to be devolved to the Scottish Assembly, it is interesting to note what the Centre was still unwilling to let slip from its grasp. There was to be no separate Scottish civil service, no autonomous sources of Assembly income free from Treasury control, and no grant of powers other than those specifically enumerated in the legislation. In addition Scottish (and Welsh) representation at Westminster remained the same and this was combined with the continued existence of both Secretaries of State, who were granted considerable supervisory powers over the new Assemblies. Thirdly, the actual institutional losers in the game were the Scottish and Welsh Offices, the Centre in general lost few important functions. The potential losers were local authorities and *ad hoc* nominated agencies in Scotland and Wales, whose functions, indeed existence, were to be subject to the authority of the new Assemblies.

It seems reasonable to conclude with the obvious. From the Centre's point of view, devolution to Scotland and Wales was not meant to represent a radical break with the traditional territorial order, but rather a reconstruction of much of the old system; hived-off territorial administration via the indirect rule of local or regional collaborators, albeit within a new institutional and constitutional strait-jacket. Once again, when it was forced to consider a new territorial constitution for parts of the United Kingdom the Centre's eventual solution revealed its continued attachment to the governmental precepts of the old Dual Polity. Of course, political practice may not have followed these precepts. Territorial duality may not have survived the potential for intergovernmental conflict contained in the legislation. A more radical 'devolution all round' may have followed because of the problems and inanities inherent at Westminster in a markedly asymmetrical union, in which the dominant section, England was omitted from the devolution design.[43] Despite this the Centre had done its best, in difficult circumstances, to maintain the old traditions: offload 'Low Politics' concerns to those that want them, keep 'High Politics' concerns within the existing Westminster and Whitehall structure.

In the event, these constitutional proposals were never put to the test. In the March 1979 referendum the devolution package was rejected by an overwhelming majority of Welsh voters. In Scotland it was supported by a small plurality but failed to meet the requirement that forty per cent of the electorate had to give their positive approval. At the very least the 'no' campaign had won a moral victory. The precise reasons for this outcome are difficult to identify.[44] Divisions within the Labour Party on the issue (especially its Scottish and Welsh organisations) undoubtedly played a part. So too, perhaps, did the argument that the Assemblies would produce yet another layer of expensive and inefficient bureaucracy. The devolution proposals also suffered from the declining popularity of the Labour government after its failure to control rank and file trade union opposition to its five per cent pay norm during the 'winter of discontent' of 1978/9; a case perhaps of one peripheral revolt adversely affecting another. Whatever the reasons, the government's refusal to implement Scottish devolution following the referendums led the SNP to put down a parliamentary vote of no confidence, an action which quickly produced a similar motion from the Conservatives. In the complex parliamentary negotiations which preceded the no confidence vote in late March, territorial issues and personalities certainly played a part and the SNP may have overplayed its hand.[45] In the end, the government lost the motion by only one vote. The subsequent general election in May witnessed a very distinctive geographical division of support between the major parties. It also saw the return of the Conservative Party to office with a comfortable overall majority. In Wales, Plaid Cymru's vote declined by two per cent and it lost one parliamentary seat. In Scotland, the SNP, which had precipitated the election, lost nine seats and its share of the vote declined from thirty per cent to seventeen per cent.

The 1979 election results possessed a certain rough justice. The Labour Party had gained and held office in the elections of 1974 largely as a result of trade union opposition to the Heath government's incomes policies, the relatively poor electoral performance of the Conservative Party in Scotland, and the unwillingness of the Ulster Unionists to continue their traditional alliance with the Conservatives in parliament. Thereafter, three major reasons why Labour managed to hold on to office were its social contract with the unions, its promise to implement devolution schemes for Scotland and Wales, and the support it drew from various kinds of Northern Ireland MPs. Labour then lost control of the Centre in 1979 because of trade union opposition to the government's pay norm, its refusal to implement Scottish devolution following the referendum result, its failure to receive support from the Scottish Nationalists and most Northern Ireland MPs in the parliamentary vote of confidence following that refusal, and the increased voting support which the Conservatives received in Scotland and Wales in the subsequent general election. At all events, whichever party won that election, it appeared that the Centre had been well and truly reprieved from its previous position of territorial weakness.

CONCLUSIONS

The period 1961 to 1979 saw a number of forces emerge which challenged the pattern of United Kingdom territorial politics as it operated during the *Ancien Régime*. The most spectacular were the advent of intercommunity strife in Northern Ireland and the rise of Welsh and, above all, Scottish nationalism. But other significant developments also took place. Principal among these were the emergence of a political culture less deferential to established authority, the formal extension of national party control over most local authorities, and the evolution of a House of Commons less amenable to the dictates of party leaders. In addition, the period also witnessed a succession of administrations at the Centre which eschewed the old autonomy code for more direct intervention in the periphery. Presented in this form, the conclusion to be drawn from the story appears obvious: the structure of territorial politics in 1979 was very different from that operating twenty years earlier. The discussion above suggests that this was not so.

Analysis of the three major phases of territorial development after the early 1960s emphasised the following points. The initial break with the Dual Polity structure came from the Centre's commitment to remodernisation. The policies associated with this commitment posed problems for the collaborative system which it was not designed to meet. It also raised peripheral expectations, which were not fulfilled, concerning the benefits likely to be obtained from remodernisation. In the mid-1970s highly favourable political circumstances, the SNP forced the Centre to initiate devolution legislation, seemingly a radical change in the territorial constitution. Even in this phase, however, the extent of the peripheral revolt and its challenge the Centre must be qualified. Political duality was sustained for Northern Ireland and much of the SNP's success stemmed from the climate of appeasement at the Centre. Moreover, no significant unrest occurred in England, the heartland of the United Kingdom periphery. Forced to face the Centre on its own, and committed to parliamentary politics, the SNP's challenge was isolated and then stifled by the Centre's improved political position after 1977. It was then killed by the unpopularity of the Labour government resulting from the industrial unrest in the winter of 1978/9. Even the devolution legislation was an ambiguous success. From the Centre's point of view it represented less a radical break with the past than a reaffirmation, in changed circumstances, of the old duality principle.

In many ways, this period's importance stems from its omissions, from what didn't happen. Despite its numerous problems the United Kingdom state did not collapse, as many on the left and right in the mid-1970s believed it would. Domestic remodernisation was initially adopted and constantly pursued to resolve the problems caused by the decay of the old external support system. The continuing failure of this strategy was the root of the system's weakness. Nevertheless, there could be no regime crisis because ultimately the external challenges were its supports as well. The interdependence of the western world, with all its problems, was a new external support system. Hence the United Kingdom survived (with its oil) as a kind of 'Cowslip's Warren', constantly bailed out by external forces unwilling to let it founder completely.[46] In these circumstances general radical change could be avoided. The absence of radical territorial change merely reflected this.

Again, although elite consensus declined in this period, the continued commitment to the primacy of parliamentary politics (behind which lurked the relative autonomy of the Centre) largely remained. Hence no peripheral revolt was directly promoted by dissident members of the national elite: the periphery still lacked friends at court or Westminster. Finally, after nearly two decades of interventionist policies, the organisational resources of the Centre, the essential basis of improved peripheral management, were still rudimentary. The principal reason for this was the lack of agreement at both the Centre and in the periphery concerning the nature of any new territorial settlement. Northern Ireland and the devolution fiasco were two obvious examples of this. But so too was the constant refusal to deal positively with the problems of local government finance and the determination to ignore proposals, such as those contained in the Layfield Report and the Memorandum of Dissent of the Royal Commission on the Constitution, which suggested the basis of a new British territorial regime.

It would be easy to conclude that the general election of 1979 marked the route to yet another 'suspended revolution' on lines similar to events after 1926. On the basis of the first two and a half years of the Thatcher administration, however, this would be a questionable assumption.

NOTES

1   E. W. G. Bill and J. F. A. Mason, *Christ Church and Reform 1850–1867* (Oxford, 1970), p. 2.
2   Giuseppe di Lampedusa, *The Leopard* (London, 1963), p. 29.
3   Three general surveys of the period, concerned primarily with nationalism and devolution, are: A. H. Birch, *Political Integration and Disintegration in the British Isles* (London, 1977); Tom Nairn, *The Breakup of Britain* (London, 1977); Vernon Bogdanor, *Devolution* (Oxford, 1979).
4   In addition there was the ambiguous concept of 'the Crown'. See Kenneth Dyson, *The State Tradition in Western Europe* (Oxford, 1980), pp. 210–12.
5   Acheson made this remark in the course of a speech at West Point in December 1962. A former Secretary of State, he was at the time an advisor to the Kennedy administration.

6   For the 1976 crisis see Stephen Fay and Hugo Young, *The Day the Pound Nearly Died* (London, 1978) and William Keegan and R. Pennant-Rea, *Who Runs the Economy?* (London, 1979), Chapter 5.

7   Ivor Crewe *et al.*, 'Partisan de-alignment in Britain, 1964–1974', *British Journal of Political Science* (1977); Committee on Financial Aid to Political Parties, *Report* (Cmnd. 6601, London, 1976); H. M. Drucker (ed.), *Multi-Party Britain* (London, 1979); S. E. Finer, *The Changing British Party System*, 1945–1979 (Washington D. C., 1980) .

8   Northern Ireland developments are discussed in Richard Rose, *Northern Ireland: A Time of Choice* (London, 1976) and I. McAllister and S. Nelson, 'Developments in the Northern Ireland party system', *Parliamentary Affairs* (1979). For Plaid Cymru and the SNP see Alan Butt Philip, *The Welsh Question: Nationalism in Welsh Politics, 1945–1970* (Cardiff, 1975); Kenneth O. Morgan, *Rebirth of a Nation: Wales 1880–1980* (Oxford, 1981), Chapter 13; Jack Brand, *The National Movement in Scotland* (London, 1978) and H. M. Drucker and Gordon Brown, *The Politics of Nationalism and Devolution* (London, 1980).

9   For general discussions of these matters see Patrick Dunleavy, *Urban Political Analysis* (London, 1980), Chapter 3 and Peter Saunders, *Urban Politics* (London, 1980), Chapters 2 and 3. Closer contact between councillors and citizens sometimes led to corruption. John Poulson's activities in the north of England were one example. Another was the operation of a building firm in Birmingham which, Mr Justice Melford Stevenson later declared, had turned the city 'to some extent' into 'a municipal Gomorrah'. See *The Times*, 21 April 1978. The corruption issue is briefly discussed, with appropriate references, in Tony Byrne's *Local Government in Britain* (London, 1981), pp. 138–43.

10 On Clay Cross see David Skinner and Julia Langdon, *The Story of Clay Cross* (Nottingham, 1974) and Austin Mitchell, 'Clay Cross', *Political Quarterly* (1974).

11 I am not suggesting that regional economic planning policies were absent prior to the early 1960s. Those that operated, however, applied to only small parts of the country and, as in the case of the industrial development certificates, were essentially negative in character. See Gavin McCrone, *Regional Policy in Britain* (London, 1969), Chapters 3 and 4.

12 See Layfield Committee Report on 'Local government finance' (Cmnd. 6453, London, 1976); J. Lagroye and V. Wright (eds.), *Local Government in Britain and France*, Chapter 4; Maurice Wright, 'Public expenditure in Britain: the crisis of control', *Public Administration* (1977).

13 This was the title given to Chapter 7 of Samuel Brittan's *The Treasury Under the Tories* (London, 1964). Brittan's choice for the year 'in which everything really happened' was 1960, not 1961. He also argues (p. 215) that in the early stages the various dimensions of the modernisation programme were the work of different groups of people. See also Trevor Smith, *Anti-Politics: Consensus, Reform and Protest in Britain* (London, 1972), and the very funny book by Harold Wilson, *The New Britain* (London, 1964).

14 Two books which played an important role in promoting this culture were W. A. Robson's *Local Government in Crisis* (London, 1966) and J. P. Mackintosh's *The Devolution of Power* (London, 1968). A succession of official committees of inquiry also drew attention to deficiencies in the provision and organisation of various local services. See Layfield Committee, *op. cit.* p. 65. For a general critique of the whole movement see John Dearlove, *The Reorganisation of British Local Government* (Cambridge, 1979).

15 In July 1966 Gwynfor Evans won the Carmarthen by-election for Plaid Cymru and became the party's first representative at Westminster. Subsequent by-elections at Rhondda West (March 1967) and Caerphilly (July 1968) produced large swings to Plaid Cymru, although no victories. In March 1967 the SNP polled twenty-eight per cent of the vote at the Glasgow, Pollok by-election. In November of the same year Winnie Ewing won the Hamilton by-election with forty-six per cent of the votes. All these parliamentary seats were held by Labour and in all of them the Labour organisation was in a bad state. At the May 1968 local government elections in Scotland the SNP won over 100 council seats.

16 For differing views on the O'Neill period see *The Autobiography of Terence O'Neill* (London, 1972); Michael Farrell, *Northern Ireland: The Orange State* (London, 1976) and Paul Bew, Peter Gibbon and Henry Patterson, *The State in Northern Ireland, 1921–1972* (Manchester, 1979).

17 James Callaghan, *A House Divided* (London, 1973), Chapter 1.

18 Tom Nairn, *op. cit.*, p. 13.

19 Ronald Robinson and John Gallagher, 'The partition of Africa', *New Cambridge Modern History*, XI (Cambridge, 1962).

20 For poll data see Richard Rose, Ian McCallister and Peter Mair, *Is There a Concurring Majority About Northern Ireland?* (Glasgow, 1978), pp. 28, 29. For elite views see Joe Haines, *The Politics of Power* (London, 1977), Chapter 6 and Cecil King, *Diary 1970–1974* (London, 1975), pp. 178, 187.

21 Robert Fisk, *The Point of No Return: the Strike Which Broke the British In Ulster* (London, 1975) and T. E. Utley, *Lessons of Ulster* (London, 1975), Chapter 10.

22 In addition to Dearlove op. cit. see Douglas E. Ashford, 'The limits of consensus: the reorganisation of British local government and the French contrast' in S. Tarrow *et. al.*, *Territorial Politics in Industrial Nations* (New York, 1978). One consultative paper on the reorganisation of water administration stated that 'the representative principle can militate against effective management'. See Department of the Environment, *Constitution of Regional Water Authorities* (London, 1972), para. 7 (iii). The corporate management approach to the internal organisation of the new local authorities embodied in the Bains and Paterson Reports (London, 1972 and 1973) was criticised on similar grounds. The boundaries of: the new local authorities in England were also attacked because it was felt they were often the result of political pressures from local Conservative parties.

23 The Government's attitude to Scotland, devolution and the Royal Commission is examined by Geoffrey Smith in 'The Conservative commitment to devolution', *The Spectator* (19 February 1977) and 'Devolution and not saying what you mean', *The Spectator* (26 February 1977).

24 This second phase of Heathite management is discussed in Denis Barnes and Eileen Reid, *Governments and Trade Unions* (London; 1980), Part III; and Stephen Fay and Hugo Young, *The Fall of Heath* (London, 1976). On the duality of power within the TUC and CBI, and its effects on corporatist strategies see D. Marsh and W. Grant, 'Tripartism: reality or myth', *Government and Opposition* (1977); More specifically, as Fay and Young indicate, Joe Gormley proved to 'be an unreliable collaborator in the grand design'. In a letter to *The Times* two noted theorists of corporatism, R. Pahl and J. Winkler, defined it as 'indirect administration through incorporated private groups'; in short, a system of functional indirect rule. See *The Times*' (18 June 1976).

25 James Margach, *The Abuse of Power* (London, 1978), pp. 160–1.

26 James Douglas, 'The Overloaded Crown', *British Journal of Political Science* (1976) provides a good general discussion of the main themes of the ungovernability thesis. Richard Rose, 'Ungovernability: is there fire behind the smoke', *Political Studies* (1979) is a useful corrective to many of the more extreme claims.

27 The manifesto entitled 'Scotland's future' was summarised in *The Times* (24 September 1974).

28 P. Norton, 'The changing face of the House of Commons in the 1970s', *Legislative Studies Quarterly* (1980) and J. Schwarz 'Exploring a new role in policy making: the British House of Commons in the 1970s', *American Political Science Review* (1980).

29 See, for example, David G. Green, *Power and Party in an English City* (London, 1981).

30 This is the gist of the analysis contained in the Central Policy Review Staff's report on *Relations between Central Government and Local Authorities* (London, 1977). See in particular paras. 5.1, 8.1 and 10.1. Para. 9.1 indicates that the representation of interests by individual local authorities suffered from this situation at the Centre.

31 James Kellas, *The Scottish Political System* (Cambridge, 1975), p. 127.

32 Richard Rose's *Understanding the United Kingdom: The Territorial Dimension in Government* (London, 1982), Chapters 3 and 8, covers many of these points. See also the editorial 'Away from the centre who wants devolution?', *The Times* (1 November 1973). Also the comments of Alan Watkins in *The Observer* (November 1976), cited in Tom Dalyell, *Devolution: The End of Britain?* (London, 1977), p. 41.

33 Ronald Robinson and John Gallagher, *Africa and the Victorians* (London, 1961), p. 468.

34 For criticisms of the Royal Commission's reports see Harry Calvert (ed.), *Devolution* (London, 1975), Chapters 3 and 4, and the editorial, 'The Royal Commission on the Constitution', *Public Administration* (1974). The Royal Commission reports were published at the end of October 1973. The SNP won the Glasgow, Govan by-election in November 1973.

35 The election also allowed those Protestants in Northern Ireland who opposed the power-sharing experiment to show their strength, an early nail placed in the executive's coffin.

36 Cmnd. 5732. *Democracy and Devolution: Proposals for Scotland and Wales*. The Labour leadership was also influenced by Mori opinion polls in Scotland which found, in response to simple questions, that over fifty per cent of those polled favoured a Scottish parliament.

37 Cited in Bogdanor *op. cit.*, p. 6. The link between the EEC and devolution issues is examined in Martin Kolinsky (ed.), *Divided Loyalties* (Manchester, 1978).

38 The Scotland and Wales Bill was defeated by twenty-nine votes on a government motion to impose the guillotine. The bill had passed its second reading by forty-five votes primarily because the government promised to hold referendums on the issue in Scotland and Wales. Progress at the committee stage was slow owing to the large number of amendments put down, hence the attempted guillotine. The government's motion was opposed by the Conservatives and all but two of the Liberals. In addition, twenty-two Labour MPs voted against and twenty-one abstained. Following the defeat of the bill, opinion polls indicated that thirty-six per cent of Scots supported the SNP, making the party easily the most popular in Scotland.

39 These conclusions are drawn from my reading of the analysis of the 1976 crisis in Fay and Young, *op. cit.* and Keegan and Pennant-Rea, *op. cit.*

40 Alistair Michie and Simon Hoggart, *The Pact: the Inside Story of the Lib-Lab Government*, 1977–1978 (London, 1978).
41 In 1975 Anthony Crosland, then Secretary of State for the Environment, told local authorities 'the party is over' in terms of their future expenditure plans. Undoubtedly local authorities entered a new period of financial restraint as a result of this changed climate at the Centre. Nevertheless they still retained considerable autonomy concerning the policies they pursued within the new climate. See Alan Budd, *The Politics of Economic Planning*. (London, 1978); David Coates, *Labour in Power?* (London, 1980), Chapter 1; Christopher Hood and Maurice Wright (eds.), *Big Government in Hard Times* (Oxford, 1981), pp. 8–11 and Chapters 3 and 4.
42 For discussions of the contents of the two bills see Bogdanor, *op. cit.*, Chapter 7 and Rose, *op. cit.*, Chapter 8.
43 An omission which gave rise to the 'West Lothian question', namely the problem that Scottish MPs would continue to vote on matters relating to England which had been devolved to the Scottish Assembly. Tom Dalyell, MP for West Lothian, constantly raised this point. See Dalyell, *op. cit.*, pp. 130 and 245–9. The problem was never resolved. See 'Government loses last battle on devolution', *The Times* (27 July 1978).
44 In Scotland thirty-two per cent of the electorate voted 'Yes', thirty per cent 'No' and thirty-seven per cent abstained. In Wales eleven per cent of the electorate voted 'Yes', forty-six per cent voted 'No' and forty-one per cent abstained. In terms of voters, however, fifty-one per cent in Scotland voted 'Yes' (Wales twenty per cent). For a preliminary assessment see Denis Balsom and Ian McAllister, 'The Scottish and Welsh devolution referenda of 1979', *Parliamentary Affairs* (1979).
45 On the SNP's role see James Naughtie, 'The year at Westminster: the Scotland Act brings down the Government' in N. Drucker and H. M. Drucker (eds.), *The Scottish Government Yearbook, 1980* (Edinburgh, 1979).
46 Cowslip's Warren was the home of some relatively prosperous well-fed rabbits encountered by Hazel and his friends in their journey to Watership Down. In theory, these rabbits were wild and independent. In practice, they were kept rabbits, kept by a local farmer who found them a convenient source of occasional support for his own domestic economy. The culture of Cowslip's Warren was one of gloom and despondency. The glories of the past were constantly emphasised and awkward questions about the present and future constantly avoided. See Richard Adams, *Watership Down* (London, 1974), Chapters 12–18. When he wrote the book Adams was a civil servant in the Department of the Environment.

chapter seven | the territorial economy of Thatcherism[1]

The Department of the Environment...visualised the possibility of pressures which would force the Department to look at more rigorous and more detailed forms of control, should the existing methods prove inadequate in the extremely difficult current situation. They made it clear it would be a matter of regret to them if such measures should prove necessary.[2]

In practice, the rules within which local government operates originate with central Government. The corner-stone of those rules is that central Government have the right to establish the macro-economic pattern of local authority expenditure. When I took on this job, local government's proudest boast was that it stuck by those rules.[3]

INTRODUCTION

We have seen that nearly twenty years after the Dual Polity began to decline, a new United Kingdom-wide territorial settlement had still to be achieved. In these circumstances the policies of the newly elected Conservative government assumed great significance. This chapter examines the territorial code of the Centre during roughly the first thirty months of the Thatcher government's life.

The Conservatives took office in May 1979 with a radical programme to implement. It is true that aspects of this programme reflected the changing intellectual climate regarding economic management goals and techniques which developed after 1975. Nevertheless, the enthusiasm with which the Conservatives publicised their acceptance of many of the new ideas was in marked contrast to their more covert adoption during the Callaghan-Healey years. The major policy themes of what can be called early Thatcherism were four. First, an emphasis on the general benefits to be gained from the disciplines of the market economy, individual liberty and rolling back the frontiers of the state. Secondly, it was constantly stressed that the defeat of inflation was the necessary basis for establishing conditions leading to sustained economic growth. Any problems resulting from the emphasis put on that goal were regarded as the short-term price to be paid for eventual economic progress. Thirdly, in pursuit of these aims the government favoured an economic policy package involving strict control of the money supply, high interest rates, public expenditure cuts, cash limits on central departments and other public bodies, direct tax reductions, the abolition of price and income controls and the hiving-off or 'privatisation' of some commercial and industrial functions of government. Fourthly, implicit in all this was a willingness to allow external forces to affect the domestic economy. The abolition of exchange controls in the autumn of 1979 was one example of this stance. Another was the decision to allow the value of sterling to be determined by international market forces.

This programme represented a sharp break with the economic management techniques accepted by most governments after the early 1960s. In terms of medium-term economic goals the government's views were at variance with every Cabinet since 1945.

What were the implications of this grand strategy for territorial politics? The government was fortunate on two counts: throughout the period it remained possible to treat the Northern Ireland problem as something separate from British politics, and, despite the instant repeal of the devolution legislation, Welsh and Scottish nationalism was strangely quiescent. As a result the government was able to focus its policy attentions on territorial governments, particularly local governments, throughout Britain. Initial comment on its actions in this arena was highly critical. The gist of the critics' case was as follows: either Thatcherism, because of its general commitment to monetarism, involved the bloody-minded pursuit of a number of policies which, in each case, were disadvantageous to peripheral interests and governments, or the government's policies reflected a more general and coherent doctrine in which local authorities were regarded as a part of the state, as subordinate state agencies.[4]

These criticisms will be assessed later in this chapter. What follows is an attempt to present a broad overview of the Thatcher Centre's territorial operations in terms of the following topics: the forces behind the Conservative Party's espousal of a 'monetarist' macro-economic strategy; the contents of the initial Thatcherite territorial code; the problems encountered by the government in attempting to implement that code and its response to those problems; an assessment of the impact of the government's policies in Britain up to the early months of 1982; and a discussion of the Cabinet's policies relating to Northern Ireland.

Monetarism and the search for Centre autonomy

Popular perceptions of early Thatcherism tended to view it solely in economic terms; to believe that the policies of the government merely reflected a set of economic nostrums given the umbrella label of monetarism. This is an over-simplification.[5] Thatcherism began life as both a remodernising anti-statist doctrine and as a piece of statecraft, an operational code to deal with the problems of governing the United Kingdom as they emerged in the late 1970s.

Thus, monetarist techniques of economic management were not adopted simply because Sir Keith Joseph and Mrs Thatcher were converted to the virtues of

Friedmanite theory. They were also adopted because such techniques represented a set of convenient political mechanisms, convenient in the sense they promised the Centre the prospect of managing the economy on the basis of policies over which it could claim, in relative terms at least, some control, namely money supply, public expenditure (at least its non-wage elements), taxation and interest rates. In other words, with such techniques macro-economic strategy would be able to re-enter the domain of 'High Politics' and, as a consequence, be less open to influence from awkward *domestic* forces, such as trade unions. The government's twofold rejection of a formal incomes policy illustrates this point. On the one hand, as Mr John Biffen, Chief Secretary to the Treasury, put it in July 1980, an incomes policy represented 'a gigantic expansion' of the state's role, 'a potentially dangerous flirtation' with corporatism, and 'a most illiberal attempt' to centralise all economic activity.[6] On the other hand, and what was not said on that occasion, earlier Conservative attempts to run an incomes policy, notably under Mr Heath, had proved unsuccessful, and most developments in the industrial relations field after 1974 had indicated to many Conservatives that any renewed commitment to such policies would not prove any more successful.

Early Thatcherism, then, was very much a *political* response to the basic governing dilemma facing both the major parties, but particularly the Conservative Party, in the late 1970s. To survive in office the Conservatives had to regain Centre autonomy in the vital field of macro-economic management. A change in economic theory was a necessary instrumental step in resolving that dilemma. On this view, despite its radical rhetoric, the political economy of Thatcherism bore a stronger resemblance to its Keynesian counterpart than many of its critics and supporters were prepared to accept. In terms of the desired *structure of politics* the Government's grand strategy was yet another exercise in reconstruction.

The initial territorial code

As indicated, political circumstances allowed the Conservative leadership to concentrate its territorial thoughts on the Centre's relations with peripheral governments in Britain, in particular elected local governments. At first glance the analysis above suggests that on this matter the government intended to rely on the governing principles of the *Ancien Régime*, with its political duality resting on both Centre and peripheral autonomy. On this basis, governments in the periphery would be granted the same freedom to manage their affairs as the Centre was seemingly prepared to allow employers and trade unions in the industrial relations arena.

At the outset of the Thatcher government's period of office the evidence suggests that this was one of the ways Conservative leaders hoped to manage territorial politics. In opposition, for example, Mrs Thatcher had told the Conservative's local government conference: 'Our aim will be to give you more responsibility for your own communities. It is time-wasting and pound-wasting for central government to spend so much time looking over your shoulders'. Again, shortly after taking office, Mr Michael Heseltine, the new Secretary of State for the Environment, addressed the Joint Local Authority Association conference in the following terms: 'My philosophy towards local government is clear. It rests on a total commitment to give you the maximum possible freedom'.[7] Moreover, in two important respects the Cabinet put these principles into early practice. In September 1979 it published a White Paper which argued the case for abolishing many of the existing central controls over local authorities and, in addition, promised a general review of local government's statutory obligations.[8] Further, the 1979 Education Act repealed those sections of Labour's 1976 legislation which had compelled local education authorities to reorganise secondary education on comprehensive lines.

All this supports the contention that, in its early days at least, the Thatcher government, as well as claiming a general autonomy for itself in the sphere of macro-economic management, was prepared to seriously consider and operate a form of reciprocal autonomy for local governments. Rolling back the frontiers of the state would benefit that institution as well. But the initial code went further than this. An important theme of the Centre's rhetoric, one which dominated its general policy pronouncements from the beginning, was the emphasis it put on the need to cut public expenditure. On this matter the Conservative Cabinet found three aspects of the existing system of local government finance defective: local government spending in aggregate was too high, a major cause of inflation, so it was argued, and something which adversely affected investment by private enterprise; the rate support grant led to high levels of central financial aid and, in addition, rewarded those local authorities which spent more at the expense of those which spent less; and the Centre's control over local government expenditure was rendered ineffective because it could not reach down to regulate the budgets of individual, high-spending local authorities. These defects of the system were annoying in themselves. Combined, they threatened, so it was argued, the success of the Centre's macro-economic strategy. Cabinet soon made it clear that this was something it was not prepared to accept. Hence the necessity for some sort of reform of local government finance became an important theme of the early code.

Another item in the initial code was the government's concern for certain aspects of the local government policy process. Two points were important here. First, Thatcherism disliked what it saw as the increasingly influential role acquired by trade unions in local authority affairs. The activities of direct labour organisations were one example of this. Another was the role of teacher organisations in determining local educational policies. The government objected to what it perceived to be an increasingly corporatist style 'carve up' of local affairs between councils and trade unions and these objections were accompanied by a more positive desire to increase the role of private enterprise interests in the local government policy process.[9] Secondly, Thatcherism was particularly concerned to improve the methods by which key local expenditure decisions were made. Reducing the level of the Centre's grant assistance to local government was justified not only on the grounds of the necessity to cut public expenditure, but by the additional argument that such action would force local authorities to make a series of explicit choices (hitherto avoided) concerning the trade-off between pay awards to local government employees, local service standards and local rate poundages. In these ways, so the government argued, the local policy making process would be improved and thus local democracy enhanced.

This interest in the nature of local decision-making and the structure of local politics reflected a more important item in the Thatcherite territorial code. Government spokesmen persistently emphasised the existence of three, not two, actors in the territorial arena, the central government, local governments (of all sorts) and local citizens. As Mr Tom King, Minister for Local Government at the Department of the Environment, put it:

> Our aim is to clarify what we consider to be a proper balance and relationship between central government and local government. But it is not only that. We also wish to clarify the relationship between central government and local government and the local elector – the ratepayer, the citizen and the taxpayer – and the accountability of local government and central government to him.[10]

An important element in this clarification was to ensure that the actions of local governments did not impinge on the rights of individuals. In the words of Mr Heseltine, Secretary of State for the Environment: 'In general terms we did not feel it correct to enhance the rights of local authorities at the expense of the individual'.[11]

This commitment to expanding the rights of individual citizens against the corporate rights of the mass of governments periphery was pursued in a number of ways. The 'tenant rights' provisions of the 1980 Housing Act, which obliged authorities to sell council houses to tenants wishing to buy, was one example; so too were the moves to increase parent choice in, and influence over local education services contained in Education Act, 1980, and as indicated, the repeated calls for a local authority budgetary process more open to citizen influence. Similar aims underpinned the reorganisation of the Health Service, involving the abolition of area health authorities (in 1982) and the emphasis on patients' rights within the service. The attack on quangos can be viewed in the same light.[12] Even the original decision to ignore the Conservative Party's 1979 manifesto commitment and not establish a separate language television channel (a decision later reversed) was presented in terms of ordinary citizen preferences against the institutionalised influence of Plaid Cymru and the language 'mafia'.

Thus, the initial Thatcherite territorial code was more complex and less coherent, than many of its critics allowed. Some reflected traditional notions inherent in the old Dual Polity; others, such as the desire to improve local decision-making and the concern for more effective Centre control over local expenditure, represented new, and in some senses more centralising attitudes. The complexities of the code at this stage were exactly reflected in the government's first major legislative exercise in this field, the Local Government Act, 1980.[13] This Act:

(a) abolished many detailed central controls over local authorities;

(b) instituted special responsibility allowances for certain local councillors, especially committee chairmen;

(c) directed local authorities, as an exercise in 'open government', to publish more data regarding local service standards;

(d) altered the planning responsibilities of local authorities in ways generally favourable to district councils as opposed to county councils;

(e) repealed the Community Land Act, instituted local authority land registers, and gave the Secretary of State for the Environment the power (with parliamentary approval) to direct local authorities to sell land 'demonstrably surplus to their requirements';

(f) established, in the first instance, two nominated urban development corporations in the Liverpool and London dockland areas, with powers to override local authority planning responsibilities in order to secure faster redevelopment and an increased role for private enterprise in those areas;[14]

(g) established new and more commercially biased regulations for controlling the activities of local authority direct labour organisations;

(h) revised the arrangements governing local government capital spending, such that on the one hand local authorities were given greater freedom in deciding *how* they would spend the Centre's annual capital blocks, and, on the other hand, made rate revenue contributions to capital expenditure illegal;

(i) instituted a new block grant system as the basic instrument of financial assistance to local government, a system which, for the first time, allowed the Centre to penalise *individual* local authorities, by cutting their grant allocation if they spent more than the *Government's* assessment of their specific expenditure requirements.

Several points need to be made about this piece of legislation. First, before it reached the statute book the Local Government Bill was severely attacked, both inside and outside parliament, on several counts. Its critics objected to a number of features: its composite nature, its retrospective clauses, the extent to which the implementation of many of its provisions lay with the ministers concerned and, finally, the degree to which it seemed to break the traditional partnership between central and local government and replace it with a system imposing central direction on many aspects, above all financial, of local authority activities. Equally important, the fact that this legislation was opposed by Conservative local councillors and MPs as well as their Labour counterparts, plus the inability of the government to list the criteria by which the Centre would assess local authority overspending (and hence the incidence of grant penalties), only served to emphasise two awkward points: the Cabinet had failed to consult adequately its own supporters and had failed to do its homework in terms of the detailed application of the bill's provisions. For a government which placed so much emphasis on efficient public sector management and maintaining relations with its own backbenchers this was surprising.

Secondly, whatever its failures regarding the politics of the issue, the government had produced a legislative measure which almost exactly reflected the themes it had consistently emphasised since gaining office and which, combined, constituted the initial territorial code described above. Further, despite the criticisms levelled at the bill, the Cabinet was able to mount a reasonably plausible case for its enactment. It admitted that such legislation, in Mr Heseltine's words, 'challenged long established habits and attitudes'. But, it argued, given the problems facing British governments, the attempt to increase the Centre's control over local authority spending was 'overdue in any circumstances and in the economic circumstances of today ... essential'.[15] Apart from constantly stressing the dangers to local democracy inherent in the legislation and the necessity for continued reliance on the traditional collaborative culture of peripheral elites, opponents of the measure were unable to suggest any viable alternative to the Cabinet's scheme. Moreover, the centralising financial provisions of the Local Government Act were neither new nor exclusively the Conservatives'. In one form or another, these ideas had been hanging around the political-administrative community at the Centre since the mid-1970s. The first epigraph to this chapter is one example of this trend; so too was the greater central responsibility model outlined (and rejected) in the Layfield Committee report. In fact, by early 1979 it had become legitimate in many circles at the Centre (including the leadership of the Labour Party) to assume that if certain economic trends continued then more specific and intensive controls over local authorities (and other types of peripheral governments) would be required. In this Thatcherism merely reflected changes which had already taken place in the Centre's official mind regarding the desired form of territorial management.[16]

It follows that the major innovative feature of the early Thatcherite territorial code was its emphasis (reflected in the Local Government Act) on the role of the ordinary citizen in the local political process. This amounted to a rejection of both the customary automatic association between local governments and local democracy and the equally popular idea that intergovernmental relations was the primary operational framework for territorial politics. For the Conservatives this new emphasis on the importance of local citizens or ratepayers was seen as a necessary counterweight to what they perceived to be the increasingly corporatist character of both peripheral politics and Centre-periphery relations. In following this line the Cabinet jettisoned the support traditionally given by Conservative *leaders* to local elites within their peripheral institutions. The link with the macro-economic strategy was twofold. On a general level anticorporatism was common to both codes. More interestingly, the increasing rate burdens placed on industrial and commercial ratepayers at the local level (which was not reflected in the displacement of those interests at local elections) were regarded as a threat both to the profitability of private enterprise and local employment prospects.[17] Clearly the hope was that by increasing the role of economy-minded local citizens in local politics the macro-economic strategy would benefit as well. As Mr Heseltine put it: 'I believe that an efficient local democracy can monitor the activities of local councils far better than civil servants in Marsham Street'.[18] Thus the long-established hostility of Conservative activists to local governors, so often embarrassing to their leaders, now corresponded with the strategic designs of those leaders. The Local Government Act (1980) was the legislative response to this change in the party's territorial code.

It is clear that the Government's initial moves in this game reflected both the changing official mind at the Centre and the interests, fears and demands of its peripheral supporters as they emerged in the 1970s. The result was a composite territorial code and the enactment of a composite piece of legislation. Hence, to view these early manoeuvres solely in terms of a planned drive for more central control and direction is an oversimplification.

Nevertheless, in two important respects the territorial economy of Thatcherism was ambiguous. Despite its severely critical attitude to the existing system of local government finance, the Cabinet made no early move to implement a comprehensive reform of the rating system. As the 1979 manifesto made clear, this was regarded as less important than general taxation reforms. In addition, the relative weighting given by the Centre to the various items in its code was not made clear. The problem here was that the easy way to induce more coherence was to accept that Centre autonomy was the name of the game. In other words, that the concern for improved local decision-making procedures and a more active role for local citizens was merely a means to a more important end, effective Centre control over its grand economic strategy. On this basis, the government would inevitably follow more interventionist and directive policies towards local government to protect its own position. In the early stages of the government's life it is doubtful whether the Conservatives (at both the Centre and the periphery) fully understood the potential problems surrounding the implementation of their complex territorial code. But a government so concerned to impose priorities on local authorities was hardly likely to avoid, for very long, a similar exercise for itself. If 'hard times' continued the code would have to be made more coherent, and the simple way out of this dilemma was for the Centre to pursue its own interests, whatever the initial code suggested, and whatever the views of some of its supporters in local government and parliament.

The code in practice
Roughly thirty months into the political economy of Thatcherism is hardly an appropriate time to attempt a comprehensive narrative and assessment of its operation following the enactment of the Local Government Act. There are too many loose ends and too many prospects of enforced changes in the government's policies to allow a systematic account of the story. Nevertheless, for anyone interested in British territorial politics the events of 1980 and 1981 mark an important phase in the development of the subject. Thus, some attempt must be made to examine this period, however tentative and superficial the exercise is bound to be. What follows, then, is concerned with just two topics: the problems encountered by the Thatcher Cabinet in attempting to implement its territorial code, and its various responses to those problems.

Problems of implementation
The implementation of the code was affected by three related problems: the performance of the British economy, party political developments and, from the

government's point of view, the failure of the Local Government Act to control local authority spending.

By the autumn of 1981 the government's broad economic strategy was in a state of disarray. In terms of its own preferred economic indicators, inflation, money supply, taxation, public expenditure and holding back the frontiers of the state, the story was one of unrelieved failure. In terms of the economy's wider performance, as reflected in the unemployment figures, business failures, profit levels and industrial production, the end product was equally gloomy. The Cabinet's explanation for this failure of the economy to respond positively to its policies was couched in the following terms: the continued propensity of the labour force to demand wage increases not matched by higher productivity; the unexpected depth and longevity of the world recession; and, later, the interest rate policy of the Reagan administration in Washington. Whatever the reasons, it is clear that for the government 1980/1 was a bad experience, one made more awkward by its refusal to consider any alternative strategy and the emphasis it put on external causes of the domestic economic crisis. Hence this was a period in which the Centre had very little room for manoeuvre; it was forced to sit things out and wait for something better to turn up. In these circumstances, the government's relations with its own supporters on the parliamentary backbenches and in the constituency associations were necessarily awkward. Consequently, any domestic institution which was both disliked by those supporters and assumed a significant role in the national economy was bound to come under increasing Cabinet scrutiny. Local government fell into that category.

Economic difficulties begat party political problems. Increasingly, and publicly, the Cabinet was divided between the so-called 'wets' and 'dries', between those who wanted changes in the economic strategy, and those who didn't. As The Times put it: 'Mrs Thatcher's Cabinet is the least harmonious Conservative administration within memory and has shown a singular inability to respond collectively to changing circumstances'.[19] Policy disputes in the government were reflected in part amongst Conservative MPs and local council groups, although not, it appeared, in the constituency parties. Conservative divisions, of course, were small change compared with developments in the Labour Party after 1979. However, Labour's misfortunes did not stop a Conservative slide in the opinion polls, nor the loss of many of its council seats in the local elections of 1980 and 1981, and the formation of the Social Democratic Party in March 1981, plus its subsequent alliance with the Liberals, only made matters worse. Conservative dissidents now had a respectable outlet for their votes as the series of disastrous by-elections (for the government) at Warrington, Croydon North-West and Crosby indicated too well.

The Local Government Act had provided an early 'catalyst' uniting opposition to the government's territorial policies. It even drew together the various local authority associations, at the time all Conservative-controlled. Changes in the party composition of many local councils following the local elections in 1980 and 1981 allowed Labour to take control of the important Association of

Metropolitan Authorities, as well as providing it with an opportunity to mount more wide-ranging local opposition to the Centre's policies. Labour's victory in the GLC elections of May 1981, for example, and the subsequent elevation to majority group leadership of Mr Ken Livingstone were generally recognised as significant developments, bound to have an adverse effect on the Government's policies. Official Labour policy, as enumerated by Mr Roy Hattersley in 1980, was to employ 'every legal means at their disposal' to resist the government's attempts to cut local services.[20] Left-wingers, such as Mr Livingstone and others, who were becoming increasingly important in local Labour council groups and constituency parties, were prepared to go much further than this in opposing the territorial economy of Thatcherism. The traditional collaborative culture which had characterised peripheral Labour party elites was breaking down.

This brief discussion emphasises one obvious point: throughout 1980 and 1981 the territorial management policies of the Thatcher government were pursued in an increasingly awkward politico-economic environment. It could be argued, however, that on the specific issue of local government finance the Centre, via the new block grant and its penalty system, was now equipped to effectively control local authority spending. By the autumn of 1981, however, the Cabinet had concluded that it had failed on that count as well.

From the Centre's viewpoint the position on this matter developed in a number of unsatisfactory ways. First and foremost, despite the new grant mechanism, local authorities continued to spend more on wages, salaries and services than the government had projected. According to Mr Tom King, Minister for Local Government, over half of the local authorities in England had failed to comply with their centrally-fixed expenditure targets.[21] In the language of the Department of the Environment, 1980/1 had witnessed a £1000 million 'overspend' by local government. In fact, the only area in which local authorities had achieved economies was capital expenditure: a point which the government felt only served to emphasise the degree to which current expenditure was still free of Centre control, and the degree to which old habits of evading expenditure cuts were still prevalent. The government's general view on this issue was expressed in the following terms:

> The fact is that a £1 billion overspend is not the marginal excess of legitimate freedom. It is the extravagant consequence of political licence. It is too large, too persistent, and too flagrant.[22]

Ideally, the government argued, it would have wished to continue the traditional system of voluntary adherence by local authorities to its expenditure policies. But, and this was the second unsatisfactory aspect of the situation, this was no longer possible. The traditional partnership was now undermined by the activities of a few (Labour-controlled) authorities determined to challenge the Centre's authority. One specific device employed by some of these authorities to raise additional revenues to finance 'overspending', one which the government (and, so it was argued, local ratepayers) found increasingly annoying, was the supplementary rate or precept. According to Mr Heseltine there was a 'growing tendency' to use this ploy. After April 1981 over twenty local authorities in England had raised additional revenue in this way, and the overwhelming majority of these were controlled by the Labour Party.[23]

The final weakness in the Centre's position in the autumn of 1981, although not one it was prepared to admit in public, was the problems it encountered when attempting to assess what counted for overspending in terms of each local authority. This particular point was crucial because it was on this assessment that the whole new system of grant penalties rested. During 1980 and 1981, much to the annoyance of local government, the Cabinet pursued no coherent line on this matter.[24] The problem was obvious: if the criteria employed were too harsh then too many local authorities, including many controlled by the Conservative party, would be penalised; if too generous they would constitute no controls at all. What the Centre required was a simpler and more effective method of curtailing local expenditure.

Thus, by the autumn of 1981, the Thatcher government had concluded that the Local Government Act had failed to solve the problem of local spending. This had occurred at a time when, as the second epigraph to this chapter indicates, it was constantly emphasising that the Centre's responsibility for macro-economic management demanded that local government conformed to its overall public expenditure strategy.

The Centre's response

These problems of territorial management produced a variety of reactions from the Thatcher Centre. The initial, and as it turned out, the major response, was the Local Government Finance Bill. After a considerable amount of prior publicity, though not, it seems, consultation with the interested parties, this was introduced in the Commons early in November 1981.[25] The principal provisions of this bill were threefold:

(a) In the first instance it provided for Centre-set initial limits to the annual rates and precepts of local councils. Any local authorities wishing to raise revenue beyond such limits via supplementary rates or precepts were required to hold referendums on the matter.[26] The questions posed would be set by the Centre. If local citizens approved such proposals then the councils were required to levy the supplementary rates or precepts in ways which discriminated in favour of non-domestic ratepayers. Councils which failed to gain citizen approval from a referendum were directed to cut their budgets to comply with the government's rate targets by the end of the financial year. If this proved impossible then they were subjected to special borrowing regulations by the Department of the Environment. In addition, strict limits would be set to their rates or precepts in the following year.

(b) The Secretary of State for the Environment (and his Welsh counterpart) were given the power, at any time during the local government financial year, to vary (that is, reduce) the amount of block grant payable to any local authority, if, in their view, it was proposing an 'unreasonable increase' in local spending in relation to Centre-set targets (primarily the grant related expenditure figure). The amount of grant reduction would be fixed in accordance with the Secretary of State's assessment of 'general economic conditions'. The government justified this proposal on the grounds that it would allow a degree of discrimination between local authorities in terms of grant penalties. In other words, good behaviour would be rewarded.

(c) The right of local authorities to choose their own auditors was abolished. A new agency, the Audit Commission, appointed by the Secretary of State, was given the task of auditing the accounts of all local authorities in England and Wales. The old District Audit Service in the DOE was hived off to become a part of the new Commission which, in turn, was to appoint all local auditors after consultation with the local authorities concerned. The new audit regime was to have several novel features. Individual auditors were to place far more emphasis than hitherto on the 'value for money' aspects of local authority spending. Again, greater use was proposed of private sector firms in the local authority audits, on the grounds that they had considerable experience in dealing with value for money issues. Finally, the accountability of local government to their electorates was to be increased by giving auditors a duty to report immediately on matters of public concern, and by expanding the occasions on which local electors could object to the auditors about local authority actions.

On the surface, the government had produced a subtle bill. In difficult circumstances it had manufactured a measure which, once again, reflected most of the items in its initial territorial code. This time, however, the emphasis was definitely on the desire for Centre autonomy regarding macro-economic management. Despite the unanimous opposition of the Local Authority Associations, the government had every reason to believe that the measure would be supported by Conservative activists and MPs. In the event it was proved wrong. A significant number of Conservative backbenchers objected to the proposals for local referendums. Although these objections were not always the same as those of the Local Authority Associations, they were sufficiently strongly presented to make the Cabinet reconsider the matter. The result was that just over a month after the bill was published it was withdrawn. The government's major response to its peripheral problems had been defeated.

The second response to these problems was in practice equally ambiguous. This was the Chancellor's mini-budget of December 1981. On the one hand this allowed public expenditure in general to rise by $4\frac{1}{2}$ per cent over and above the targets set the previous March. More specifically, local authority expenditure was set to rise by £1.4 billion, an amount which almost equalled the total overspend by local authorities in 1981/2. On the other hand, housing subsidies to local authorities were cut and a £2.50 per week rise in council rents suggested. Again, the rate support grant contribution to local authority revenues in England was reduced from an average of fifty-nine per cent to fifty-six per cent. Similar reductions were made for Wales and Scotland. It was estimated that this grant cut would cause rates to rise by an average of fifteen per cent in England.

Shortly after this mini-budget the government produced the Local Government Finance (No 2) Bill. In terms of the new audit arrangements and the provisions for mid-year grant penalties this was exactly the same as its predecessor. The difference was that the proposals for referendums and differential treatment for non-domestic ratepayers were dropped. In their place was a more simple plan: supplementary rates and precepts were abolished. On this occasion the government had made strenuous attempts to consult its own backbenchers regarding the provisions of the new bill. Nevertheless, it was still unpopular with many Conservative MPs. In particular, that section of the bill which allowed the imposition of grant penalties after local authorities had fixed the one and only rate now allowed them was severely criticised. Once again, out of fear of losing the whole Bill, the government gave way. Early in February 1982 it promised to drop the offending clause.[27] Thus, after two attempts, its legislation strategy was reduced to a ban on supplementary rates and precepts and a new audit service.

A major criticism of the Local Government Finance Bills was that they were merely tinkering with the problem. MPs on both sides of the House, plus interested parties outside, argued that what was required was a wholesale reform of the rating system. These criticisms provoked the Centre's final response to its territorial management problems. It accepted (whatever its initial views) that the Finance Bills could only be temporary measures, that a general reform of local government finance was required. As a result, in December 1981, it published a Green Paper on the subject.[28] Following consultations, legislation on this matter was promised before the end of the 1979 parliament. Even here, however, it was forced to admit defeat. The Green Paper made it clear that none of the reform options discussed were particularly attractive; nor was there any agreement outside the government as to what form any changes should take. More important, the Cabinet realised that reforming the rates was not a vote winner: whatever it suggested would be time-consuming and unpopular. The result was that in February 1982 this proposal was dropped.[29] Whatever else the Thatcher government did, it appeared its territorial economy would not include a general overhaul of the local government finance system.

Assessment

The story detailed above can be interpreted in three ways. One popular view is to stress what two academics commenting on the first Local Government Finance Bill called 'continual panic *ad hocery*'. Put somewhat differently: 'In the urgency of its need to reassert control of the economy, the Government is allowing itself to be drawn into a misconceived constitutional attack on local government'.[30] Combined, these comments suggest that the Cabinet's primary concern for success in its macro-economic strategy caused it increasingly to adopt a number of ill-prepared radical policies which, whilst threatening the traditional central-local relationship, were yet ineffective in achieving the government's aims.

Evidence to support this viewpoint is not hard to find. As one Conservative

MP argued: the constant introduction of new legislation concerning local government 'says little for the depth of initial thinking and – at least as bad – it is a recipe for chaos and uncertainty'.[31] Government defeats on key aspects of their legislative initiatives in parliament undoubtedly suggested a degree of chaos and uncertainty. Equally significant were the number of occasions on which ministers seemed incompletely acquainted with the details of their own proposals.[32] Another common criticism was that the government was employing sledge-hammers to crack nuts. Only a few local authorities were actively resisting its local spending policies and, it was argued, electoral considerations, or the judiciary, would soon ensure that most of those qualified their intransigence. Moreover, for many people, the government's opposition to higher rates was difficult to understand since these had no adverse effects on its preferred economic indicators, the money supply and the public sector borrowing account. Finally, all this legislative effort amounted, in practice, to very little. Shorn of its ideas for local referendums and mid-year grant penalties, the Centre still had insufficient control over local authority expenditure. The postponement of rating reform only served to emphasise the futility of the whole exercise. Hence, the only practical result of the government's policies was the politicisation of local government, a politicisation which took a number of forms. Controversies over expenditure cuts and rate increases affected the internal operation of individual local councils, set local authority against local authority, both united the Local Authority Associations against the government and on other occasions divided them, brought judicial intervention into the local political process, and forged closer links than hitherto between some MPs and local authorities in their constituencies. Whatever the form, the politicisation of local affairs was hardly a traditional Conservative goal.

An alternative interpretation would stress the relative success of the government's efforts. Put another way, it is remarkable what the Centre, in this short period, managed to get away with.

We have seen that the government encountered many problems when attempting to legislate on the subject of local government finance, and it is true that, like public expenditure generally, local authority spending continued to rise. The difficulty, of course, is that we will never know what the level of local expenditure would have been under another administration at the Centre. What is certain is that the Conservatives created a culture of retrenchment and change within local government quite different from the culture prevailing when they came to office. Equally important, in terms of the mechanics of the Centre's controls over local government three important developments had taken place. No matter how inefficient and discriminatory the procedures, the Centre had achieved some sort of influence, via grant penalties, over the budgets of individual local authorities, something it had never possessed before. In addition, supplementary rates/precepts had been abolished and the district audit service was to be radically restructured. These steps certainly fell short of the Centre's aims. Nevertheless, in terms of the 1979 position they can be counted as small successes.

Thus far the discussion has concentrated on the financial affairs of local government. But a glance at some of the non-financial aspects of the Centre's relations with territorial governments, including non-elected ones, gives additional support to this particular interpretation. First, the government pursued a number of significantly interventionist policies with regard to territorial *ad hoc* agencies. Following the early abolition of the regional economic planning councils, a reform of the National Health Service structure was enacted, regional water authorities were brought under greater government supervision and radical changes in the structure and personnel of these authorities promised.[33] Secondly, despite the rhetoric concerning the desirability of increasing the autonomy of local education authorities, the DES and successive ministers in this period continued to take considerable interest in, and even veto, local plans to reorganise secondary education, especially if they involved sixth-form colleges.[34] Nor did the autonomy of local councils count for much when, as in the case of council house sales, it clashed with another item in the government's territorial code, namely the desire to increase individual citizen's choice. Councils which objected to such policies, for example Norwich, found their responsibilities in this field taken over by DOE-appointed commissioners, an action later supported by the courts.

Thirdly, despite the Cabinet's stated intentions, the steady drip of government by circular continued; indeed, in some ways it intensified. Two examples from the DOE were circulars 22/80 and 7/81: the former requested more favourable responses from local authorities to development schemes sponsored by private building firms; the latter 'advised' local councils to draw up five-year housing plans and housing land 'banks'. The DES played the same game. Circular 2/81 requested that local education authorities inform the Department by the end of 1982 of their plans to reduce the number of schools relative to falling rolls, another policy which made a significant contribution to the politicisation of local council affairs.

On the basis of this sort of evidence the Thatcherite Centre was willing and able to intervene effectively to protect and promote its territorial code. Of course, the government encountered considerable opposition to its policies from local government interests. Nevertheless, as indicated, most local authorities tried to collaborate with the Centre; old habits died hard. No Labour council group, for example, resigned office, refusing to carry out the policies, and the uncomprehending bleatings of some local Conservative groups were largely ignored.[35] The Local Authority Associations, particularly the Association of Metropolitan Authorities, campaigned against many of the policies, but as one commentator pointed out, 'the strength of party loyalty triumphed over loyalty to local government'. In other words, the government was able to divide and rule. As correspondents to the Labour Party's new house magazine complained, it was difficult to defy the government because its strategy was more subtle than that of the previous Heath administration![36] The government's most dangerous enemies were found inside the House of Commons, on its own back-benches. These dissidents were certainly appeased. But, it should be stressed, most Conservative MPs supported the Cabinet or were indifferent to its proposals. And the dissidents followed no coherent line: some, it is true, objected to the attack on local autonomy as a matter of principle, but others were more interested in rating reform, and others only opposed the local referendum proposals because they were seen as a threat to *all* representative government, especially parliament itself. On this basis, then, what is remarkable is not how much opposition the government encountered, but how little.

The focus of the final interpretation is somewhat different. It is concerned less with the relative success or failure of the Thatcher government's policies in this period than with the emergence of a threefold ambiguity concerning the Centre's position in relation to territorial management in Britain.

The first ambiguity relates to the organisational resources of the Centre. We have seen that the Conservatives entered office in May 1979 stressing the need to roll back the frontiers of the state. It was also argued above that 'monetarism' was taken up primarily for political reasons. It offered the prospect of running the economy at arm's length from the interests involved and, as a consequence, the possibility of reconstructing the Centre's autonomy in relation to macro-economic management. In the event, the promise of this twofold scenario was not fulfilled. In particular, monetarist techniques of government did not work as easily or as effectively as was hoped. As a result, a government committed to non-interference was forced to interfere in order to pursue its policy objectives.[37] If this was the general picture, it also applied to the Centre's management of territorial governments. Here the Cabinet was forced to learn two unpalatable lessons. The more it emphasised the legitimacy of the Centre laying down the parameters of local government expenditure, the more it was necessary to supervise the details of that expenditure. Secondly, the organisational resources of the Centre (at least in England and Wales) were such that the supervisory policies followed were bound to be confused, arbitrary and heavy-handed.[38] This was because, in terms of departmental co-ordination at the Centre and their contacts with governments in the periphery, the position in the early 1980s was pretty much the same as it was described (and criticised) in the report of the Central Policy Review Staff published in the late 1970s.[39] The Thatcher Cabinet, however, was not interested in the machinery of government matters. Its interests were confined to introducing business principles into public sector management and cutting down the size of the civil service. Yet the policies it followed demanded a quite different approach. If, for example, the supervision of local expenditure was to be handled efficiently then the DOE needed to be expanded in size. Specifically, it needed to develop a more extensive and more efficient field administrative structure. In short, there was a lack of congruence between the territorial policies of the Thatcher Centre and its attitude towards the territorial resources of the Centre.

The second ambiguity concerns the attitudes of both the Conservative and Labour party leaders towards territorial management in the 1980s. We have seen how the initial Thatcherite territorial code was subtly altered by circumstance. Its original composite nature was developed over time to a point where the various items in the code were subordinated to the Centre's grand strategy, its pursuit of

autonomy in economic management. The paradoxical result was that a party traditionally committed to the Dual Polity (or local autonomy, as Conservatives preferred to put it) jettisoned those traditions for a more interventionist directive
approach.

Similar conclusions can be drawn regarding the attitudes of Labour Party leaders. Inside and outside parliament, Labour leaders were easily able to criticise
Conservative policies as a threat to local democracy. At the same time they suggested that such policies were unnecessary; territorial management could still be
run on the old system of collaborative local elites. Whether the country's problems
allowed the Centre to continue with the free and easy methods of the past is open
to question. More important is the fact that Labour's new commitments to the
Alternative Economic Strategy and withdrawal from the European Community
hardly suggest that, in office, their position would be any less ambiguous than the
Conservative's. Both these policies would involve a more directive Centre; the
one to promote industrial rejuvenation and social justice, the other to protect the
United Kingdom economy from the initial adverse effects of withdrawal from one
of its major institutional supports. On these grounds alone it is difficult to envisage a future Labour administration adopting a substantially different stance
towards territorial management from the Thatcher government, and Labour's
position was further complicated by its continuing adherence to some form of
devolution for Scotland.

The doctrinal splits within the Labour Party, which intensified following the
1979 electoral defeat, compounded this problem of Labour's future attitudes.
What remains of the centre-right, plus the Tribunites, in the parliamentary party
are still firmly committed to the traditional primacy of Westminster politics. But
the same cannot be said of the so-called Bennite left. Its doctrines of intra-party
democracy and action represent a direct threat to that primacy behind which, of
course, has developed the autonomy of the Centre or court. The precise territorial
implications of this new code of the Labour Party are difficult to specify. Clearly,
if adopted, local council groups and Labour representatives on *ad hoc* agencies,
will be far less free of local party control than previously. The possible impact on
Centre-periphery relations however is less clear. Nevertheless, simply because it
attacks the primacy of Westminster politics, 'Bennism' must be regarded as a
potential major threat to the continuance of the traditional territorial order. The
conclusion must be that Labour attitudes to future territorial management are even
more ambiguous than those existing in the Conservative Party.[40]

The third and final ambiguity concerns the nature of the British territorial constitution. Since the mid-nineteenth century the British have lived with a constitution structured around the principle of the sovereignty of parliament. It was this
principle which obstructed the development of a 'written' constitution and any
meaningful concept of the state. And it was from this principle that the unitary
nature of the territorial system could be inferred. In theory, both the principle and
the territorial system firmly relegated elected local governments to a subordinate
position in the body politic, a subordination which was often bolstered by the

behaviour of judges, who usually took a restrictive attitude towards the activities of local councils. On the other hand, over the same period, the British also developed the twin concepts of local self-government and the central-local 'partnership'. In theory, these concepts placed elected local councils in a more favourable position than that occupied by their counterparts in other unitary systems.

It was pointed out in Chapter 1 that very little serious discussion of the theory and practice of unitary systems has taken place. Hence the contradiction detailed above exists, more or less, in most non-federal countries. Nevertheless, it can be argued that other countries have advanced further down the road towards the resolution of this contradiction than Britain. Resolution has come via a number of devices: written constitutions which often give certain formal guarantees to local governments; the Napoleonic administrative system, which accepts that local governments are subordinate agencies of the state and yet, at the same time, allows them adequate representation at the Centre through the Ministry of the Interior; and political structures which, again, permit local interests and governments to effectively penetrate the Centre to articulate their demands. The British, however, developed none of these devices. Instead they resolved the contradiction of local self-government and 'partnership' within the unitary system by manufacturing a common culture at both the Centre and in the periphery; a culture in which the 'chaps' involved (both bureaucrats and politicians) would behave themselves, would not overstep the mark. In short, everything depended on an elaborate system of compromise and mutual deference between political and administrative elites at the Centre and in the periphery.

During the territorial economy of Thatcherism this system began to break down. As a result the basic constitutional ambiguity was revealed. In general terms, the decline of the old territorial constitution occurred because the 'chaps' were not behaving themselves. For many it was the brutal inconsistencies of Mr Michael Heseltine which were at fault. For Mr Heseltine the fault lay, as he constantly emphasised, with the new sort of Labour 'chaps' in the periphery, 'chaps' who simply would not collaborate with the Centre on the traditional lines.

This general problem produced, or exposed, a number of more specific 'squeak points' in the territorial constitution. One was the increasing public insistence by government spokesmen on the traditional constitutional subordination of local authorities to the central government. Hitherto, this piece of 'logic' had been left to the imagination of those involved in the 'partnership'. Another was the Conservatives' unwillingness to accept that local authorities were political as well as administrative institutions, that they might produce party majorities with local mandates, which could claim a legitimacy for their policies to rival that of the national government. In other words, to accept the viewpoint expressed by a Labour MP during one parliamentary debate: 'I believe in the right of a Labour council to defy within the law the will of a Conservative Government, as I accept the right of a Conservative council to do the same when we are in power'.[41]

Finally, and perhaps most interesting of all, was the doctrine of the 'fiduciary duty' of local authorities to their ratepayers, enunciated, or rather re-enunciated, by the Law Lords in their decision on the GLC's transport subsidies.[42] This duty required that local councils should not expend ratepayers moneys 'thriftlessly', but 'economically' and on 'business principles'. In other words, local authorities were not like other elected governments: they were mere trustees of their ratepayers 'donations', a strange concept of local self-government and one linked to Mr Heseltine's view that: 'we may feel that democracy as we know it depends on the sovereignty of Parliament and its duty to protect any one group in society against another that overburdens it'.[43]

In these various ways the basic ambiguity of the British territorial constitution was exposed.

Northern Ireland

In opposition, Conservative leaders had given relatively little consideration to Northern Ireland. There were three major reasons for this. First, policy proposals for Northern Ireland lacked electoral appeal in Britain, and any radical stance risked breaking the crucially important bipartisan line with Labour leaders at Westminster. Secondly, the experience of the early and mid-1970s had shown that the accepted Centre strategy for the Province – no return to the Stormont regime, a power-sharing executive, and some sort of 'Irish dimension' – was not acceptable to Protestant leaders. Thirdly, under the tough management of Roy Mason's Secretary of Stateship, Northern Ireland had experienced a period of relative quiescence after 1976. As a result, two advantages of direct rule were highlighted: the very absence of elected regional institutions served to dampen the domestic politics of the Province and this further sustained its arm's length position from British politics. In these circumstances radical initiatives were best avoided. Hence, Northern Ireland formed no part of the initial Conservative territorial code. Apart from a vague commitment to reform local government in the Province, the Conservative leaders, prior to taking office, promised very little indeed.

However, following their general election victory several significant shifts in the environment of Northern Ireland politics took place which forced the Conservative leaders to pursue a number of more positive policy initiatives. These were as follows:

(i) The so-called Atkins constitutional initiative: first announced in October 1979, this amounted to a further attempt to reach agreement, via a constitutional conference, on a scheme for devolved government in the Province. Described as 'a triumph of hope over experience', the conference was boycotted by the Official Unionist Party, caused a serious split in the mainly Catholic SDLP, and produced nothing concrete in terms of agreed action. By the spring of 1980 this particular policy initiative was dead.[44]

(ii) The Anglo-Irish summits: these began with the Thatcher-Haughey talks in May 1980 in London. At this meeting it was decided to hold the summits 'on a continuing basis'. They provided a convenient device whereby relations between the United Kingdom and the Republic could be discussed in general terms, as well as the specific problem of Northern Ireland. Further summits took place in

December 1980 and November 1981: the former instituted a series of study groups and the latter announced the formation of an Anglo-Irish 'intergovernmental' council. This was to be composed of ministers and civil servants from London and Dublin, but not Belfast. At the time of writing the precise role of this council is unclear. Potentially, however, it represents a significant innovation.

(iii) The government successfully resisted the demands by Republican detainees in the Maze prison for political status. This campaign, backed by a hunger strike, began in October 1980. It collapsed a year later.

(iv) The Prior policy package pursued in the early months of 1982: this involved an extra £91 million in economic aid to the Province and a further political initiative. This time the strategy was labelled 'rolling devolution'. In other words, following the election of a regional assembly its powers would be confined, initially to discussion and advice. Additional functions, and the formation of an executive, would only be granted if a certain majority in the Assembly (say seventy per cent) favoured such action.

These policies require some comment. First, both the early Atkins proposals and the initial Anglo-Irish summit were largely the result of external pressures. The former was Mrs Thatcher's response (dutifully carried out by a sceptical Northern Ireland Office) to two major developments: the recommencement of Republican para-military operations (the assassination of Mr Airey Neave, the murder of Lord Mountbatten and the Warrenpoint ambush) and the increasingly vocal protests of the Irish lobby in the United States at the lack of any policy initiatives on the part of United Kingdom governments. Given these circumstances (and an inexperienced Secretary of State) it is not surprising that this first exercise was badly managed. The constitutional conference was announced before the publication of the government's thoughts on the matters to be discussed, a state of affairs which led *The Guardian* to describe the whole affair as 'an insubstantial plan without sufficient consultation and without sufficient evidence to back Mr Atkins' assertion of its potential'.[45] Similar criticisms, of course, were levelled at the Local Government Bill: 1979 was not the Conservative government's year for territorial consultations. The first summit meeting was equally a response by Mrs Thatcher to external pressures, in this instance the replacement of Mr Jack Lynch as Irish premier and leader of the Fianna Fail party by Mr Charles Haughey in December 1979. Mr Haughey, and important elements in his party, wanted a much harder line towards London over Northern Ireland. The failure of the Atkins' initiative, and the need for intergovernmental security discussions, provided the new Irish leader with an opportunity to pressure Mrs Thatcher's Cabinet. In a speech to a Fianna Fail conference, he declared: 'Northern Ireland as a political entity has failed and a new beginning is needed. The time has surely come for the two sovereign governments to work together to find a formula and lift the situation on to a new place'.[46] Secondly, the advent of the summit meetings had important implications for all the actors involved in the Northern Ireland problem. They did draw 'the two sovereign governments' closer together, although there was always scope for disagreements about what actually had been decided at the meetings.

But if Dublin and London grew closer, this was at the expense of raising the suspicions of Protestant politicians in the Province and re-emphasising the peculiar nature of its position within the United Kingdom. Moreover, summitry meant that London governments became increasingly sensitive to political events in Dublin, at a time of growing instability in the Republic's politics. Perhaps the most important aspect of this particular development was its potential impact on Dublin's official mind regarding unification. In a sense the summits can be regarded as a subtle device to offload some responsibility for Northern Ireland on to Irish governments. The problem here was that for years Irish politicians had talked and dreamed of unification. In practice, however, they had given relatively little consideration to the mechanics of the process. Thus, rather late in the day, there occurred a gradual realisation in certain sections of the Republic's political elite that some thought needed to be given to the key question of the whole problem: the terms of the future contract which Dublin would offer the majority community in Northern Ireland to bring about unification.[47]

Finally, back at the ranch in Northern Ireland, it must be emphasised that the government's victory over the Maze hunger strikers was bought at an awkward cost. The Provisional IRA gained considerable favourable publicity in the western world and an increase in funds from certain groups in the United States. In addition, the victory of the H-Block candidates in the two by-elections in the Fermanagh and South Tyrone constituency in 1981 further polarised opinion in the Province and weakened the grip of the SDLP on the minority community. The government's victory was also followed by a renewal of IRA hostilities in both Northern Ireland and London. In the former, the attacks on Protestants in the border areas and the murder of the Unionist MP, Robert Bradford, in the autumn of 1981 resulted in renewed criticisms from the Protestant community of the security services. Mr Paisley raised the question of a 'third force' and threatened to make Northern Ireland 'ungovernable' if security measures were not improved. All this provided an awkward background for the Prior policy package of early 1982 (from which the Dublin government was excluded). The extra financial aid was welcomed, although regarded as a tip to a waiter in relation to the Province's growing economic problems.[48] Perhaps its main purpose was a political one: to put a stop to growing Protestant suspicions that the government was allowing the economy of the Province to run down in order to make unification with the Republic more attractive. At all events the concept of 'rolling devolution' faced considerable problems of implementation. An indication of the Government's continued commitment to the indirect rule collaborative code, it faced increasing opposition from politicians in both communities, the very people designated as the future collaborators.

CONCLUSION

In Britain, the territorial economy of Thatcherism marked an important stage in the development of Centre-periphery relations. The government's initial territorial code represented an interesting set of variations on the traditional stance of the Centre. Over time, and under the pressure of perceived economic problems, the Thatcher Cabinet's code became more radical, involving a direct attack on the traditions of the Dual Polity. This development served to highlight two important points. First, under the impact of 'hard times', the Conservative leaders, (and there is no reason to believe their Labour counterparts would behave differently) put the primacy of the Centre's autonomy above that of the traditional autonomy allowed peripheral interests and governments. Secondly, in the process the fundamental ambiguities of the British territorial constitution were revealed. If to these points is added a third – the partial politicisation of the periphery resulting from the implementation of the Thatcher code – then it is clear that a new territorial settlement in Britain is not only required, but, on the evidence of this period, shows all the signs of being very difficult to achieve.

In Northern Ireland the government's activities were less dramatic, at least in terms of their initial impact. Lacking, at the beginning, any considered code for the Province, and subject to a series of rapid and awkward changes in its political environment, the Thatcher Cabinet was associated with two important measures: the Anglo-Irish summits and the defeat of the Maze strike. Whether the second devolution gambit for the Province will succeed is open to question. It may be pushed through because Mr Prior's political future (though not the Cabinet's) depends on it. In this light perhaps the most important feature of the Conservatives government's Northern Ireland operations was its maintenance, in difficult circumstances, of the status quo. In this context the status quo means the continuation of the bipartisan line at Westminster (even over the Maze strike). This 'line' is important because it is the key to the successful achievement of every United Kingdom government's medium-term Ulster strategy since 1968 – keeping the problems of the Province away from British politics. Where Northern Ireland is concerned Mrs Thatcher did her duty by the Dual Polity.

NOTES

1 The title requires some explanation. The word 'economy' is used not because of the importance of economic theory to this Conservative government, but, as the argument below emphasises, because economic problems had a considerable impact on the government's activities. 'Thatcherism' obviously overemphasises the importance of one individual. Nevertheless, like most Prime Ministers, Mrs Thatcher was the most important member of the Cabinet and her determination to be a 'conviction politician' had a considerable impact on both the content and style of its operations.

2 Layfield Report, *Local Government Finance* (Cmnd. 6453, 1976), p. 244, para. 25.

3   Mr Michael Heseltine, Secretary of State for the Environment, H. C. *Debates*, (12 November 1981), col. 684.
4   On this point see W. J. Meadows, 'Local government: discretion accountability?' in P. M. Jackson (ed.), *Government Policy Initiatives 1979–80: Some Case Studies in Public Administration* (London, 1981), p. 58.
5   Compare, for example, the interpretation of Thatcherism in Bryan Gould, John Mills, Shaun Stewart, *The Politics of Monetarism* (Fabian Tract 462) with Mrs Thatcher's own views expressed in the interview 'The first two years', *The Sunday Times* (3 May 1981).
6   H. C. *Debates* (1 July 1980), col. 1396.
7   Both these statements were cited by Mr Gerald Kaufman, Shadow Minister for the Environment, during the second reading debate on the Local Government Finance (No 1) Bill. See H. C. Debates (12 November 1981), col. 682.
8   Cmnd. 7634 (1979), *Central Government Controls Over Local Authorities*.
9   Labour's manifesto for the 1979 election had contained a commitment to remove the automatic disqualification on local government employees standing for election to councils and a promise to allow local authorities to co-opt employee representatives on to committees, as non-voting members. For the government's ideas see: DOE, *Local Authority Direct Labour: Consultation Paper* (August 1979); and DOE, *Service Provision and Pricing in Local Government* (November 1981).
10 H. C. *Debates* (5 February 1980), col. 368.
11 *Ibid.*, col. 246. Opposition to Scottish devolution was justified on similar grounds. See Mrs Thatcher's comments on the matter cited in N. Drucker and H. Drucker, *The Scottish Government Yearbook*, 1980 (Edinburgh, 1979), p. 98.
12 For NHS reorganisation see Department of Health and Social Security, *Patients First* (London, 1979). For an assessment of quango policy see Christopher Hood's 'Axeperson, spare that quango...' in Christopher Hood and Maurice Wright (eds.), *Big Government in Hard Times* (Oxford, 1981).
13 For descriptions and criticisms of this legislation see Meadows, *op. cit.*, Society of Local Authority Chief Executives (SOLACE), *The Local Government Bill* (Lewes, 1980); Richard McAllister and David Hunter, *Local Government: Death or Devolution?* (London, 1980); and Tony Travers 'Local Government, Planning and Land Act, 1980', *Political Quarterly* (July-September 1981). The best source of information, however, is the second reading debate on the bill in the Commons. See H. C. *Debates* (5 February 1980), cols. 244–380.
14 To these proposals must be added the provisions for enterprise zones in certain depressed areas. They were added to the Bill after the Chancellor's budget speech in March 1980. See Stan Taylor, 'The politics of enterprise zones', *Public Administration* (winter 1981).
15 Mr Heseltine, H. C. *Debates* (5 February 1980), cols. 244–5.
16 On this point see Meadows *op. cit.*, p. 60; Travers *op. cit.*; and Tyrrell Burgess and Tony Travers, *Ten Billion Pounds: Whitehall's Takeover of the Town Halls*. Mr Tom King, Minister for Local Government, defended the new financial provisions on just these lines. See H. C. *Debates* (5 February 1980), cols. 370–1. One problem for the Conservatives was what to call the new grant, since they had objected to the very similar unitary grant proposals when in opposition.
17 The problem of non-domestic ratepayers is examined in Cmnd. 8449, *Alternatives to*

Domestic Rates (December 1981), Chapter 10.

18 Speech to the Annual Conference of SOLACE (18 July 1979). Marsham Street is the London address of the Department of the Environment.

19 *The Times* (8 September 1981), editorial, 'A shuffle to some purpose'.

20 *The Guardian* (3 May 1980).

21 H. C. *Debates* (12 November 1981), col. 743.

22 *Ibid.*, col. 687. The speaker was Mr Heseltine.

23 H. C. *Debates* (18 January 1982), cols 48 and 49.

24 For a discussion of the problems encountered by the government see *The Times* (11 May 1981), Diana Geddes, 'Penalising overspenders could hit Tories'.

25 One problem of analysis concerning this legislation should be mentioned. Its critics directed their attacks at Mr Heseltine, who was regarded as the architect of the bill. An alternative view is that the Treasury, supported by Mrs Thatcher, determined its main outlines. See, for example, Hugo Young, 'The inside story of a Cabinet meeting', *Sunday Times* (14 February 1982) and *The Economist* (26 December 1981), 'Diary of a Dry'.

26 These new rules were to apply only to local authorities in England and Wales. Scottish local authorities were already forbidden to levy supplementary rates.

27 See *The Times* (1 February 1982 and 3 February 1982); also *The Economist* (13 February 1982), which pointed out that the government's new clause left the position extremely ambiguous.

28 Cmnd. 8449, *Alternatives to Domestic Rates*.

29 *The Times* (19 February 1982).

30 See the letter from Professors G. W. Jones and J. Stewart printed in *The Times* (7 November 1981). Also, that paper's editorial on the same day entitled, 'No way to police the parish pump'.

31 Mr Charles Morrison, H. C. *Debates* (18 January 1982), col. 73.

32 For some splendid examples see *ibid.*, col. 55. Also Tony Travers, *op. cit.*

33 The government employed the Monopolies and Mergers Commission to investigate the pricing policies of regional water authorities. In addition, their audit arrangements were changed to those operating in the nationalised industries. See H. C. *Debates* (7 December 1981), cols. 581–7 and DOE (January 1982), *The Membership of Regional Water Authorities: A Consultation Paper*.

34 *Times Educational Supplement* (20 November 1981), 'The message from Manchester'.

35 For an excellent example, see the passage from the memorandum produced by the Conservative-controlled Kingston upon Thames council cited by Mr Gerald Kaufman, H. C. *Debates* (12 November 1981), col. 682.

36 *New Socialist* (November/December 1981), pp. 51 and 63.

37 For a general comment on these lines see the leader in *The Economist* (8 December 1979). A similar story occurred in terms of the government's relations with the nationalised industries. See *The Economist* (6 March 1982).

38 There is some debate as to whether the Centre's position in relation to Scotland is any better. See J. M. Ross, *The Secretary of State for Scotland and the Scottish Office* (Glasgow, 1981); and David Heald, 'The Scottish rate support grant: how different from the English and Welsh?', *Public Administration* (Spring 1980).

39 Central Policy Review Staff, *Relations Between Central, Government and Local Authorities* (London, 1977), especially para. 5.1.

40 This seems to be the most plausible conclusion to emerge from a reading of Mr Kaufman's speeches in many of the parliamentary debates cited above; David Kogan and Maurice Kogan, *The Battle for the Labour Party* (Glasgow, 1982) especially Chapter 9; Francis Cripps *et al.*, *Manifesto: A Radical Strategy for Britain's Future* (London, 1981), especially p. 156; Evan Luard, *Socialism at the Grass Roots* (Fabian Tract 468); David G. Green, *Power and Party in an English City* (London, 1981). Curiously, Mr Tony Benn devotes very little time to an analysis of local government.

41 Mr Guy Barnett, H. C. *Debates* (5 February 1980), col. 310.

42 *The Times*, Law Report (18 December 1981). Two previous cases cited to support this doctrine were Roberts v. Hopwood (1925) and, Prescott v. Birmingham Corporation (1955).

43 H. C. *Debates* (12 November 1981), col. 690.

44 See *The Observer* (28 October 1979), 'Margaret's other island'; Cmnd. 7763 (November 1979), *The Government of Northern Ireland: A Working Paper for a Conference*; Cmnd. 7950 (July 1980), *The Government of Northern Ireland: Proposals for Further Discussion*; Derek Birrell, 'Northern Ireland: the obstacles of power sharing', *Political Quarterly* (April-June 1981).

45 *The Guardian* (26 October 1979).

46 Mr Haughey's speech is cited and discussed in *The Times* (18 February 1980) editorial, 'Mr Haughey and Irish unity'. This editorial argued that Irish politicians were over-influenced by the Thatcher government's willingness to withdraw from Rhodesia.

47 Professor Lyons has argued that over time southern politicians ingeniously reversed Gambetta's dictum concerning the desired French attitude, after 1870, to the recovery of Alsace-Lorraine – 'Think of it always, speak of it never'. See F. S. L. Lyons, 'The lessons of history', *The Spectator* (20 June 1981). One Irish politician who tried to change matters was Garett Fitzgerald. As Prime Minister he promised 'a crusade' to change attitudes and the constitution in the Republic. See the article by David Morrison in *The Times* (9 November 1981).

48 On these problems see Brendan Keenan, 'Ulster: an economic disease which may yet prove fatal', *Financial Times* (17 March 1982).

| conclusions

We live under a system of tacit understandings. But the understandings themselves are not always understood.[1]

If you want to stop fearing doomsday, sell raffle tickets.[2]

This concluding chapter deals with three topics: a summary of the principal arguments contained in each of the preceding chapters; a recapitulation of the major general themes to emerge from this analysis concerning the nature of the Centre; and a brief exercise in political astrology, an attempt to discuss the future of territorial politics in the United Kingdom.

SUMMARY

The specific arguments contained in the previous chapters can be detailed as follows:

1. The existing approaches to the general subject of central-local relations – territorial systems analysis, the centralisation/decentralisation dichotomy and the internal colonialism thesis – were examined and found to suffer from a number of common weaknesses. The most important of these were: their failure to take sufficient account of the political process surrounding central-local relations; their obsessive determination to regard elected local/regional governments as the sole instruments of local democracy; and their constant tendency to over-emphasise the resources of the central authorities. It was concluded that descriptions of the United Kingdom as a unitary state, a centralised or decentralised system, or an internal society were highly suspect.

2. It was argued that if the subject was relabelled territorial politics and the analytical framework expanded to take account of the politics of Centre-periphery relations, viewed over time and from a Centre perspective, then the weaknesses of the existing approaches might be avoided. However, any study of the United Kingdom on these lines would encounter new problems: the concept of 'territory' was ambiguous; abstracting the politics of Centre-periphery relations from the wider political system would be difficult; and the emphasis on the techniques of

Centre 'estate' management might skew the analysis towards certain conclusions.

3. The initial Union of the United Kingdom was not inevitable. It was a reluctant creation, manufactured to resolve a particular set of recurring problems faced by English politicians at the court, or Centre. As a result the post-Union structure of territorial government was not designed to be innovative: it was a reconstruction of as much of the old informal Empire as was possible in changed circumstances. The Unions involved the transfer of the English Centre's territorial code to the three 'celtic' peripheries. Hence a relatively weak Centre continued to rely on the system of indirect rule, through local collaborative elites, to manage its expanded periphery. Within this structure parliament played a key role: it legitimised Centre policies, socialised peripheral elites, and acted as the main location for the articulation and settlement of peripheral interest demands.

4. Social and political modernisation between 1870 and 1926 produced, in the end, neither a more powerful Centre nor a more politically awkward periphery. The principal changes which did occur – the Irish settlement of 1920/1, the rise of the Labour Party, and the decline of parliament as an effective articulator of peripheral interests – had a profoundly conservative impact on territorial politics.

5. Between 1926 and the early 1960s the main features of United Kingdom territorial politics combined to produce what was called a Dual Polity; a state of affairs in which national and local politics were largely divorced from one another. Those contacts which existed between Centre and periphery were, for the most part, bureaucratic and depoliticised. In this period the Centre achieved what it had always desired – relative autonomy from peripheral forces to pursue its 'High Politics' preoccupations. Peripheral affairs, 'Low Politics' from the Centre's viewpoint, were left to collaborative local elites to manage.

6. After 1961 this Dual Polity was seemingly challenged by a number of forces – a more interventionist Centre, inter-community strife in Northern Ireland, Scottish and Welsh nationalism and problems concerning local authority spending. However, the strength of the peripheral challenges was less than many people either feared or hoped for. Duality survived, for a variety of reasons, in Northern Ireland. In Britain, only the SNP, assisted by highly favourable political circumstances in the mid-1970s, mounted any serious challenge to the traditional territorial order. Nevertheless, by 1979 the SNP and the Centre's response to it, devolution, had been defeated. In retrospect, the greatest challenge to the Dual Polity in this period came from the Centre itself, from its constant attempts to pursue remodernisation programmes and its considerable efforts to appease peripheral dissidents for reasons of electoral expediency.

7. The territorial economy of Thatcherism represents a new and important phase in the development of United Kingdom territorial politics. It illustrates both the increasing problems of peripheral management faced by the Centre and the changes in the Centre's territorial code in response to those problems. In Britain, Thatcherism began its life with a composite code, the most innovative feature of which was its concern to increase the role of the ordinary citizen and private enterprise in the local political process. Under the stress of continuing economic problems,

of 'hard times', this code was altered to emphasise the Centre's ultimate responsibility for macro-economic policies and hence the legitimacy of its attempts to increase its control over local authority expenditure. The stress of events produced similar, though less dramatic, changes in policies for Northern Ireland.

GENERAL THEMES

The principal themes to emerge from this historical survey concern the location, problems, and intentions of the United Kingdom Centre. Three points need to be made here.

First, the United Kingdom can be considered an example of a 'system' with a single predominant Centre, located in London. This predominance can be traced back to eleventh-century England, and hence predates the Union. Of course, subordinate 'provincial' centres have existed, but they have never rivalled, for any length of time, the constitutional, political, administrative and cultural importance of London. Significantly, this has been accepted by peripheral dissidents, as well as collaborators. *Within* London, the precise institutional location of the Centre has varied. Over time, the Centre has been located successively in the court, the court plus a political administration drawn from and ultimately responsible to parliament, the Cabinet, and, since the mid-1920s, a political-administrative community composed of senior ministers and top civil servants. It follows that England, as a territorial section, has never been *the* Centre. More important, whatever the precise location of the Centre in London, an incipient court ethic has always influenced its thinking and activity. The traditional role of parliament has been to act as an intermediary between this Centre and the periphery. As a consequence, in operational terms, United Kingdom territorial politics (and much else besides) has been run on the basis of a separation of powers, something enormously facilitated by the Westminsterisation of British MPs which took place after about 1870.

Secondly, the creation of the Union meant that the Centre was forced to assume responsibility for a difficult 'estate'. The perennial problem of Ireland is one obvious example. But in Britain, especially since the extension of the franchise, Wales, and above all Scotland, have always represented potential sources of trouble. A less obvious problem, though in many ways a more intractable one, has been that posed by England and the English. In terms of population and wealth the English have dominated the United Kingdom, making it a markedly asymmetrical Union. Moreover, the English have never taken the Union seriously. They have either ignored it, or regarded it as a mere extension of England and Englishness. The English problem, however goes further than this. England has always been an incredibly localised society, exhibiting a strong distaste for positive peripheral government from any quarter. At the same time, since the late nineteenth century, the bulk of its inhabitants have been increasingly unwilling to treat territorial politics seriously. Indeed, they have often sought to trivialise political thought and behaviour in this arena. Combined, these matters have posed an awkward dilemma for the Centre: how to run a territorial Union not taken seriously by this peculiar dominant section.

The intentions, the territorial code of the Centre, must be viewed in the light of these problems and the continuing influence of the court ethic. The analysis has emphasised the traditional propensity for the Centre to draw a distinction between 'High Politics' and 'Low Politics'. This was accompanied by a desire, furthered by constant preoccupation with a fragile external support system, to seek a relative autonomy for itself in matters relating to 'High Politics'. Once all this is understood it enables us to answer the interesting question of why the Centre has been unwilling to construct for itself a ruling territorial ideology (on the lines of 'the UK one and indivisible') or an extensive and effective bureaucratic machine to govern its 'estate'. In other words, we can explain the constant reliance on indirect rule, involving in practice the granting of considerable reciprocal autonomy to collaborative local elites in matters of 'Low Politics'. The fact is that until recently the Centre sought not to govern the United Kingdom, but to manage it; the code of an absentee landlord with reasonably efficient local agents. Yet, paradoxically, the Centre provided one of the few sources of Unionist sentiment in the system. It was prepared to brandish the symbol of the Crown (the regal Union) when needed and, at all times, it attempted to relate to (or distance itself from) *all* parts of the periphery in similar fashion. For the Centre then, if not for the English, England was a part of the periphery.

Thus, the structure of territorial politics in the United Kingdom can be best described, over time, in terms of a one-Centre, one-periphery model. Or, in terms more appropriate to the country's history, territorial politics was based on a court/country dichotomy. It should be emphasised that this was the system's predominant bias, it did not always work that way in practice. The joke, however, is that this bias was facilitated by the advent of electoral democracy. For reasons explained above, it achieved its fullest expression in practice with the Dual Polity, which operated between the mid-1920s and the early 1960s. It even survived the troubles of the 1960s and 1970s. Whether it will survive the territorial economy of Thatcherism is open to question.

One further obvious point needs to be made. The supporting data for many of these arguments is much less than perfect. And, of course, the Centre autonomy/collaboration theses are untestable, they cannot be disproved. These, however, are drawbacks inherent in all macro-political studies.[3] The exercise, then, represents a 'case', a plausible reading of United Kingdom territorial development, and no more.

POLITICAL ASTROLOGY

What does the future hold for territorial politics in the United Kingdom? We have seen that in the twentieth century this particular political arena has been remarkably free from successful radical challenges to the traditional order. Even when the

Centre itself pursued or promised radical changes, as in 1912–14, 1920–1, and 1977–9, a variety of forces intervened to save it from the consequences of its own actions or rhetoric. There are several reasons for thinking that this state of affairs cannot continue. The next decade may well be one when either the salience of particular aspects of territorial politics in the system increases, or, more radically, a general territorial crisis will develop.

The specific challenges to the existing territorial order could come from the following sources:

The Centre
We have seen how the territorial economy of Thatcherism broke with many of the traditional conventions of British territorial politics as a result of the increasing problems encountered by the government regarding its macro-economic strategy. It is likely that similar problems and responses will afflict any future party administration at the Centre, especially a Labour one with its commitment to the Alternative Economic Strategy and withdrawal from the European Community.

Northern Ireland
The British commitment to Northern Ireland, to retaining its position in the United Kingdom, has weakened considerably since 1968. In a sense, the key question regarding the Province is now, further experiments in devolution notwithstanding, when and how a future British government will try to 'offload' the problem. This could come about in a number of ways: by a formal commitment (for example, from a Labour government) to Irish unification; by creating a state of affairs in the Province which either forces Protestant politicians to accept unification, or react violently against it; or by persuading a Dublin government 'to pop the question', to make public the sort of contract it would offer the Protestant community within a united Ireland. In short, whatever the morality of the issue, Protestant fears of a 'sell out' seem justified.[4]

Scotland
Devaluation and the SNP were defeated, somewhat fortuitously, in the referendum and general election of 1979. However, this may be only a temporary reprieve for anti-devolution forces. Despite, or because of, its new explicit commitment to secession, the SNP is still a force to be reckoned with. The events of the 1960s and 1970s cannot be swept under the table. Equally important, the pressure of British electoral competition, in an increasingly unstable party system, may well force renewed commitments to Scottish devolution from the SDP/Liberal alliance and the Labour Party at the next general election. Once granted, it may be difficult to avoid a further instalment of devolution 'all round' to Wales and the English regions.

'Bennism'
As pointed out in Chapter 7 the emphasis placed an intra-party democracy, and extra-parliamentary activity generally, by movement represent a considerable

potential challenge to Centre autonomy and territorial duality. The SDP/Liberal alliance's commitment to decentralisation, although vague, may involve the establishment of elected regional councils throughout Britain.

Race

The political demands of black minority groups may 'come of age' in the 1980s. Previously, this particular challenge was avoided because black communities allowed their politics to be organised by white politicians and because the major opponent of the black presence, Mr Enoch Powell, eschewed populism for a continued commitment to parliamentary politics. Black riots in various inner city areas in 1980 and 1981 represent, perhaps, a new phase in the development of this issue. These minority groups show signs of demanding for themselves a much greater displacement in the political system. Local government, and its relation with the Centre, will be affected by this. Whether the traditional system of government in English urban areas, particularly as regards the police and education, can take the strain of United States style 'ethnic politics' is open to question.

Parliament

The partial renaissance in the influence of the House of Commons, which has taken place over the last decade, has been welcomed by most liberals. However, if continued it could have awkward repercussions for territorial politics. The more the Commons seeks to influence the Centre's policies, the more it may wish to interfere, or suggest that the Centre interfere, in various aspects of local government. Once again, education and the police are obvious examples.

This is one possible list of the major specific challenges to the traditional territorial order in the 1980s. Their potential impact must be viewed in the light of the two further points: the rules of the territorial 'game' are becoming increasingly unclear; and most of these challenges affect the heartland of the United Kingdom periphery, England. In other words, they cannot be hived off and dealt with by the Centre as separate 'celtic' problems. Finally, in previous chapters it has been argued that the general conditions necessary for a territorial crisis in the United Kingdom are the combined appearance on the scene of (a) a perceived decline in the external support system; (b) a decline of elite consensus at the Centre; (c) a collapse of peripheral collaborative arrangements; and (d) the development of plausible alternatives to the existing structure of the Union. In the present situation (early 1982) it would be foolish to argue that the reappearance of this particular combination is not a serious possibility. The qualification that has to be made to this view is given us by history: the remarkable facility shown by the British for avoiding radical developments in territorial politics. And this facility, of course, merely reflects that shown in many other aspects of the political system.

NOTES

1   Sidney Low, *The Governance of England* (London, 1927 edition), p. 12.

2   Alexander Baron, *The In-Between Years* (London, 1971), p. 55.

3   Another possible objection is that the conclusions drawn are an example of 'imperialist historiography in the age of post-imperial frustration'. See W. Ferguson, *Scotland's Relations With England* (Edinburgh, 1977), p. 60. I suspect that this particular criticism will be levelled at any English account of the United Kingdom.

4   Consider, for example, the following scenario. A future Labour government in London withdraws from the European Community and threatens to withdraw from NATO. The United States and its NATO allies then put pressure on the Irish Republic to become a member of NATO. The price is a united Ireland. Labour would be prepared to accommodate this demand. The only doubt is whether Dublin politicians really want a united Ireland. The Labour Party's annual Conference in 1981 accepted a motion declaring that Irish unification was the long term aim of the party.

index

www.ingramcontent.com/pod-product-compliance
Lightning Source LLC
Chambersburg PA
CBHW050708280326
41926CB00088B/2877